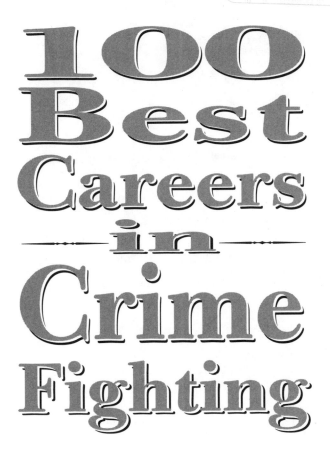

100 Best Careers in Crime Fighting

ARCO

100 Best Careers in Crime Fighting

Law Enforcement, Criminal Justice,
Private Security, and Cyberspace Crime Detection

Mary Price Lee • Richard S. Lee • Carol Beam

MACMILLAN • USA

Macmillan Reference USA
A Simon & Schuster Macmillan Company
1633 Broadway
New York, NY 10019-6785

Macmillan Publishing books may be purchased for business or sales
promotional use. For information, please write: Special Markets
Department, Macmillan Publishing USA, 1633 Broadway, New York,
NY 10019.

An Arco Book

ARCO is a registered trademark of Simon & Schuster Inc.
MACMILLAN is a registered trademark of Macmillan Inc.

Library of Congress Cataloging-in-Publication Data: 97-80221
ISBN: 0-02-861397-X

Manufactured in the United States of America

10 9 8 7 6 5 4 3 2

DEDICATION

for my loving family
Tom, Jon, Robin, Kim, and Meri
and for Tig

—C.B.

for Monica and Chris and
for Gwyn, Miles, Kelsey, Kira, Brigid, and Meredith Rays,
and Jane and Bob

—M.P.L. & R.S.L.

CONTENTS

ACKNOWLEDGMENTS

So many thanks to Barbara O'Neill, who helped with the research on this book and showed a continuing and enthusiastic interest in its progress.

Philip Howe, detective (retired), Haverford Township, Pennsylvania Police Department. Detective Howe helped us in an immeasurable number of ways.

Paul Fischer, young and dynamic president of Surveillance Systems, Inc., Limerick, Pennsylvania. Mr. Fischer gave us invaluable time on the now very sophisticated world of private security.

William Little, marketing manager, Vance International. Mr. Little stayed with us through our entire private security adventure and was kind enough to read our manuscript on that segment of crimefighting.

Judge David Keightly, district justice of Lansdale, Pennsylvania. Judge Keightly gave us an interesting and sometimes unorthodox view of the court system.

Many thanks to Chief of Police (Retired), Bedminster Township, Pennsylvania, David Stevens. Mr. Stevens is now a Regional Security Coordinator.

We appreciated the help of Lieutenant, Philadelphia Police Department (Retired), Donald Nypower, now director of the Department of Criminal Justice and director of the Police Academy of Montgomery County Community College in Gwynedd Township, Pennsylvania.

Kudos to Mr. Jon E. Clark, chairman of the Department of Criminal Justice at Temple University, Philadelphia, Pennsylvania, and director of Criminal Justice Training programs at Temple University. Mr. Clark kindly reviewed the Law Enforcement section of our book, and in an informal afternoon get-together, the authors enjoyed exchanging ideas with Mr. Clark's savvy and enthusiastic students.

Judge Sandra Schultz Newman serves on the Pennsylvania Supreme Court. We take pleasure in *her* pleasure at helping us to make this the most accurate, interesting, and forward-looking book of its kind.

Miles Thompson, juvenile counselor, offers compassion and discipline to his charges at St. Gabriel's Hall in Audubon, Pennsylvania. We thank him for his help with this book and for his friendship.

Thanks to:

Jill Bigden of Lancaster, Pennsylvania, and Lori Morse and Andre Milteer of the Free Library of Philadelphia for invaluable source material.

Monica Lee and Barbara Lee Wysochanski, for their interest and help.

Joe Morsello, freelance photographer, who has followed our "lead" for over 24 years.

Sandy Howe, who finally managed to get her police family to pose for this book!

Mary Carr, who has come to the fore again to provide us with a picture of Pennsylvania's first female Judge of the Supreme Court.

Susan Keightly, who enrolled her brother, Judge David Keightly, in the undertaking of this book.

Marg Eldredge, who provided valuable information in the writing of this book.

And finally, the staff of the Flourtown, Pennsylvania, Swim Club, who provided one author with her special "working corner" while writing this book.

—M.P.L & R.S.L.

• •

My sincere thanks to the following for the time, help, guidance, leads, expertise, information, and abundant encouragement and good nature they shared with me during my work on this book:

David Bernstein, editor of *Infosecurity News,* for critical information delivered quickly.

Jay Bloombecker, of the National Center for Computer Crime Data, for quick data and leads for more sources.

Dave Dasgupta, of the American Institute of Certified Public Accountants, for staying in touch through my longest game of phone tag to date.

Alan Fedeli, of IBM's Computer Emergency Response Service, for his extraordinary command of his material and the kindness of sharing it with me twice (due to technical failure during the original interview), as well as for reading through our chapter on cyberspace crime.

Joan Feldman, of Computer Forensics, for a wonderful look at how an innovative mind can function and succeed—and still keep a sense of humor.

Ken Geide, of the FBI's Computer Investigation and Threat Assessment Center, for taking the time to make a complicated subject understandable to a novice.

Rick Koenig, of the International Information Systems Security Certification Consortium, for his timely response.

Rich Petillo, manager of Network Security for AT&T, for taking time out of his very busy schedule to share his knowledge and experience.

Richard Ress, of the FBI's Computer Crime Squad, for presenting a chilling overview of their task and an eloquent and organized presentation of the facts.

Neal Schiff, of the National Press Office, for being my link to such fine information and interviews, for being consistently helpful and great to talk to, and for reading our sections of the book relating to the FBI.

Kurt Stammberger, of RSA Data Security, for responding so efficiently and thoroughly to his e-mail.

Ira Winkler, of the National Computer Security Association, whose background knowledge and familiarity with the field helped me start making progress in the vast subject of cyberspace crime.

Charles Cresson Wood, of Baseline Software, for his perceptive overview of the challenges facing those who opt for fighting computer crime.

—C.B.

• •

Thanks to Dr. Kathleen Rex Anderson, Ed.D., associate dean and director of the Accelerated Program at Chestnut Hill College in Philadelphia, Pennsylvania. We thank her also for reading the criminal justice segment of our manuscript.

Thanks to Sara Kitchen Benn, division chair of Social Sciences, Chestnut Hill College, in Philadelphia, Pennsylvania.

Thanks to Chris Kratz, victim advocate, Network of Victim Assistance (NOVA) in Bucks County, Pennsylvania, for clarifying the court system in the book's early stages.

Thanks to Dianne Freestone, first female assistant public defender in Saratoga County, New York.

B.O'N.

CAREER INDEX

continues

continues

INTRODUCTION

This book describes over 100 crimefighting careers in the public and private sectors. Law enforcement (section 1) is the firing line of crimefighting—city/town, county, state, federal. Criminal justice (section 2) is the "umbrella" that covers all the above. It also includes every level of the court system that determines the guilt or innocence of criminal suspects.

Private security (section 3) is its companion field; however, private security is just that—a private enterprise. Although it may include some forms of crime prevention and investigation, it does not seek "justice" but protects private property.

Computer-based cyberspace/Internet crime detection (section 5) can be a law enforcement or a private security function. This field is so new and different that we have devoted a section to it.

When you enter any of these exciting, promising, and challenging career fields, your job will relate directly or indirectly to the apprehension and punishment of criminals.

WHY CRIMEFIGHTING?

Our country has grown more caring and environmentally sensitive in recent years. And although crime rates are easing somewhat in some segments of our society, we are also combating more of certain forms of crime and violence. (For instance, the higher the number of teens to early 20s in the population, the higher the crime rate.) The need for crime control has grown, from desert border crossings to vice-plagued cities, from airports to college campuses.

Police, especially in some urban areas, may confront crime levels unequaled in recent years. Today, no city, town, or suburb escapes random violence. The issues breeding crime often cannot be addressed by those in criminal justice since they may relate to education, the economy, and a breakdown in family structure and social institutions. The task of law enforcement and the criminal justice system is to deal with the consequences.

The *Montgomery County* [Pennsylvania] *Record* newspaper put the problem succinctly in a 1996 article: "When restaurant managers are gunned down for a couple of bucks; when bank tellers are shot in broad daylight; when husbands beat their wives and children, and children assault one another over the sneakers they're wearing, we have a very serious crisis on our hands. We need . . . drastic, visionary [preventive] measures."

Rightly or wrongly, television gets blamed for much current violence. While the transfer from viewing to action may not be traceable, there is no denying the fact that by their teen years, the average young person has seen thousands of acts of violence on TV and in movies.

The TV industry seems uninterested in policing itself, but this lack of responsibility shocks others. The National Television Violence Study conducted by the University of California analyzed 2,693 TV programs from 23 channels. These programs all depicted "harmful violence," according to the study's authors. We may now be living in a violent society, shoot-'em-up television or no, but the small screen does not improve the big picture.

The nation has become increasingly shocked by teenage violence. The kid who might once have battled with his fists now uses a shotgun. *Newsweek* magazine (December 4, 1995) stated that, "Hundreds of thousands of American kids are being pushed toward adolescent criminality by neglect, abuse and just plain bad parenting. The rampant drug problems are also a controlling factor."

Newsweek said that the teenager with a gun is far more dangerous than an adult because the teen does not consider the consequences. "He'll pull a trigger over a leather jacket, pair of sneakers or a joke."

Police hope to reduce teenage and adult criminal activity with community outreach programs and closer surveillance. But violence is something each police department must deal with every day, even though individual officers may go for months, even years, without drawing their weapons. Police try to involve communities in the problem. (In fact, police departments spend 90 percent of their time on social services and regulations.) Violent crime is dropping in many cities because of this cooperation. (Perception of violence is greater than actual violence, a fact that does little to reduce the level of fearfulness.)

In August 1996, the Justice Department reported that juvenile crime rates had dropped for 1995 compared to the previous year. Overall arrest rates for violent crimes declined 2.9 percent among youths aged 10 to 17. And the murder arrest rate for this age group dropped by 25.2 percent. Violent crime arrest rates for those over 18 continued to climb slightly, but murder rates also dropped 9.7 percent from the 1994 figures for this group.

At a news conference called to announce the findings, Attorney General Janet Reno spoke cautiously: "What is so important is that we not relax and we not take credit for victory yet, because the number of young people is going to increase significantly in the next 15 years. So, the actual number of crimes, unless we work real hard, is going to go up."

Law enforcement faces other dilemmas besides juvenile crime. These range from misuse of the Internet to an apparent increase in natural disasters with their need for public assistance and crime control. The realities and perceptions of crime and violence would make it helpful for all law enforcement agencies to beef up their forces. But few areas can afford to expand. The same factors are fueling the growth of private security. Crime, unpleasant but inarguable, makes the market.

TECHNOLOGY AND EDUCATION

Law enforcement and private security people today are just as likely to be sitting at computers or analyzing laboratory data as operating security desks or driving patrol cars. We have emphasized the high-technology elements of many public safety jobs and have covered their tech-related careers. From bomb detectors to sticky foam, from infrared night vision binoculars to speedy fingerprint IDs, crime-fighters employ the latest technology. Those who invent, perfect, and market these anti-crime tools are just as legitimate crimefighters as those who use them.

Today's security desk person and patrol officer (as well as detective and forensic pathologist) must understand technology to get the most from it. This is why today's law enforcement professional needs more education and better training than was true even a few years ago. It explains why an associate degree in law enforcement is fast becoming the career minimum, and why a bachelor's degree gives any job applicant a distinct advantage.

Technology has also fueled the increase in "civilian" employees within the largely paramilitary law enforcement structure. Computer operators and data processors, photographers/videographers, and crime laboratory technologists are among the many enforcement-related careers that are part of the tech revolution.

FEDERAL LAW ENFORCEMENT

As you will read in chapter 6 of this section, the Federal government operates many agencies devoted to varied forms of law enforcement.* For example, the Secret Service, operated by the Treasury Department, is both protective and investigative. The agency protects the President and First Family and other high-ranking government officials. It works with other federal agencies to prevent acts of terrorism against our officials and visiting foreign dignitaries. The Secret Service is also responsible for currency violations and investigating counterfeiters of U.S. money.

---

*Strictly speaking, the Central Intelligence Agency (CIA) is not part of law enforcement, since the agency is prevented by law from conducting intelligence-gathering within the United States. The CIA secretly tracks the activities of those in other countries who could carry out terrorism and sabotage against us. We owe much of our national security to the exciting, often dangerous work of the agency's worldwide network of agents and informants. Since most CIA activity is classified (restricted), we may never know the extent of their protective actions.

The Federal Bureau of Investigation (FBI) pursues all who commit crimes across state lines, or whose acts are federal offenses. (Example: bank robbery in any state is a federal crime because all banks are insured by a federal agency. However, the majority of bank robberies are solved by local police.) The FBI uncovers information and pursues suspects ranging from drug dealers to racketeers. They investigate accidents such as airline crashes and train wrecks that involve interstate commerce or international terrorism.

Job Variety, Personality Traits

Finally, one exciting element of law enforcement is its scope. Perhaps no field has as many interesting careers and diverse areas within its careers. (Private security is also becoming more varied.) Hostage negotiator? Bounty hunter? SWAT team member? Our times demand widely varied law enforcement skills.

It is not always easy to work in law enforcement. Those of you who will deal with the public need to be caring yet firm. You will have to be involved in your communities, and always remember that you are public servants. If you are working behind the scenes, you need wisdom and training to beat criminals at their game. You must be dedicated to problem-solving and pursuit. However, most patrol work—which most of those in law enforcement do most of the time—has often been called 90 percent boredom, 10 percent terror.

Among the less-than-ideal conditions you will have to be prepared for are the changing shifts that most local police must work, and the limits the work places on other aspects of life. Mr. Jon E. Clark, head of the Department of Criminal Justice at Philadelphia's Temple University, described the life this way in a letter to the authors:

> "Rarely do police officers get to be home on Christmas morning to open presents with their kids. Or, as a federal officer, you serve the needs of the service and can be moved temporarily or permanently, on short notice, and as often as the service needs to move you, anywhere in the country.
>
> "Police marriages undergo considerable strain with rotating shifts and the six [days] on, two [days] off or other kinds of schedules that are so at odds with the rest of society. The spouse of a law enforcement officer has to be pretty independent and self-sufficient because the officer-spouse is often not around to make some of the important decisions. To a degree, a person doesn't join the police force. His or her whole immediate family does. . . .
>
> "Because of your very different working hours and unusual duties, often the only friends you have are other cops. Also, many of your contacts with the public are negative. All this can give some police a pretty jaundiced view of the world. [Law enforcement] has high rates of alcoholism and domestic discord. It is not for everyone."

Salaries

Salaries vary widely according to geography for local police sheriffs and probation and parole officers. As law enforcement jobs require more skills and as opportunities grow, salaries throughout the field are becoming increasingly attractive; however, they are still far too low in many jurisdictions. (Many salary ranges are part of individual career descriptions.)

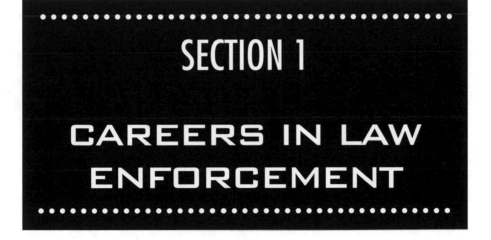

SECTION 1

CAREERS IN LAW ENFORCEMENT

CHAPTER 1

Becoming a Law Enforcement Officer

EDUCATION

If you enjoy public service and want to make this country safer, you can start to fulfill your wishes as early as high school. High schools have broadened their curricula, so you may find you can take courses such as business law, communications, economics, laboratory sciences, psychology, sociology, and urban problems. If your school does not offer every course, plan to take them in the future at any of three places: a community college, a four-year college, or a police academy. (You will ultimately attend at least one as a law enforcement careerist.)

Also, develop computer proficiency in high school, or on your own. Computer skills will serve you well in any law enforcement career.

College experience will give you an advantage in applying for a law enforcement post. You can major in police science or law enforcement and earn an associate degree at a two-year community college. Or you can make criminal justice or law enforcement your four-year college major. If you wish to enter a law enforcement career other than police officer, you may need a college degree plus job training or attendance at a specialized academy.

In most community colleges, you will find the first of your two years to be more general: English, government, introduction to law enforcement. The second year's courses may stress police supervision and department operation, police/community relations, criminal investigation, and narcotics enforcement. A bachelor's degree from a four-year college will put you well ahead with courses in all law enforcement areas.

BASIC REQUIREMENTS

You must be a United States citizen to apply for law enforcement training in most jurisdictions and all federal careers. You will need a valid driver's license and a good driving record (no DUIs, few or no moving violations). Residence require-ments differ among states; you may or may not need to live in the state where you wish to work after training. You also must have a high school diploma or GED (equivalency certificate), and be 21 years old to begin most careers. (You can be trained before age 21.)

You must be dedicated to your future career. According to James Stinchcomb, author of *Opportunities in Law Enforcement and Criminal Justice Careers* (VGM Career Horizons, 1996, rev. ed.), a candidate must show leadership, maturity, per-ception, good judgment, decisiveness, and adaptability. He or she must be skilled in clear, effective verbal and written communications. Other requirements are good general intelligence and reasoning ability, mental and emotional stability, and good health.

Attitude is important, too. According to Jon Clark of Temple University: "A good law enforcement officer must hold to a higher standard than the public at large . . . but then must be gracious and tolerant enough to understand the failings of others. This is not easy. A strong value system and tolerance, physical capabili-ties, emotional stability, intelligence, integrity, and commitment to service is . . . a rare combination. . . ."

TESTS

A police academy will put you through many steps even before you start to train as a police officer, deputy sheriff, state trooper, or FBI agent. Entrance require-ments and academy training will differ depending on the job for which you are preparing. But the tests you must take are essentially the same.

You must first complete an application. In doing so, it is essential that you pro-vide facts about yourself and your past that "check out" because the academy will investigate your background. It will help if you have a detailed resume of your accomplishments. You can use it to complete the application, or attach it. Even if you are two years past high school, you need such a resume to list your academic achievements and sports interests, summer employment, and character references. At any age, you may not make it if you have unexplained gaps in employment, more than minor encounters with the law, a poor credit history, or other personal discrepancies.

If you are an older applicant, you may not make it either. Many agencies do not want officers working past age 55, yet they want people to work for 20 years before retirement.

Background checks take time and cost money. Yours probably will not be con-ducted until you meet all the other requirements for police academy admission, but you may be asked for the information when you first apply. It's essential that you describe your life and accomplishments fully and honestly.

You will probably have to pass a written test, but a few jurisdictions do not have them. Many people who take these written law enforcement examinations do not enter the field. This is because the tests are intentionally stressful and difficult. The exam will reflect your talents for clarity of expression, reading comprehension, recollection, management of detail, and your ability to make decisions. Although you do not need to know the details of law enforcement to pass a police academy written test, knowledge of the field should improve your score. Do not expect a "snap" test. Police departments are looking for those who can take the heat!

Some departments have oral tests and panel reviews either along with or replacing written exams, according to Jon Clark. These are opportunities for the department evaluators to test your specific knowledge, to determine how you think, or—probably—both. There may not be "right" answers to certain oral questions, but the response you make will show the examiner how you approach a problem logically and emotionally. The same questions may then be asked differently, to judge your response from a different perspective; again, no answer is "right." Since the chief of the department must answer for the officers' attitudes and activities, interviewers look for candidates who are committed to certain ideals but who are balanced in their attitudes ("neither extreme, unpredictable nor dogmatic," says Clark).

Physical examinations are, of course, required. You need more than general good health. You must demonstrate stamina because your training will be rigorous, and the job will call for long hours without rest. You must show good lifting ability and upper body strength, good coordination, and above-average physical condition. Height and weight requirements are less rigid than they used to be. Your weight must be in proportion to your height. Your vision probably will be fine if it is correctable to 20/20 with glasses.

As an example of meeting physical requirements, James Stinchcomb listed the Miami, Florida, Police Department's test of physical condition: a short-distance run, running to aid another officer, running after and subduing a suspect, climbing stairs, gripping a firearm or other weapon, pushing a disabled vehicle, climbing a six-foot fence, carrying 50 pounds, climbing through a window, climbing to a roof on a ladder, and swimming a moderate distance.

You can expect to be tested for drugs before, during, and probably after training. Positive test results will usually result in academy rejection and job probation or dismissal. You should be prepared for a polygraph (lie-detector) test, although you probably will not have to take one unless your drug tests raise questions about you.

Whether or not you have had an oral exam, a personal interview will review your mini-history. Here is where you should express your sincerity about a law enforcement career. It is your chance to show your all-around competence, your communications skills, and your demeanor and appearance.

Psychiatric and personality tests will complete the picture. These tests will show if you have the mental makeup and the personality traits you need for success on a police team: calmness under stress, judgment and decisiveness, ability to follow instructions, physical and mental courage tempered by defensiveness against danger, and "people" skills.

Despite the sophistication of law enforcement tests, authors Coulton and Field wrote in the summer 1995 issue of *Public Personnel Management* magazine that no single measure can accurately identify police officer candidates. But law enforcement testers are finding that the Assessment Center (a method, not a place) can offer insight into future officers' behavior.

The Assessment Center uses extensive role-playing. Would-be officers must make suitable choices in police-versus-suspect situations. In the hypothetical examples, candidates take part in skits carefully designed to show "ability to deal with the public, the ability to maintain emotional stability under stress, teamwork, communication skills, and the proper use of force," according to Coulton and Field. The Assessment Center also uses interactive videos. In these, a candidate selects among computerized options. Police officers judge these selections to see if the candidate made the wisest move for a given crime situation. In some Assessment Center evaluations, other police officer candidates—your peers— judge and vote on their fellow prospects, giving the exercises an added dimension.

Proof of the value of Assessment Center evaluation is in the impressive clarity and quality of testimony given by police officers who have had Assessment Center experience.

ACADEMY TRAINING

Once the police department accepts you as a candidate, you will undergo the rigors of training. Here are two views of what happens.

Russell Bintliff, author of *Police Procedural: A Writer's Guide to the Police and How They Work* (Writer's Digest Books, 1993), believes that at the start, you leave the civilian world forever. He has noted that "Recruits must be stripped of their identity and taught to assume a police identity." Temple University's Jon Clark disagrees: "I had hoped we had gotten past that 'stripping of identity' stuff! In my opinion, the most useful tools any [officer] has is the good sense of self, level-headedness, regard for others, common sense, integrity, humanity and humility that he or she learned—more than likely—from Mom."

Bintliff wrote that three traits make up the police personality. The first is defensiveness, which he has described as ". . .to be alert to the many dangers of police work and to build defenses against them. . . ."

The second characteristic is professionalism, taking pride in your work and developing an esprit de corps or group loyalty and unity similar to that found in military service. Public friendliness is fine to a degree, but professionalism must take over if you are to be an effective officer.

Finally, you as an officer candidate should develop what Bintliff has called "depersonalization." You may feel that you are losing a sense of self as both the public and your instructors and superior officers tuck you into a no-name category.

Bintliff wrote: "Recruits . . . learn that some occupational demands require them to deny personal qualities such as compassion. . . . Police officers learn quickly that personalizing their official relationships with the public, even when it seems the right thing to do, can be twisted and used to get them in trouble. . . . Police officers must walk a thin line between prudence, common sense and impartiality. . . ."

Jon Clark takes issue, to a point. He wrote: "Professionalism does not have to equate to detachment from the public. The perception by police that they are 'a thin blue line' is exactly what gets a lot of [them] in trouble."

Academy training (or a mixture of regimentation and college courses) will eventually turn you into a beginning police officer. It is a long and rigorous process—and continues beyond formal training. You will have a period of probationary duty under the watchful eyes of superiors. Even when you have graduated and earned your badge, many cities and states require periodic refresher training sessions to maintain your position on a police force.

Length of Training

Until the 1950s and '60s, few states had minimum police training standards. Now, all states do, and most minimums have increased dramatically since the early 1980s. Although minimums differ by state, all states have higher minimums than ever. This shows the increasing importance of police training and certification and the growth of professionalism in the ranks.

You can expect to undergo at least 400 hours of police training, and perhaps up to 1,000 hours. (Also, many departments purposely exceed state minimums.) Basic training may take from eight weeks to six months. Police academies can be part of community colleges and other academic settings. You may receive essential training to join a small town police force, or more detailed instruction to become part of a large city department. Logically, a large city police department has more police functions and needs more specialists. This is why a city police academy may require more hours and offer more sophisticated training.

Scope of Training

Police training covers all the basics of duty. You will learn in the classroom, at the target range, in the gymnasium, and behind the patrol car wheel. This training will let you handle varied duties such as traffic enforcement, evidence securing, courtroom testimony, and confronting an armed suspect.

California created the POST (Peace Officer Standards and Training) program, which has become a model for police training in many departments nationwide. As of 1995, POST courses included 664 minimum hours of basic training. Here is the basic POST training curriculum. (Source: State of California, Commission on Peace Officer Standards and Training, Commission Regulation 1005, POST Administrative Manual, (Sacramento, CA: POST, 1995.)

Basic POST Training (664 minimum required hours)

History, Professionalism, and Ethics	8 hours
Criminal Justice System	4 hours
Community Relations	12 hours
Victimology/Crisis Interventions	6 hours
Introduction to Criminal Law	6 hours
Crimes Against Property	10 hours
Crimes Against Persons	10 hours
General Criminal Statutes	4 hours
Crimes Against Children	6 hours
Sex Crimes	6 hours
Juvenile Law and Procedure	6 hours
Controlled Substances	12 hours
ABC Law	4 hours
Laws of Arrest	12 hours
Search and Seizure	12 hours
Presentation of Evidence	8 hours
Investigative Report Writing	40 hours
Vehicle Operations	24 hours
Use of Force	12 hours
Patrol Techniques	12 hours
Gang Awareness	8 hours
Weapons Violations	4 hours
Hazardous Materials	4 hours
Vehicle Pullovers	14 hours
Crimes in Progress	16 hours
Handling Disputes/Crowd Control	12 hours
Domestic Violence	8 hours
Unusual Occurrences	4 hours
Missing Persons	4 hours

Traffic Enforcement	22 hours
Traffic Accident Investigation	12 hours
Preliminary Investigation	42 hours
Custody	4 hours
Physical Fitness/Officer Stress	40 hours
Person Searches, Baton Use, Etc.	60 hours
First Aid and CPR	21 hours
Firearms/Chemical Agents	72 hours
Information Systems	4 hours
Persons with Disabilities	6 hours
Crimes Against the Justice System	4 hours
Cultural Diversity/Discrimination	24 hours
MINIMUM INSTRUCTIONAL HOURS	599
TESTING	
Scenario Tests	40 hours
POST-Constructed Knowledge Tests	25 hours
TOTAL MINIMUM HOURS	**664**

In *Police Procedural*, Russell Bintliff has listed these typical police instruction subjects:

Arrest	Crime scenes
Authority and jurisdiction	Directing traffic
Basic law	Defensive driving
Choke defenses	Drug abuse
Club techniques and defenses	Elements of proof
Communications	Ethics
Conduct of search and seizure	Examinations
Court testimony	Fingerprinting

Interviews and interrogations

Investigative procedures

Legal rights, warnings, waivers

Note taking

Patrol operations

Police information

Practical exercises (day, night)

Records and forms

Report writing

Restraints and use of force

Search and seizure

Traffic accident investigation

Traffic accident reports

Traffic control operations

Unarmed defense and self-defense

Weapons and firing ranges

Today's training also includes relevant skills and public interaction. Computer use, understanding different cultures, dealing with terrorist acts—all are recent elements of police activity and are sometimes (but not always) included in law enforcement training.

Classes must be disciplined if you are to absorb all this information and acquire the skills needed to be an effective police officer. Most instruction outside the classroom is what military schools call "competency-based." This means you must show you can disarm a gun-toting suspect, not just write about it. Your demonstrations may be videotaped for review as part of your instruction. Your instructors probably will be people who know their subjects firsthand: veteran police officers.

Firearms training is a key part of academy instruction. You will be taught to use those weapons that will be assigned to you as a new officer, usually the service revolver or—more likely—a 9mm or .40 cal semiautomatic pistol, and police shotgun. You also will learn when and when not to use a firearm. (This may include computer-interactive shoot/don't shoot training.) Gym time will include lessons in self-defense, disarming and subduing suspects, and rescue techniques plus strength-building exercises and workouts. You will learn defensive and performance driving at the classroom desk and behind the patrol car wheel.

You also may be taught by guest lecturers at the police academy. These can be attorneys, prosecutors, court staff, fire department officials, even federal officers. Each will teach a specialized subject related to your future, such as arson investigation, tactical techniques, and how police use helicopters.

Colleges are helping police academies by expanding their curricula. In college (or community college) classrooms, you may learn the finer points of human behavior and psychology and successful communications and report writing, among other subjects. Such classes may be taught by civilians and can humanize the police training. You also may earn college degree credits.

Getting into a police academy or college program does not mean you will automatically graduate. It's essential that you keep up with daily instruction, take complete notes, and study for the frequent tests. Your academy performance becomes part of your permanent record as a police officer—so will all the performance reviews you will later receive on the job.

LIFE AFTER GRADUATION

Once you graduate from a police academy or otherwise complete your police department's officer requirements, you will go to work, but you will remain on probation. Ideally, this will be for one year, perhaps two. Also in an ideal situation, you would work under the watchful direction of experienced police officers. In this field training, you at first observe police patrol and station-house activity as you absorb even more instruction in police procedures. Then, under the direction of the field trainers, you apply what you have learned. You begin to handle police duties and make decisions first under supervision, and increasingly for yourself. This is when you learn the "street smarts" that will help you balance law enforcement theory and real-world crime.

Reality may differ. You may train for a shorter time and be on your own sooner, assuming full responsibilities. With departments being shorthanded, as most are, you may not receive full "textbook" supervision. Divide the staff of any police department by four (three shifts a day, plus a shift with time off), and you have the effective strength at any moment. Such strength, or its lack, makes probationary training harder for a department to do. The chief and your other superiors may put you more fully in charge earlier.

In any case, you will be continuously evaluated by your field training officers and their superiors. They can decide at any time whether or not you will make it as a police officer.

After the probation period, assuming you have performed satisfactorily, you will become a full-fledged officer. You will then have the security and chance for career advancement open to all "sworn" police officers.

Continuing Training

Training does not end when you receive your badge. As an officer, you will receive additional training in specialties, or to meet your state's continuing education minimums. In *Police Procedural* (1993), Russell Bintliff mentioned the types of training you may receive. In *Law Enforcement and Criminal Justice Careers* (1996), James Stinchcomb described some special subjects for added training:

- **Advanced training**—additional policing and administrative skills needed to meet department objectives.

- **Specialized training**—includes bomb squad, canine operations, community relations, crowd and riot control, harbor patrol or helicopter patrol work, emergency/rescue, street crime patrol, SWAT (Special Weapons and Tactics) team training, and youth crime, among others. (Specialized training is not for all officers but for those part of or moving to special groups or squads.)

- **In-service training**—for reviewing earlier training and learning new skills. Often related to state-required continuing education and meeting community needs. The most important in-service training most police officers receive consists of legal updates, revised case law, and new statutes. Officers must be up-to-date on legal matters related to their dealings with the public and with suspected criminals, such as use of force, search and seizure, arrest, investigative procedures, etc.

- **Seminars/workshops**—Offered by police academies and colleges, these courses usually cover investigation techniques, patrol officer topics, and qualification courses for detective examinations.

- **Video training**—used for in-service and in-department training on nearly all law enforcement subjects.

RISING IN THE RANKS

James Stinchcomb has noted that a typical police department is 75 percent police officers, 12 percent first-line supervisors (usually sergeants), and 13 percent management and command-level officers.

If you remain a police officer, you will pursue an honorable, respected career, receive good employment benefits, and retire with a pension after 20, 25, or 30 years.

To advance through the ranks, you will need continued study beyond minimum requirements, favorable career reviews from your superior officers, and high scores on competitive examinations held periodically for department openings. "You will also need the good fortune of those above you retiring," wrote Jon Clark of Temple University. "Police agencies are pyramids, and advancement is limited to the complement authorized at each rank." (Invariably there are many applicants for each advanced post, and test scores plus performance evaluations will determine who gets the job.)

Frank Schmalleger reported in *Criminal Justice Today* (Prentice-Hall, 1997) that growing numbers of police departments are requiring some college courses for advancement. A San Diego police officer needs at least two years of college to be promoted to sergeant. The New York Police Department mandates at least 64 college credits for promotion to any supervisory job. And a bachelor's degree is the minimum for entry-level jobs in many federal law enforcement agencies. Jon Clark stated the case this way: "I tell [law enforcement] students that they may be absolutely certain that required educational credentials will become higher rather than lower. This rise may be dramatic over a 20-year career. A particular degree might get you the job today, but you might be competing with people with far more education when it comes time for promotion. Those . . . hired after you are likely to have more advanced degrees as the years go by."

The Dark Side

The overwhelming majority of police officers are professionals dedicated to controlling crime and serving the public. But there is a "dark side" that a few police embrace —corruption. A good definition is "improper conduct for personal gain." Corrupt officers break the laws they are sworn to uphold.

Some police departments tell officers that corruption even includes accepting a free cup of coffee from the operator of a diner on the beat. This is debatable. But there is total agreement that taking bribes; pocketing confiscated drug money (or drugs!); withholding, altering, or stealing evidence; false arrest; framed (fabricated) charges; and similar actions are corrupt. Any abuse of power fits the corruption mold.

Of officers led astray, Jon Clark wrote: "How is it that these idealistic [officers] end up in such straits? Where and when does the change occur? A lot of people, myself included, suspect that characteristics of the organization breed cynicism and, ultimately, corruption. It requires a particularly secure and adept person to withstand the pressures to conform—even then conformity to some norms is flat-out wrong. Separation from the community and society at large is often a part of the problem, which is why I object to the characterization of professionalism [as being detached]."

Proven corruption charges bring dismissal, criminal prosecution, possible lawsuits, and jail terms to officers who are tried and convicted. Worse yet, the corruption of the few casts a long shadow over all the "good cops" out there.

This is not the image with which you should end your introduction to a career as a police officer. In a 1995 nationwide survey of more than 3,600 police conducted by *Parade* magazine, 83 percent answered "yes" when asked, "Do you find your job satisfying overall?" These fine professionals who often serve "beyond the call of duty" find the job tremendously rewarding.

CHAPTER 2

How Local Police Officers Work

Many people in other law enforcement areas began as police officers. The officer is the basic rank of the military-like command structure of the police system in every town, suburban township, and city. There are about 40,000 town, city, and state police departments. Department size ranges from the chief and no officers at all in a rural area or small town to the 25,000 officers and their many supervisors who protect New York City.

These are the usual police department ranks. In large departments, each upper rank may include several deputies or assistants. In small towns and rural townships, many intermediate ranks do not exist:

Commissioner or Chief— highest in command

Deputy Commissioner or Deputy/Assistant Chief

Commander (usually of a geographic segment or a department)

Captain

Lieutenant

Sergeant

Police Officer

POLICE OFFICER

Most police officers carry out patrol duties on one of three eight-hour shifts that divide a day into equal parts. The patrolling police officer is (sometimes literally) the *foot soldier* of a city's or town's police department. He or she may walk an assigned *beat* for part or all of the shift time. Some foot patrol officers walk part-time and ride in police cars for other shift hours. Foot patrol officers usually walk a manageable area of a few city blocks. In the course of their work, they get to know their neighborhood residents and businesspeople and come to count on them for information about goings-on in the area.

Mobile police officers patrol larger territories by bicycle, scooter, motorcycle, or usually by car. They work singly or in pairs in high-crime areas. Two-way radio links foot patrol and vehicle police officers to each other and to their headquarters.

Other officers on the street, particularly those on traffic detail, may occupy a *post*, directing traffic at the same street corner during a specific time of the day.

In a few cities, some police still patrol on horseback. Horses can go where cars cannot and can control crowds. City harbor patrol officers cover waterfront beats by powerboat. In some big cities, helicopter patrols monitor large areas or spot difficult situations from the air.

No matter how he or she gets around, the police officer is the first link in the chain that protects the public from crime and danger. Police enforce the law. They do so mostly by questioning people, by arresting those suspected of crime, and by checking out suspicious places or unusual activities. Many authorities, including Professor Jon Clark of Temple University, believe that the amount of police presence has relatively little effect on crime. (Police discover few crimes; most are reported by victims or witnesses.) Most police work involves routine patrol with a moderate dose of community interaction. Yet, danger is ever present, and the smaller the department, the more jobs each member must do.

Police officers are alert to suspicious activities as they patrol on foot or by car. They also answer radio calls, either to investigate reported troubles, settle domestic disputes, and even rescue children—or, in the case of two Middletown Township, Pennsylvania, officers, to free a frantic Rottweiler ice-trapped in a pond! Officers also respond to each others' calls for backup. They aid firefighters with crowd control at fire scenes. They investigate reported robberies and accidents, and respond to whatever neighborhood problem comes crackling over their radios.

Patrol officers are usually first on a crime scene. They keep the curious away and preserve all evidence for detectives and other specialists to investigate. They question everyone—neighbors, coworkers, family members, and witnesses. The police can arrest anyone if they have *probable cause*. (That is, if they have reason to believe a person is involved in a crime.) Police officers (on foot or in vehicles) spend lots of time in on-the-spot situation management. This can range from neighborhood parking-space disputes to fallen tree limbs, from convenience store holdups to student protests. Police are front-and-center for rock concert shenanigans, drug busts, and bomb threats. Officers get some assignments at the roll call that starts their shift. Many events just happen during a supposedly "routine" eight hours on the street.

Sometimes, local police receive unusual assignments. Recently, a public school in the Philadelphia, Pennsylvania, system with a history of violence, added a new employee to help its nonuniformed security force: a Philadelphia police officer. Some students had been terrorizing classmates and teachers, carrying knives and guns with their school books. The school asked for help, and a uniformed officer began patrolling classrooms and halls. On his first day, he disarmed a gun-toting student who was ready to fire at two of his classroom companions.

Police and students are not always confrontational. Philadelphia's PAL (Police Athletic League) has a long history of positive police/juvenile relations. In Horsham, Pennsylvania, police officers are trying to gain the respect of kids on their beats. Compassionate, caring detectives and police officers are playing a legitimate card game with the township's youngsters, ages six to fourteen. Boys and girls get credit points for each police officer they sight. Young people who earn the greatest number of points receive bicycles and U.S. Savings Bonds. Police departments all over the country are playing this game to encourage friendship and trust between young people and law enforcement officers.

TRAFFIC OR HIGHWAY PATROL

Police officers assigned to traffic duty may work on foot directing traffic at an assigned corner. Or they can cruise the streets looking for parking and traffic violators within a given territory. They also may patrol superhighways within their jurisdictions and respond to traffic accident reports. But the majority of highway patrol officers are state police (see chapter 4). Many cities and towns do not have separate highway patrols—the same officers manage all police tasks. Every police officer and traffic patrol officer keeps a log of each shift's activities. When officers make arrests, they must complete all the paperwork related to the criminal suspect. They must be ready to appear in court and testify if the arrest leads to a criminal case.

LINE AND NON-LINE OFFICERS

All police officers on the street are *line* officers, but police departments have *non-line* officers as well. They are just as much police officers as their compatriots who walk the streets or cruise the neighborhoods. Some have desk (support) jobs. These include (in some departments) dispatchers and station house officers. In other departments, civilians handle some of these duties, particularly dispatching and operating 911 emergency systems. Other non-line officers carry out special assignments such as vice squad or dealing with juvenile offenders. Sometimes line officers unable to work the streets carry out non-line responsibilities.

THE POLICE IMAGE

In 1962 (before women were involved in patrol work), Charlotte Epstein, an author and police instructor at the University of Pennsylvania, wrote in her book, *Intergroup Relationships for Police Officers* (Williams and Wilkins): "The [police officer] is repeatedly called upon to deal intelligently with conflict situations, using his judgment, offering his services as arbiter, placating, calming, and comforting disturbed citizens. Although he realizes that he is neither social worker nor psychologist, that he cannot assume the function of physician or minister, he is often forced into situations in which it would be very useful to have some of the concepts and skills developed by these professions."

Although "he" would read "he or she" today, those words are as true now as when they were written more than 35 years ago. While police may not be trained in advanced situation management, nearly all officers, men and women alike, are patient and caring in the face of unexpected, difficult, and often dangerous situations.

High Tech: The Crimefighter's Ally

Modern technology is a crimefighter's best friend. But the latest developments—many based on military technology—are not always available. Cost is the number one reason. A police department may wisely decide to spend its limited funds on bulletproof vests instead of advanced electronic devices.

However, when dollars are available, the technology is at hand to make crimefighting faster and more effective.

Here is a "laundry list" of new devices that patrol officers, detectives, non-line officers, and police-employed civilian technologists can use to fight crime:

- **Mobile Data Terminals**—Straight out of *Terminator 2: Judgment Day*, these MDT laptop computers cost $6,540 each. With an MDT in the car, a police officer can tap into the National Crime Information Center and into their state criminal data banks. Even minimum data entered on a suspect will call up whatever computerized information there might be, including arrest records and outstanding arrest warrants. Data will come up on the officer's computer screen in seconds. The speedy response reduces officers' radioed requests for information, makes police more productive, and improves their safety.

  MDTs have already helped police arrest several major criminals, some with records going back many years.

  A variation on MDTs transmits auto license tag information—including owner, outstanding violations, and whether the car has been reported stolen—in seconds to police officers in pursuing patrol cars.

- **Live-scan system**—This advanced system can help officers in police cars immediately and positively identify suspects they see on the street.

- **Vehicle-mounted video cameras**—These give the police officer a visual and audio record of street apprehensions and arrests. Cameras put date and time on the film. Most courts accept such film as evidence.

- **Infrared technology**—This takes many forms. With infrared glasses (or eyepieces), police can see fleeing subjects even in total darkness. Police can photograph fugitives with infrared cameras, or view them on screens in real time through infrared camera lenses. Officers in helicopters use infrared videography with microwave downlinks to track and show suspects that officers on the ground cannot see.

Fireflies are blinking lights that officers wear during night pursuit with infrared viewing. Only fellow officers can see the lights through infrared lenses, and thus keep track of one another.

- **Computerized fingerprint files**—By imitating human reasoning powers, a program called AFIS (Automated Fingerprint Identification System) can scan over a million recorded fingerprints in minutes. It then delivers a short list of likely matches in answer to a technician's input of a suspect's fingerprints. The technician completes the matchup. If done entirely by hand, the job would take years.

- **Paperwork-shortening computer systems**—These are designed to shorten report generation and filing time for police officers, thus increasing their time on the streets. (One such system is at Los Angeles Police Headquarters.)

- **CAD (Computer-Aided Dispatch)**—A system that tells officers the locations of 911 emergency calls. CAD gives each call a priority (aided by a dispatcher). It then finds the police car nearest the location and describes the problem. CAD is 400 times faster than conventional response and dispatching. It also profiles 911 call-intensive locations. (In one midwestern city, CAD told police that half the 911 calls were coming from 3% of all households.)

- **Computer-generated composite photos**—These are replacing police sketch artists with more detailed images of suspects.

- **Digital enhancers**—These help officers fight crime by adding needed detail such as house addresses and license numbers to photographs.

- **Inkless fingerprinting**—A system that lets police record fingerprints and check them instantly against a fingerprint database.

- **Restraining foam**—An officer can fire this material from a special *goo gun*. It sprays a suspect with a gluey mess that stops their flight. A launch net, first used to subdue animals, works on the same principle. Fired from a launcher, it enmeshes the subject.

- **Rubber ball launchers**—These can be used for crowd control.

- **Personal monitors**—These can tell headquarters exactly where each officer is. Each monitor sends back a picture of what the officer is viewing, from a tiny transmitter he or she is wearing.

- **A tagger**— When fired by police, this electronic transmitter adheres to a fleeing car and constantly signals its location. This is a safe alternative to a high-speed chase.

- **An electronic pulse**—This can disable a fleeing car by zapping its electrical system. The Road Patriot is a rocket-powered device launched from a pursuing patrol car. It runs far faster than the car being pursued, gets underneath, and short-circuits the car's electronics, stopping the engine.

- **Virtual-reality driving simulator**—Uses computer-driven virtual-reality scenes based on filmed events to train highway patrols in performance driving techniques and situation management. Wrong responses to the virtual-reality situations can cause "accidents" (without injuries, of course).

- **"Smart" guns**—These have handgrips that "recognize" only their owners. They will not fire for anyone else—protecting a police officer, and civilians, if someone steals his or her gun.

- **Composite bullets**—These are made of powdered metal. When fired they will penetrate tissue, but will shatter instead of ricocheting if they strike a hard surface. This safety feature protects police and civilians.

- **Robots**—Officers remotely direct these tracked devices.
  A robot has a controllable arm and gripper, loudspeaker, floodlight, video camera/transmitter, and a shotgun. Officers use them to grasp and move suspicious packages, move or explode bombs, and even to pursue fugitives holed-up in buildings—almost any situation that would put an officer in harm's way.
  With or without the advanced technology, the police officers of tomorrow will continue to protect the public in the dedicated traditions of the past.
  Many other law enforcement careers begin at the police officer level. Officers advance to other assignments through capable job performance, favorable evaluations from their superior officers, and high scores in competitive examinations for department openings.

SALARIES

Salaries for beginning police officers vary widely by jurisdiction and section of the country. Those of three departments recruiting new officers in 1997 in a suburban eastern Pennsylvania county can be considered typical for the northeastern United States:

Abington	$32,640
Horsham	$32,640
Upper Merion	$28,010 to $30,344, depending on training.

The maximum salaries for police officers in these departments ranged from $44,980 to $46,683.

FOUR-LEGGED PARTNERS

In many jurisdictions, police officers share their duties with four-legged partners: horses for mounted patrols or specially trained "K-9" dogs. In both partnerships, the animals help control situations more forcefully than the officers could without them.

Horsepower was once the only way for police officers to move with any speed, so virtually every department used horses. Many larger cities still do so, on a limited scale. A few officers on horseback can control crowds far more effectively than many police on foot. The sheer size of a police horse, and the fear their hoofs can engender, are effective deterrents. On the positive side, the horses and their mounted officers often receive friendly response from the public as they go about routine patrol. For the officer with equestrian interest and talent, the mounted patrol offers a rewarding career option.

K-9 dogs are more personal "partners" than horses, since they may live with the officer who patrols with them. These dogs are breeds that the public respects for their size and perceived ferocity. This characteristic is controlled by K-9 trainers and by the partnering officer. A so-called "police dog" is trained to react and respond only to the commands given it by its partner-handler.

Dogs, like horses, aid with crowd control, especially in hostile situations. Unlike horses, however, many K-9 dogs have the ability to sniff out the hiding places of drugs. They can also pursue suspects into cramped areas and intimidate them into staying still until their human partners can bring them out for interrogation or arrest. (Also, see chapter 4, "State Police Careers.")

Police Careers at the County Level

County government falls midway between cities and other local jurisdictions (towns, boroughs, townships), and law enforcement careers at the state level. Some counties operate police departments, but a county sheriff and deputy sheriffs, or sheriff's deputies, carry out the police duties in most areas. (For related county jobs, see section 2.)

The sheriff's duties traditionally include serving the county's courts. The sheriff may operate the county prison system as well, and a sheriff's office must maintain 24-hour prison staffing and security in any prison facilities it operates.

SHERIFF

The sheriff is the commanding officer of many a county's law enforcement arm. Those counties with police departments are operated by chiefs and officers, not sheriffs and deputies. A few counties have both forces, with the sheriff and deputies assigned primarily to court and prison tasks. But most American counties use one force—sheriffs and deputies—as law enforcement officers.

The title of sheriff goes back to early English law (remember the sheriff of Nottingham in *Robin Hood?*). In our country, sheriffs are nearly always elected. A funeral director, hardware store owner, or someone else without a legal or law enforcement background, could run for sheriff and win. A sheriff must be as much an administrator as a law enforcer, so a business background is helpful.

DEPUTY SHERIFF

In the Old West, the sheriff could deputize any law-abiding citizens he needed to help him "make this town safe for decent folks!," but today's deputies are a far cry from the suddenly badged good guys of yore. Increasing numbers need to meet the basic requirements of city and town police officers—physical and mental qualifications, background checks, and formal law enforcement instruction including weapons training. Many, like their city and town police counterparts, operate within a civil service system, with opportunities for advancement within the county's law enforcement structure. (This may include a detective bureau, crime lab, and other specialized offices.)

It's fairly accurate to think of a deputy sheriff as doing the same law enforcement jobs as a city or town police officer. Deputies drive patrol cars (usually alone) and enforce the law, often over far larger chunks of geography than city or town police. They, too, are in touch by radio with the equivalent of a headquarters. Deputies can carry out any law enforcement job from stopping a highway speeder to answering a 911 distress call. Many sheriff's departments serve as law enforcement bodies under financial contract to unincorporated towns or rural areas that do not have police forces. Sheriff's deputies, if called on, can also go into towns or even cities to reinforce local departments, since deputies have full law-enforcement powers.

But deputies do additional jobs that police officers normally do not. When they are part of a county's court system, they often serve in the court house as court bailiffs. They may guard prisoners, help with the security of sequestered jurors in court cases, and secure the court house. As court officers, deputies may do legal tasks such as serving court papers, posting properties designated for Sheriff's Sale, and transporting county prisoners to and from court. Criers, clerks, and other court officers (not all with law enforcement training) are usually part of the county sheriff's department, along with the deputies.

These court-related jobs mean that county sheriffs and their deputies are law enforcement officers and part of the criminal justice system. Since county sheriffs and deputies carry out court duties, they are part of both systems.

"Criminal justice" includes law enforcement and the court system: the local district justice's courtrooms, the county courts, and the federal judiciary, ending with the Supreme Court of the United States. (See section 2.)

In earlier times, sheriffs and their deputies collected a fee for each service they completed or court paper they served. Today, most sheriff's deputies are county employees, with salaries generally competitive with police officers of equal training and experience.

Our suburbs and rural areas are growing as greater numbers of people move away from cities. More businesses are finding that they can operate without a metropolitan infrastructure of harbors, rail yards, and sources of supply. Also, America is increasingly becoming a nation of service industries that can exist wherever qualified employees live. This growth is creating opportunities in small towns and in counties for those interested in becoming deputies. The duties are essentially the same as those of the police officer in a city or large town. Deputies usually have more space to cover, but perhaps with less pressure.

CHAPTER 4

State Police Careers

Forty-nine of America's 50 states operate state police departments. (In Hawaii, county police perform state police duties.)

The Texas Rangers (1835) were the nation's first state-based law enforcement officers. Massachusetts was next, in 1865, and Connecticut had formed a state police department by 1900. Most other states were operating police departments by 1939, mostly for highway law enforcement. The California Highway Patrol is the nation's largest state police force. North Dakota has the smallest state police contingent.

Since the Texas Rangers and other early statewide departments began long before the days of the automobile, their members rode horses. They called their smallest unit a *troop*, the same name used for a U.S. Army cavalry unit. Pennsylvania is one state that still operates a mounted patrol. The 24-member unit is always on the lookout for donated horses that meet certain requirements. They can be ex-race horses or family steeds. The patrol even had one horse left to them in a person's will!

The gift horses must be from 5 to 15 years old. Those that pass a veterinarian's examination undergo rugged training. They learn to build trust with their police officer riders. Since they fear injury, horses avoid unusual surfaces. At the State Police Academy in Hershey, Pennsylvania, they receive confidence training until they can walk fearlessly over mattresses and black plastic. They even go through a discouraging tunnel hung with black plastic ribbons. And their stables are next to the police academy's firing range, so they learn not to be wary of gunfire.

The police horses and their skilled state trooper riders control crowds, often at sporting events and outdoor fairgrounds. Crowds respect the imposing-looking animals. And the troopers can see what is going on over the heads of the crowd.

Although few of today's state police officers ride horses, most are still called *troopers*. Many state police stations are called *barracks*, another military term. And state police officers base their ranks on their army equivalents (captain, major, colonel). In most states, the top-ranking state police officer is a colonel.

STATE POLICE TROOPERS

The state trooper is the beginning rank in the system. Most state police troopers work with car and truck traffic. They patrol state highways and interstates, enforce speed and safety laws, issue citations (tickets) to apparent traffic law violators, take command of accident scenes, and help stranded motorists. They also can operate truck weigh stations, spot-check truck safety, and monitor the transportation of toxic materials. Other duties may include directing traffic at highway construction or accident/emergency sites, investigating auto thefts, and (in Pennsylvania, for example) overseeing the state motor vehicle inspection system. In many states, troopers and higher-ranking state police officers serve as state police academy instructors.

Some states have both state troopers and state highway patrol officers. In such states, the state troopers assume all the duties of a police officer, while the highway patrol officer's duties may be primarily auto-based law enforcement. This can be broadly interpreted, since criminals use cars for almost every type of crime. Police officers performing highway traffic duty must testify in court. If the case is heard in a local court (district justice, magistrate, justice of the peace) where there is no prosecutor as such, the officer must present the case for the state. He or she must testify and question any witnesses.

Most troopers drive specially equipped patrol cars complete with two-way radios and first-aid equipment. A few may be helicopter pilots, or may ride in helicopters to observe and report on traffic to troopers in cars below.

On top of being a skilled driver (or pilot), a state trooper—like any other police officer—must know the proper use of firearms, handcuffs, nightsticks, mobile communications, and computers.

Troopers usually work alone, although they can often be in touch with their radio room or barracks and with other officers. Troopers must think through difficult or troublesome situations. Troopers must make swift, correct decisions. They have full arrest powers. Since they are constantly dealing with the public, they must show they are in charge, yet remain courteous and unruffled.

Most state troopers work eight-hour shifts. These include weekends and holidays. Shifts usually rotate, so a trooper will not always work from 4:00 p.m. to midnight. After a certain time, a trooper switches to the midnight to 8:00 a.m. shift, and later, he or she will work from 8:00 a.m. to 4:00 p.m. (or whatever that state's shift hours may be).

In states with limited county law enforcement (see chapter 3), state troopers are also all-around law enforcement officers. They work with local police or perform all police duties in rural areas without police departments. If ordered by the governor of their state, troopers and highway patrols can quell riots, control crowds, or aid the public and protect property following disasters. They can fight crime in any area of the state and even work in large cities to reinforce local police forces.

The trooper is the equivalent of an army private. Just like a town or city police officer, the trooper can rise through the ranks (trooper first class, corporal, sergeant, lieutenant, etc.). Troopers advance through good job performance, continuing education, commendations from superior officers, and high scores on competitive examinations for each successive rank.

BECOMING A TROOPER

The basics include the ability to pass a rigorous physical examination and an intelligence/aptitude test. All states require United States citizenship. Some require legal residence (usually for a year). A good character (no criminal convictions), good credit, and a good driving record are necessities. So is a high school diploma or GED. An associate degree in law enforcement or police science is an advantage. A four-year degree, earned before enrolling or part-time in the years after police academy graduation, will help the trooper to advance.

Most state police officers must be at least 21 years old when they complete their training, and many states have a maximum starting age of 30.

Training is intensive. Depending on the state, it can take from 12 weeks to six months. It includes instruction in the motor vehicle code, enforcement/arrest procedures, and basics of criminal law. Cadets also train extensively in criminal investigation/evidence management, weapons use, first aid, self-defense, communications skills, courtesy, and advanced driving techniques. They may also ride with and learn from mentor troopers. After graduation, most troopers remain "on probation" in a troop, usually for a year. Then, if they have performed satisfactorily, they become permanent state police officers.

SPECIALTY AND CIVILIAN JOBS

In many states, troopers and higher-ranking state police officers carry out special assignments. These include cargo theft detection (see chapter 20), arson investigation, and anti-narcotics work, often undercover. State police can serve as bodyguards to the governor and as escorts for dignitaries. State police specialists can conduct polygraph examinations, operate crime laboratories, and provide law enforcement services not part of local or county government.

State police departments are joining the high-tech revolution that is affecting most major job areas and improving law enforcement of all kinds. The impact of advanced technology has been overwhelming throughout law enforcement and private security. Crimefighters are alert to cutting-edge technology and are making the most of it. For example, the Pennsylvania State Police are replacing a 1987 computer system with a $6-million mainframe computer to keep records on convicted sex offenders and on gun buyers. The new system will immediately check the background of anyone purchasing a handgun, rifle, or shotgun. It also records and maintains DNA samples of sex offenders in one computer database, while another tracks their whereabouts after they leave prison. The Pennsylvania legislature provided a $1.2-million start-up fund for the computer and authorized 10 additional computer-related state police jobs.

Civilians hold many state police jobs and other administrative posts. In some states, the state police are responsible for motor vehicle licensing and registration. In other states, a department of transportation handles these responsibilities. Either way, jobs may exist within these departments for computer-trained civilians.

In addition, in most states, regulatory departments cover virtually every aspect of life and the law. Regulatory jobs may include wildlife agent (game warden), state park ranger, and areas such as dairy herd inspection, factory safety checks, and regulation of legalized gambling. Regulatory jobs, although not strictly law enforcement in the "police" sense, generally require a similar attention to detail and interest in enforcement and compliance that motivates the state trooper or other police officer.

State Police Opportunities

These depend largely on individual state budgets. Recent emphasis by the federal government on state and local law enforcement—and the funding to hire more officers—has improved the job outlook for state police candidates as well as local officers. However, state police examinations are very competitive, and in most states, there are more candidates than state police academy openings.

But if you join the ranks and successfully complete your state police training and probation, you can expect a career that is challenging and varied. The financial rewards are not spectacular—salaries for Pennsylvania state troopers, as one example, range from about $23,000 to $35,000—but there are long-term advantages. State troopers have job security, periodic pay raises, good benefits, advancement opportunities, community respect, and retirement pensions.

CHAPTER 5

Police Detectives and Private Investigators

Both these careers have many variations. Police detectives investigate crimes, prepare reports, and testify in court. They work for police departments in cities, larger towns and suburban townships, and at the county level. (Some state police forces also have detective divisions.)

Although private detectives (investigators) share many characteristics with police detectives, they are either self-employed or work for security companies. They sometimes cooperate with police detectives, but private investigators (PIs) usually work independently. (A private detective hired by a family to track down someone who has disappeared may share discoveries with the police detectives on the case.)

Private detectives may gather information for companies coping with theft or fraud. They also may work as fact finders for insurance firms, attorneys, or parties to a divorce. Private investigators often work undercover. Since they are part of private security (see chapter 18), private detectives/investigators can only probe for information; they cannot enforce the law. Both kinds of detectives wear plain clothes, not uniforms.

Background investigators use computers to run their independent businesses or franchises. Bounty hunters (bail enforcement agents) also earn by-the-job—but for capturing fugitives, not checking histories.

HOW POLICE DETECTIVES GET THEIR JOBS

Most police detectives begin their careers as uniformed police officers, generally with one to five years of experience. Police officers do not qualify for promotion to detective any more than they automatically advance to corporal or sergeant. They must apply for the job and pass proficiency tests.

The uniformed officer's regular performance reviews should reflect the motivation, education, and organizational and communications skills needed for detective work. Future detectives should show disciplined self-management because they will often work with little supervision.

Police detective positions come about through retirements, promotions within a department's detective division, and department expansions. There are usually more applicants than openings. In most departments, the would-be detective needs to pass a written test. The detective candidate should study hard for the detailed written civil service tests.

He or she must also sit for a review board interview conducted by detectives and other superior officers. In smaller departments, those who review detective candidates may know their potential capabilities by having worked with them. In larger departments, few if any members of the detective division will know all the police officers who take the tests for detective.

The review board rates the candidate's answers to penetrating questions. These let the candidate show verbal skills (especially important during court testimony and cross-examination). Questioners probe the prospect's motivation and abilities. The review board tries to determine how well a detective candidate will react to job stresses—the review is highly stressful, but some candidates' experience as uniformed officers helps them hide exam jitters well.

CHARACTERISTICS, PROBATION, ADVANCEMENT

In *Police Procedural* (Writer's Digest Books, 1993), Russell Bintliff has written that a good detective should be:

- Observant
- Skilled at report writing
- Able to make arrests without the stature of a uniform
- Aware of the usefulness and importance of the job
- Able to talk to and gain confidence of strangers quickly
- Confident in professional abilities
- Keenly interested in investigation; curious; inquisitive
- Able to work unsupervised
- Open-minded; able to avoid rushing to judgment
- Patient enough to cope with myriad details, lengthy reports, complex court proceedings
- Logical yet imaginative in analyzing crime situations
- Above average in intelligence, memory/recall
- Impartial; beyond bribery/corruption
- Knowledgeable of arrest procedures and court proceedings
- Inconspicuous; physically average in appearance

New candidates usually team with experienced detectives during several months' probation (the length varies by department). During this time, fledgling detectives also may attend police academy or college classes, or receive instruction in department-led classes. If the candidate does well during probation, he or she earns the title of detective.

Despite good written test scores and review board approval, not all probationary detectives adapt well to the demands of the job. Those who do not make it usually return to their former police officer duties at their previous rank and pay.

Detectives can advance within their specialty to titles such as detective first class, detective sergeant, or detective lieutenant. Those with exceptional administrative, management, and interpersonal skills may eventually be promoted to head of a detective division or chief of detectives of a police department.

PHILIP HOWE

For 25 years, Philip A. Howe was a patrolman and later, a detective, for the Haverford Township, Pennsylvania, police department. A township resident whose family was well-known locally (his father worked for the township), Howe could not attend college because he "became head of the family" after his father's early death. (Howe had barely graduated from high school.) But he passed all his police tests and joined the force a few years later. His continuing departmental education has included courses in some 20 subjects, from firearms proficiency and SWAT (Special Weapons and Tactics) team techniques to alcohol abuse management and community relations.

Philip Howe (retired) dons his Haverford Township police uniform for this family picture with his stepson, Mark Boggs, a campus police officer at West Chester University.

(Photo: Sandy Howe)

Not surprisingly, he received scores of commendations during his police career because Howe is a man of principle and courage. He also approaches life with rare good humor and loves to relate stories of his career. He has solved murders and burglaries, and managed confrontational situations with calmness and common sense. He has been wounded and hospitalized in the line of duty. He has also performed the less heroic duties (such as retrieving stolen bicycles for grateful youngsters!) with equal fairness and professionalism.

Like many police officers, Howe comes from a law enforcement family. His brother, William, is a retired California police officer who attended the FBI Academy at Quantico, Virginia, and was a college campus police chief and Air Force Reserve lieutenant colonel. His late brother, Roy, was a

Philadelphia police officer. And Philip Howe's children are following in the tradition. His oldest son, Todd, teaches criminal justice at Pennsylvania's Lincoln University.

Howe's wife, Sandy, is also part of a police family. Her father was a police officer. Her son (Philip Howe's stepson), Mark Boggs, is a campus police officer at West Chester University of Pennsylvania. Her daughter, Crystal, is both a criminal justice major and a member of the campus security force at the same college. Another of her sons is a prison security officer. To bring the story full circle, Detective Howe's son-in-law expects to join the Haverford Township police force. If he does, he will be only the fourth black officer in the department—Philip Howe was the first.

Detective Howe's "retirement" is anything but relaxation and reminiscence. He is the full-time protector of a well-known American philanthropist—a job that puts all his policing skills to work in a far different but equally exciting environment.

POLICE DETECTIVE DUTIES

Most police detectives work eight-hour shifts. In theory, they keep regular hours, but in fact they often work heavy overtime (sometimes with overtime pay—the primary reason many seek the jobs) when deeply involved in a case. Detectives working in smaller departments may be generalists. They investigate every type of crime. They can be called at any hour. They help prepare every case for prosecution. This is a less efficient way of managing than any of the systems used in larger police departments, but it is often more rewarding in terms of accomplishment.

A city department's detective force may operate by geographic location, by time of day/night (shift), or—usually —by types of crime. Detecting by location or by shift is often as inefficient as operating a small, general detective department.

When a detective department assigns cases by type, the detectives who pursue those cases become specialists in that kind of crime. The more examples of a given crime a detective handles, the better he or she becomes at recognizing similar crime patterns.

Detective divisions operated by specialists fight *people* crimes, *property* crimes, and general and specialized crimes. People commit people crimes against each other, or against themselves. Examples: assault, robbery, extortion ("shakedown"), murder, and sex-related crimes. Although not a crime as such, detectives may investigate natural deaths that at first appear suspicious. The aptly named homicide division also investigates suicides.

Property detectives pursue an alphabetical list of crimes related to goods or property. Such crimes can include auto theft, burglary, credit card theft, receiving stolen goods, robbery, shoplifting, vandalism, and writing worthless checks.

Detectives in general and special divisions deal with all other crimes. General assignments include every crime not falling into the person or property categories. Examples: accidental injury and animal bites or misconduct. Other general crimes include disorderly conduct, drunkenness, and traffic-related offenses. In street slang, detectives of the "bunco squad" pursue criminals who operate confidence ("con") games, embezzlements, and swindles.

A large department also may have separate juvenile and drugs/narcotics squads or divisions if there are many crimes of these types in the community. The detectives assigned to these units or squads often receive specialized training and also learn on the job.

How Police Detectives Work

Since they are already on the street, uniformed police officers are usually first on a crime scene. They secure the area to keep people from disturbing evidence. They conduct a preliminary investigation that includes questioning suspects and witnesses and writing as complete a report of events as possible. Detectives generally arrive at the scene after it has been secured.

The police officers and detectives can examine the crime scene without a search warrant; there are, however, some exceptions. They may seize evidence and make an arrest for evidence found "in plain view" in a vehicle, house, office, or street, if the view is from a vantage point they can legally use. (They need a search warrant or *probable cause* to conduct any search that goes beyond plain view. The exceptions to needing a search warrant are those incidental to an arrest, with permission (consent) of the person, including a "pat-down" or vehicle search for weapons that could endanger the officer's or detective's safety. Another exception is when police believe evidence can be destroyed, removed, or damaged if a search is delayed as officers wait for a warrant.

Police officers and detectives can arrest anyone if they have probable cause (this is when they can articulate facts that would lead another person viewing the same circumstances to conclude that a suspect has committed a crime).

Once detectives arrive at the crime scene, they work with uniformed officers to move the investigation forward. According to Jon E. Clark, head of the Department of Criminal Justice at Temple University, this means (1) recognizing those items that constitute evidence, (2) photographing the scene and the evidence, and (3) sketching the crime scene. Depending on their training and the presence of department specialists (see page 36), the on-scene detectives may use evidence-gathering kits. Or crime photographers and other specialists may arrive in a mobile crime lab containing everything needed. In *Police Procedural*, Russell Bintliff identified these kits used by detectives or specialists:

- **General evidence kit**—contains plastic bags, tweezers, scissors, and other items used to pick up and preserve most physical evidence.

- **Photographic kit**—35mm day/date imprint camera, Polaroid color camera, video camera (in some departments).

- **Fingerprint kit**—everything for securing and recording fingerprints. (There is also a postmortem fingerprint kit, used for retrieving prints from bodies.)

- **Cast/mold/impression kit**—for making casts of footprints, tire tracks, and other possibly crime-related impressions.

- **Document kit**—materials to protect papers, letters, notes, and other documents and preserve them as found.

- **Sex offense kit**—for preserving evidence of alleged sexual assault or related crimes.

- **Arson/explosives kit**—tools and containers needed to store what Bintliff called "the often charred and fragile evidence" at a fire or explosion scene.

Detectives and specialists use these evidence-gathering and protective materials plus their work experience to help assure proper collection techniques and to establish and maintain what Jon Clark calls the "chain of custody"—being able to document the source, whereabouts, and safekeeping of evidence until it gets to court.

The detective has more to do than gather evidence and interview witnesses, victims, family members, neighbors, and others affected by the crime. He or she has to review and add to the reports written by crime scene police officers. Later, the detective must draft a detailed crime report. As the case grows, he or she adds new information. Again with probable cause, the detective can ask a judge to issue a search warrant based on the belief that there may be certain evidence hidden in a particular place. The detective can serve the warrant, enter the property, and search for the evidence named in the warrant. Speed is essential in securing and serving search warrants. Criminal suspects are likely to remove the evidence if police waste time in getting the warrant and searching the scene.

At this point in any crime, the real work begins. It may be what Jon Clark of Temple University called "a slam dunk"—a simple case with obvious results. Or it could become a baffler in which the items of evidence point nowhere. Detectives, often in teams, evaluate the evidence and try to build a case leading to an arrest and, later, to a successful criminal trial. They will receive the evidence reports from specialists who have extracted every crumb of information from crime scene clues. The detectives may have to search public records and criminal histories, interview or re-interview witnesses or suspects, or speak with informants to whom they may pay cash for information. Once they narrow the search for suspects, they can ask witnesses to identify possible crime participants. Police can show *mug shots* (pictures) of those with criminal records, or ask witnesses to select from a *lineup* in which one or two suspects stand among nonsuspects (lawyers, social workers, plainclothes officers). The hope is that witnesses can identify the suspects. Police take great care to ensure that a lineup is an identification—not a selection—process.

Technology is coming increasingly to the rescue. For example, the *Montgomery County Record* newspaper reported how Detective Lieutenant John Durante of Montgomery County (Pennsylvania) Detectives uses one of the state's three Automated Fingerprint Identification Systems (AFIS) to identify any suspect whose prints he receives. Identification takes place in minutes if those prints are on file with the state. AFIS just needs a single print—not a set of 10. The 1996 newspaper article described how Lieutenant Durante's work nailed a robber who left a soda bottle at the crime scene. The bottle held one latent fingerprint. Lieutenant Durante put the print through AFIS and identified a suspect. When arrested and questioned, the thief admitted to 12 other robberies.

Montgomery County District Attorney Michael D. Marino called AFIS an entirely new capability for law enforcement. Authorities can identify a suspect from one print, something they could not do without AFIS. "Prior to this machine, we had to develop a suspect, get his 10 [finger]prints, and then identify him," Marino said.

Things do not always go this easily. Detectives working on a case may have to ask the help of departments in other cities, or nationwide. In certain cases, detectives must bring in the FBI. For example, bank robbery is a federal offense; so is kidnapping, if the kidnappers have crossed state lines.

Although emotional detachment is part of the police detective profile, detectives may become attached to an apparently unsolvable case. This is especially true of a crime involving a child. Some detectives have continued their investigations for years after officials have closed the files on such cases. And in every investigation, fresh or old, perseverance is the hallmark of the professional police detective.

If an investigation leads to an arrest on criminal charges (which does not always happen), the detectives involved must help prepare the case for criminal prosecution. In doing so, they review the evidence with the prosecuting attorney (or district attorney) who will present the case in court. Detectives and prosecutors make the case as airtight as possible. In America, every alleged criminal defendant is presumed innocent until proven guilty. Thus "the people" (the prosecution) need to prove the culpability of the accused person "beyond a reasonable doubt." (If a person of reasonable judgment is not convinced that the defendant is guilty as charged, then the defendant goes free.)

The detectives' case notes and testimony on the witness stand are keys to convicting an alleged criminal. Of all who testify in a criminal prosecution, the detective's testimony is often the most important. He or she may know more about the supposed crime than anyone else. The detective's presentation and testimony often win or lose the case. And the detective has a strong opponent in the defense attorney.

The defense attorney is a lawyer who has either been retained by the defendant in a criminal trial, or who has been assigned by the court to defend an alleged criminal who cannot afford a private attorney. In this instance, the lawyer serves as a public defender, and is normally compensated by the state for his or her legal services. (For more about public defenders, see chapter 11.) It is the defense attorney's job to create doubt about the prosecution's case in the eyes of a jury (or the judge in a bench trial). A big part of creating this doubt is to make prosecution witnesses appear uncertain of their facts. The detective—often the chief witness—must remain calm, unwavering, forthcoming, and truthful in the face of what may be tricky cross-examination conducted by an expert in verbal attack. It's all part of the job!

The courtroom can become "theater" when both the detective and the prosecuting attorney come face-to-face with the defense attorney. In crimes-of-the-century such as the O. J. Simpson murder trial, these fine minds are like actors on stage. The jury is the participating audience. But in the majority of criminal cases, theatrics don't happen. These cases are plea-bargained, with prosecution and defense working out the results together. "Events" such as the Menendez and Simpson trials are relatively rare.

State and county detectives can receive strange assignments that go with their territories. In New Jersey, some unusual jobs are opening up for law enforcement officers in Atlantic City's casinos. To stop skilled gamblers from bilking the casinos of big bucks, Garden State detectives and police learn to cheat so they can catch cheaters! The Casino Careers Institute of Atlantic City Community College offers a course in gambling trickery. It teaches undercover police and casino employees the ways gamblers cheat and how to spot them in the act.

THE CRIME LABORATORY (FORENSIC SCIENCES)

"Civilian" forensic scientists and technicians operate police department crime laboratories. They help detectives make arrests and prepare court cases by recovering, preserving, and evaluating the evidence in each criminal investigation. Whether technicians or detectives gather the evidence at the crime scene, the crime lab staff will eventually process every item. They will reach specific conclusions about each piece of evidence.

Most departments operate crime labs with "sections" or "units." These are related careers. Experts deal with:

- **Fingerprints**—Members of this unit lift or photograph fingerprints at the crime scene. They identify the people who left the prints. They do this by comparing them with prints of people involved (family, visitors, strangers). The unit members also may search fingerprint files manually or by computer to match the prints with any on record. They identify footprints and palm prints, and, if necessary, identify deceased persons by fingerprints.

- **Photography**—Members of this unit provide photographic services to the department. These include taking crime scene photographs and videos (even aerial photographs) and supplying photo equipment to detectives for their use. Unit members develop and print all photos, maintain photo files, and make photocopies of sketches and drawings. In some departments, the photo unit artists make composite sketches of suspects from witness's descriptions. Photo unit members with computer expertise and hardware can computer-enhance photos for detail and prepare "wanted" composites. Some specialists make computer-imaged pictures of how children missing for years could look today.

Large departments, such as the Los Angeles Police Department (LAPD), have crime scene photographers whose job it is to visually document every item at a crime scene. As Jeff Wong wrote for the Associated Press, "They [photographers] jump from one crime scene to another, camera in hand. They see more criminal violence up close than anyone—except perhaps the county coroner. The work can be grueling, monotonous, funny and sickening all in the same day." In the LAPD unit, there are 24 civilian staff photographers. Their unit processes about 3,000 rolls of film a month. Remaining impersonal or professionally detached from their often gruesome duties is not always an option; crime photographers often burn out or elect other duties.

- **Forensics**—(Also known as the crime lab or scientific investigating unit.) Most crime labs employ these specialists:

  - Biologists or forensic pathologists—Specialists in evaluating human tissue. Their work includes blood typing, electrophoretic analysis, and bloodstain pattern analysis. They also analyze bodily fluids and hair and make comparisons among samples related to a case.

  - Criminalists—Specialists in chemical analysis of organic and inert materials. They analyze flammables or accelerants in arson cases and identify the content of fibers, poisons, paint scrapings, and metals among many materials. (A criminalist can often learn the make and year of the vehicle involved in a criminal case from a small piece of its metal or a chip of paint.)

  - Document specialists—These professionals analyze written materials related to crimes. They can restore missing or erased segments, determine document age, and make other discoveries that can turn papers into useful evidence.

  - Ballistics (firearms)—These experts investigate all aspects of criminal firearms use. They can often identify the weapons used in a crime from shell cases or bullets. They interpret all gun-related evidence. They work on identifications with gun and ammunition manufacturers and cooperate with other police departments' gun-related crime investigations.

  - Drug analysis—Members of this unit analyze drug samples for their content.

  - Polygraph—Members of this unit administer polygraph (lie-detector) tests. They need to know human psychology so they can phrase questions and understand the second-by-second readings produced by the polygraph equipment. The operator interprets these "blips" to determine how true or untrue the tested person's answers are. Crime laboratory staffers need the same abilities to testify in court cases as detectives and police officers. They must prepare evidence reports completely, accurately, and clearly. They must be ready to interpret and defend their findings at trial.

You need English and communications courses to enter this field. Accurate and complete report writing is a key element. A bachelor of science degree in biology, chemistry, or physics with courses in related natural or physical sciences is a virtual necessity. Many crime lab careerists serve internships as part of their college training. Others follow their academic courses with on-the-job training.

Career opportunities in all branches of forensic science are excellent. The field needs more than 200 additional staffers each year. Salaries range from $25,000 to over $35,000 for those with the required education. Salaries will increase with time on the job.

PRIVATE INVESTIGATOR

The private investigator (PI or private detective) is anything but the trench-coated tough guy portrayed on TV. Private investigators can be of either sex, and almost any age. They can be physically fit or deceptively plump. (They come in all sizes!) As we mentioned, they work either for security firms or detective agencies as employees, or operate freelance (often one-person) agencies.

Private investigators should have the attributes of police officers and detectives: patience, attention to detail, deductive capabilities, and communications skills. As for qualifications, many police officers and detectives who have retired on pensions go back to work as PIs. Others go to work for a detective agency or security firm after taking law enforcement college courses. (A degree is helpful but not mandatory.) Rarely do private investigators launch detective agencies without several years' experience working for others.

In most states, investigators must pass a background check and be licensed. Those carrying guns or working with dogs may need additional certification.

Most of their work is unglamorous, tedious information gathering. This can include a *stakeout*, where the investigator spends hours lurking in a parked car, watching for a supposedly disabled accident victim to appear, and then secretly videotaping him hopping out of his wheelchair and hiking briskly to the supermarket! It can include finding and interviewing witnesses to a bus crash.

In the first case, the PI might be employed by the insurance company being sued for injuries by the supposed accident victim. Besides staking out the alleged victim, the investigator probably would search public records for background information about that person's character and past activities.

In the second instance, the investigator might be hired to gather evidence for a lawyer defending the bus driver against charges of speeding. In his investigation, the PI would look for pedestrians who might have seen the bus in motion before the accident and would testify that it was not speeding. He or she might interview passengers who had been riding in comfort on the bus, unaware of its speed. Or the investigator could just as easily be on the other side of the case, working for the personal injury lawyer representing someone hurt in the bus crash.

Corporations often hire particularly skilled private investigators to pose as employees or otherwise to work undercover. To make the cover complete, they may earn a regular paycheck in addition to their detecting fees.

Their job is to find those within (or outside) the company who are stealing. The theft can be real property (such as inventory) or intellectual property (the ideas stored on computer disks). Syndicated columnist Jack Anderson wrote that a group of computer company CEOs estimated financial losses from computer theft alone would reach $80 billion by the year 2000. (See section 5, "Cyberspace Crime" for more information.)

Private detectives often work on missing persons cases. Their clients are victims' families who do not think the police are making progress. (In any case related to law enforcement or the courts, private investigators share information they receive with police.)

Major PI jobs are in the emotional and financial areas of a divorce case or settlement. The investigator may be hired by one spouse (or his or her attorney) to learn what the other is really doing, and with whom. Or the investigation may be financial with one spouse trying to learn if assets that should be shared are being siphoned off or hidden. Child custody cases are another area of private investigation.

Private detectives also work for hotels and resorts to protect guests, control and investigate thefts, and reduce employee-generated losses.

The private detective reports regularly on the case to his or her client. These reports can range from short phone messages to detailed activities reports covering every minute of a lengthy case. They can include reports by outside experts that might be needed to complete an investigation. (The PI usually hires and pays them. Or their bills may be sent to the detective's client.)

Private investigators charge fees by the case or for a per-hour rate, plus expenses. Hourly rates can range from a low of $25 to over $150, depending on the complexity of the case and the value of the information. Chronicle Guidance Publications has written that an investigator might be paid $1,000 for a few minutes of work. The fee would be justified if securing the information depended on the PI using sources developed over many years or if the sources and the PI ran risks when getting the facts.

Private detectives working for agencies earn salaries or work by the hour. Hourly rates are comparable to private security personnel of equal experience. (See chapter 18.)

Private investigation does not have the budget limits usually imposed on police departments. Private security is growing faster than law enforcement (12 percent a year versus 7 percent), according to *Private Security Trends, 1970–2000, Hallcrest Report II* (Butterworth-Heinemann, 1990). Thus, jobs for trained PIs will be plentiful in the future.

BACKGROUND INVESTIGATOR

This is a new, growing field. Companies such as Personal Profile and National Information Company (NIC) conduct background checks. They are part of a new investigative breed—those who run personal checks on job seekers, prospective tenants, supposedly qualified educators, and even potential boyfriends and girl-friends. (Someone renting or sharing a house does not want to learn that her friendly, outgoing renter deals in drugs!) And companies need background checks because they are legally responsible for their employees' actions.

Personal Profile charges about $150 to check a person's criminal record (if any), education, employment history, driving/accident record, and credit standing. (The American Civil Liberties Union has said that such checks are legal if they are not conducted by the federal government.)

NIC franchises entrepreneur investigators such as Joseph and Cindy Stratton. This Feasterville, Pennsylvania, couple play computerized detective for a living. Through their company, InfoCheck, Inc., the Strattons can tap into NIC's data banks and retrieve information for their clients. NIC franchisees can computer-check a person's background much more easily than they could by searching records themselves.

The Strattons can check almost any personal data that is a matter of public record. The truths they unearth can range from the accident history of a would-be interstate bus driver to the poor credit rating of a prospective financial officer. Companies like Personal Profile and InfoCheck are making it harder for those with shady pasts to fool all of the people all of the time.

Background investigators need computer skills more than law enforcement experience. They also need the perseverance of anyone operating a franchise or small business. Earnings depend on the success of advertising and promotion, repeat customers and referrals, and the amount of time devoted to selling the ser-vice and operating the business.

BAIL ENFORCEMENT AGENT (BOUNTY HUNTER)

This statement appears at the start of the TV show, *American Bounty Hunter*:

> *Bounty hunters are civilians empowered by the Supreme Court to arrest defendants who have skipped bail or had bail revoked. They may cross state lines and use whatever force necessary to make an arrest.*

The bounty hunter is officially a bail enforcement agent or fugitive recovery officer. Sometimes called a "skip tracer," the bounty hunter has a colorful history. Such Western lawmen as Wyatt Earp and Bat Masterson were bounty hunters. Today, this career is an anomaly—neither criminal justice nor law enforcement, but important nevertheless.

Bail bondsmen hire bounty hunters. A bondsman posts bail for someone charged with a crime. The bondsman puts up as much as 90 percent of the bail—the fee assessed to ensure appearance in court. The suspect produces the other 10 percent. (A wary bondsman can put up a far smaller percentage if he or she believes the suspect might not appear in court.) With bail posted, the suspect can stay out of jail until trial.

If the suspect fails to appear in court, the bondsman can hire a bounty hunter to find and arrest the "skip." Bounty hunters receive their expenses plus a percentage of the bond amount as a fee—but only if they protect the bail bondsman's investment by delivering the fugitive. Speaking on American Bounty Hunter, Alan Jacobs, a Greensboro, North Carolina, bounty hunter, said, "We are the only part of the criminal justice system that costs the taxpayer nothing."

Bounty hunters are not law enforcement officers since they are not enforcing laws or seeking justice, but are protecting the bondsman's financial investment. Nevertheless, they have the power to arrest, which most private detectives do not. They can work alone or ask for (and receive) law enforcement backup. On TV, Alan Jacobs voiced the credo of the profession: "If you fail to appear in court, we will find you." (Some bounty hunters wear sweatshirts reading, "You can run but you can't hide.")

Bounty hunting calls for many skills. Dennis Kieran, a Las Vegas, Nevada, bounty hunter, attributed part of his success to being "a good con artist." (On the TV show, he located one fugitive by making repeated phone calls to where the suspect was expected, pretending to be someone setting up a deal.) Other skills in this dangerous occupation include patience, knowledge of appropriate use of force, courage, and especially, surprise.

A bounty hunter uses a fugitive's description, criminal record, photos, and copies of the arrest warrant to trail him or her. They may follow a suspect for days and weeks, asking questions, tracking down tips, and going wherever the trail leads. They can stalk a fugitive to find out exactly when he or she may be in a certain place. They can use "con" skills and subterfuge—whatever it takes to learn where the fugitive is, or will be. The bounty hunter and support team must be 100 percent sure of where the fugitive is before they can enter the property, surprise the suspect, and make the arrest. (The bounty hunter must be licensed to carry a weapon; not all do so.)

There are moves underway to create new legislation governing this career following a tragic case in 1997 when one-time bounty hunters turned to burglary. Posing as the bounty hunters they once had been, they broke into an apartment, tied up everyone inside, then killed the occupant during a gunfight. The burglars at first claimed to have been legitimate bail enforcement officers who had accidentally broken into the wrong apartment to apprehend a bail jumper.

Bob Burton is a true bounty hunter who lives in—of all places—Tombstone, Arizona, site of the famous 1881 shoot-out at the OK Corral. Tombstone is a fitting setting for a man whose missions range from run-of-the-mill captures to near-death encounters. Bob Burton, the bounty hunter, is also Bob Burton, the teacher of prospective bounty hunters. The detective-gunman lives up a dirt road not far from town. A sign in a window of his house reads, "If you come through that door, you'll be killed." Not so. He is more hospitable than that, but his job is deadly serious.

When not arresting bail jumpers, Burton teaches future bounty hunters the facets of bounty work. His pupils range from construction workers to those on assembly lines—people who want to put some drama into their lives.

As for his own work, "I have a touch of Robin Williams and a big chunk of John Wayne or Clint Eastwood. . . ." He described his mission matter-of-factly: "It's exciting, profitable, and you get to travel." (Yes—right into a lair of 10 armed men who don't plan to let the bail jumper go!)

Burton can claim a mind-boggling 3,400 bounty arrests. He described a typical one: "Maybe the guy's gone into a restaurant with his buddies. I have to wait until he's alone for my own protection. I'll park across the street, watch until he leaves his friends, then arrest him."

As for something more challenging, Burton said, "Fugitives often flee across the border to Mexico and I have to follow them. Now that's exciting!"

Law enforcement is seldom dull. Bob Burton described his life amusingly. "You get to meet strange and interesting people—and arrest them."

CHAPTER 6

Federal Careers: Capitol Police, U.S. Marshals, and Secret Service

The Capitol Police, U.S. Marshals Service, and the Secret Service are three of the more than 100 federal agencies, bureaus, and departments that offer careers in various forms of law enforcement or criminal justice. These three are good examples of the variety and opportunity to be found in federal service. We profile those federal careers related to drug enforcement in chapter 8 and devote chapter 10 to the FBI. For a complete picture of those we lack the space to describe, the authors recommend another ARCO book, *Federal Careers in Law Enforcement* by John W. Warner Jr. (ARCO, 1992).

FEDERAL PAY AND BENEFITS

According to *Federal Law Enforcement Careers—1996 Employment Guide* (CFCB Jobs, Brunswick, Georgia), most Federal law enforcement careers pay on a General Schedule (GS). GS grades range from 1 ($12,895) to 15 ($72,162). GS figures for each grade quoted in this book are RUS (Rest of Us) salaries. They are the lowest for any GS grade and apply to the federal workers who live in sections of the country with low cost of living indexes. GS salaries at any grade may be up to 30 percent higher in those areas where it costs more to live.

Most law enforcement careerists begin at either GS-5 ($19,869 minimum) or GS-7 ($24,610 minimum) depending on experience, education, and evaluation by the Office of Personnel Management and the federal law enforcement agency doing the hiring. Law enforcement promotions usually occur yearly and move the officer or agent two grades; that is, from GS-5 to GS-7, or if hired as a GS-7, to GS-9 ($30,106). There are also "step" promotions within each GS grade. Those not promoted to the next scheduled grade in a year automatically advance one step in their existing grade. (Example: a GS-7 step 1 pays $24,610; a GS-7 step 2 pays $25,431.) There is also a Merit Promotion System with rules too complex to state here. Merit promotions are based on the results of competitive examinations.

Federal law enforcement jobs include benefits such as paid overtime, annual leave (vacation), federal holidays, sick leave, life and health insurance, and a retirement plan. Federal law enforcement people may retire at age 50 if they have worked for 20 years or more. They must retire at age 57.

CAPITOL POLICE

There is an unusual police unit based in our nation's capitol. The U.S. Capitol police force protects the Capitol complex—the Capitol, House of Representatives and Senate office buildings, and the Capitol grounds.

Within its jurisdiction, this federal agency has every law enforcement power. Its officers also protect members of Congress and their staffs wherever they travel.

But the force works primarily in Washington, D.C. It includes several units, each doing interesting work. The uniformed and plainclothes officers of the Gallery Security Section keep order in the visitor's galleries of the House and Senate. They have the enforcement capability to eject or arrest those who would disrupt lawmakers' proceedings. (Protesters in the Senate galleries can be charged with disrupting Congress. Conviction entails a $500 fine and up to six months' prison time.)

The Capitol, House, Senate, and Patrol divisions patrol buildings within the 250-acre complex and on the surrounding streets. Plainclothes officers and others using unmarked cars go undercover to prevent and fight street crime.

If there is a hostage-taking or a barricade situation, the CERT (Containment and Emergency Response Team) swings into action. Its Hostage Negotiations Unit uses solid law enforcement strategies and tactics to resolve any impasse.

Other Capitol police specialists are in the K-9 Explosives Detection Section with its bomb-sniffing dogs, and its relative, the Hazardous Devices Unit. There is a First Responder Unit for exterior building security and a Civil Disobedience Unit for crowd management. Also, detectives in the Threat Assessment Unit join with the FBI to investigate any threat received by a member of Congress. The Electronic Countermeasures Division controls unauthorized electronic snooping in congressional offices. Other detectives work in the Criminal Investigation Division. The Intelligence Division monitors data on subversive groups, civil disobedience, and criminal activity within the Capitol complex. Members of the Special Events Division coordinate Capitol-related activities including protecting distinguished visitors and policing concerts, demonstrations, etc.

The health and background requirements are similar to those of others entering law enforcement. They include being age 21 to 40, passing a written test, interview, medical and psychological examinations, background check, and polygraph examination. An applicant must have a high school diploma or GED equivalent. A recruit becomes a Capitol police officer after successfully completing 20 weeks of concentrated training. Starting salary (on its own pay scale, not GS grades) is $28,886, rising to $31,010 when all training requirements have been completed successfully.

President John Quincy Adams founded the Capitol Police in 1828. He could not possibly foresee the many jobs today's Capitol Police have to do!

For information, write:

Recruiting, U.S. Capitol Police
119 D St., NW, Room 601-P,
Washington, DC 20510

U.S. MARSHAL

Thirty-nine years before President Adams founded the Capitol Police, the first United States marshals rode across the then-small United States, supporting the rulings of the federal courts. The Marshals Service and the federal judiciary date from 1789 and were established by George Washington. The marshals are the oldest federal law enforcement agency. In those days, horseback-riding marshals and their hired deputies served court papers, made arrests, executed court orders, and managed federal prisoners. Until 1880, federal marshals conducted the U.S. population census. Marshals, previously political appointees and often very independent law enforcers, became a federal agency only in 1969. U.S. marshals are still presidential appointees, but their deputies are trained in their own academy.

Except for census-taking, today's marshals and deputies perform the duties they always have, plus many not even imaginable 200 years ago. Today's marshals and deputies provide security in all federal courts. They also protect members of the federal judiciary, except for the Supreme Court, which has its own police force. Marshals apprehend escaped federal prisoners, supervise those arrested (some 13,000 in an average day!), and determine which federal fugitives should be among the "15 most wanted." They travel to retrieve federal prison escapees apprehended in other countries and arrest those wanted in other nations who have entered the United States. The Marshals Service transports all federal fugitives. (Its airline fleet serves 33 cities.) This is the service that operates the federal witness protection program, providing new identities and fresh starts in life to certain people (some involved in crime) who have testified against others in federal trials.

The Marshals Service manages all assets—from cars to houses, boats, and almost anything of value—seized in federal prosecutions. These include drug-related assets, often acquired with cash that has been "laundered," or processed to conceal its illegal origins. Marshals cooperate with other law enforcement agencies in a variety of activities.

There are three levels of training for marshals. Basic training lasts for 14 weeks and covers all aspects of their work. Deputy marshals must complete a four-week advanced course in which they study assets seizure, witness and court security, and other needed subjects. Deputies can also attend two-week specialty courses. The Service offers intensive training in special operations for those who qualify.

The requirements for deputy U.S. marshal are similar to those of other federal law enforcement careers. Deputies must be American citizens, aged 21 to 35, able to pass written tests, an interview, and a background check. They must be in excellent physical health and have a bachelor's (four-year) degree, or three years of "responsible" experience (preferably law enforcement related), or an equal period of work experience and academic training. Beginning deputy marshals earn $19,869 (GS-5) or $24,610 (GS-7) depending on their experience level when hired. Deputy marshals can rise to GS-12 ($43,658). They receive the 13 days paid sick leave, 10 federal holidays, paid vacations, and retirement pensions earned by most federal employees.

For more information, write:

U.S. Marshals Service
600 Army-Navy Dr.
Arlington, VA 22202

SECRET SERVICE

Until 1863, United States currency was printed by each state—and no two states' bills looked the same. That year, the government replaced the welter of state-issued bills with federal "greenbacks." Although the Constitution specified punishment for anyone counterfeiting government money, there was no agency to enforce any threat. (And there was plenty of counterfeiting!) The Secret Service was formed in 1865 as a division of the U.S. Treasury. Its purpose was—and is—to catch counterfeiters.

President Abraham Lincoln authorized the creation of the Secret Service on what turned out to be his last day in office, April 14, 1865—he was assassinated that evening. President Lincoln did not envision the new government department as the source of presidential protection it later became. At Ford's Theater that fateful night, the president had one policeman (said to have been drunk) as a bodyguard.

Recently, the image of Benjamin Franklin on the U.S. $100 bill was enlarged and moved to the left in the first redesign of American currency in decades. Other measures were also taken to control the huge increase in counterfeiting of "C-notes." Recent counterfeit bills of the earlier design seemed so genuine that they fooled electronic currency scanners at 12 Federal Reserve banks. The Secret Service believes that $2 billion to $3 billion of these bogus bills were printed in Syria. The goal was to destabilize our economy.

Foiling counterfeiters is still a Secret Service priority. But now, this busy federal agency has many other law enforcement duties. Because Secret Service agents were given so many tasks, President Theodore Roosevelt transferred eight agents to the Department of Justice in 1908. They formed the Federal Bureau of Investigation (see chapter 10).

Today's Secret Service operates as uniformed and nonuniformed groups. Both groups are responsible for protecting the families of the president, vice president, the president-elect, vice president-elect, and former presidents and their families (spouses for life; children until age 16). They also protect major presidential and vice presidential candidates and their families and visiting international diplomats and dignitaries during their time in the United States. The Uniformed Division of the Secret Service maintains a Foreign Missions branch. Its members protect foreign diplomatic missions (and embassies) in Washington. All such Secret Service agents are armed and fully trained in protection techniques.

These agents and other department specialists work with representatives of dignitaries and celebrities to chart their every move while in the public eye. A *lead advance agent* forms a team to oversee every minute of the VIP's activities, public and private. The Secret Service then puts all needed protective measures into place to see that nothing befalls their important "guest."

The Secret Service still performs its first duty, that of protecting American currency. Anticounterfeiting is still the number one job of most of the Secret Service's 2,000 agents and specialists. American currency is guarded and protected not only here but worldwide. The Secret Service maintains offices in Paris, Rome, London, Bonn, and Bangkok. All these protective functions demand research. Some Secret Service agents are specialists in developing, testing, operating, and maintaining advanced surveillance equipment needed for protection. The department's activities have expanded to battle techno-thieves as well as forgery and illegal use of U.S. Government bank notes, certificates, and identity devices. The Secret Service has the technical knowledge and personnel to combat fraud related to "federal-interest" computers. This activity arose from the 1984 Comprehensive Crime Control Act, nicknamed the Credit Card Fraud Act and the Computer Fraud Act. This law allows the government to pursue anyone tampering with an "access device" such as a credit card personal identification number (PIN number), cellular and long-distance phone access code, or computer codes related to access devices.

The Secret Service long ago developed a Master Central Index (MCI). This MCI allows Service personnel at any of the 100 offices to cross-reference any Secret Service investigation taking place elsewhere. The MCI also allows the Secret Service to gain access to the database of any other law enforcement agency. The Secret Service investigates techno-crimes and other illegal activities through its Technical Security Division. This division employs experts in chemical, biological, radiological, and nuclear crime detection and is involved in water security, hazardous materials, fire protection, and similar disciplines. The TSD also develops advanced security systems and new investigative equipment for Service use. A Forensic Services Division employs agents specializing in fingerprinting, visual data, graphics, audiovisuals, and other evidence management methods. This division is even experimenting with computerized handwriting and voice recognition technology.

The Secret Service selects only the cream of its applicants, and becoming accepted for training may take a long time. You cannot begin work after age 37. You must pass a written examination, physical exam (with vision at least 20/40 in each eye, correctable to 20/20), a drug screening, and a polygraph test. The Service will use the time between application and a possible availability to investigate your background.

You must have at least a high school diploma to join the Uniformed Division and a bachelor's degree from an accredited college to become a special agent. You may have your degree in any subject, but courses in criminal justice, pre-law, law enforcement, police science, police administration, or criminology may give you an edge. You may substitute three years of work experience (at least two being in criminal investigation) for a college degree.

Beneficial high school subjects—in addition to keyboarding/computer science—might include accounting, business law and economics, English, foreign culture and/or language, psychology, and social studies.

Once you are accepted for training, you will complete eight weeks of general investigative training at the Federal Law Enforcement Training Center in Georgia. Next will come a nine-week course for special agents in Washington. This course covers intelligence, investigations, protective methods, psychology, procedures, criminal law, arrest processes, and defense and firearms training. There will be many tests and lots of simulation training. Next will come a field assignment and on-the-job training until you have completed your first year. At that time, the special agent in charge of your field office will decide whether or not you remain a special agent.

Uniformed Division Secret Service members have a pay scale not tied to GS tables. Officers earn about $30,000 a year to start, with annual raises for three years. Promotion after that is based on competitive test results and available openings.

Special agents begin at GS-5 ($19,869 or more) or GS-7 ($24,610 or more). The starting grade depends on education and experience. On-the-job performance governs promotions and increased earnings. Special agents can rise to GS-12 ($43,658 or more). Promotions beyond GS-12 are based on merit and available openings.

Benefits for Secret Service uniformed officers and special agents are similar to those for other government law enforcement personnel.

For more information, write:

United States Secret Service
Personnel Division
1800 G St., NW
Washington, DC 20223

Drugs and Law Enforcement

Authors' Note: We have gathered much of this and the next chapter's information from chapter 15, "Drugs and Crime," of *Criminal Justice Today* by Frank Schmallenger, Ph.D. (Prentice-Hall, 1997) and from *Federal Jobs in Law Enforcement* by John W. Warner Jr. (ARCO, 1992). We have also used the other sources quoted in the text.

THE SCOPE OF THE PROBLEM

In an open letter to George Bush when he was president, former U.S. Attorney General Richard Thornburgh wrote, "Drug trafficking is the number one crime problem facing our country and the world."

True then, truer now.

For years, the Executive Branch of the federal government and the press called our constant, costly anti-drug effort a "war" against drugs. This view does not go down well with Ross Deck, a senior policy analyst at the Office of National Drug Control Policy. In opening a conference on controversies in criminal justice, Deck said in part: "We are not fighting a drug war anymore. To have a war you must have enemies. In this situation, we are our own enemy. And, we cannot declare victory simply because we killed ourselves."

After a drop some years ago, drug use is on the rise, especially among young people. Many, psychologically affected by early drug use, will not become competent, effective adults.

Here are some chilling statistics showing the extent of America's drug problem:

- In a mid-1996 federal report, drug use among teens had risen 78% from 1992 through 1995, jumping from 5.3% to 10.9% of 12- to 17-year-olds surveyed.

- 10.4% of teens used drugs monthly.

- Teen use of hallucinogens rose 183% from 1992 to 1995 and 54% between 1994 and 1995.

- An estimated 0.8% of American teens used cocaine in 1995, a 166% increase from 1994 to 1995.

- Marijuana use for teens jumped 105% in the 1992–95 survey period and grew by 37% between 1994 and 1995. (An estimated 2.3 million people started using marijuana in 1994. The number of new users has grown every year since 1991.)

- 11.7 million Americans of all ages used illegal drugs (9 million using marijuana) within a 30-day survey period in 1995.

- Illegal drug sales total $50–$100 billion yearly.

- The percentage of federal inmates imprisoned for drug-related offenses has risen from 25% in 1980 to 38% in 1986 to 58% in 1991, and stands at more than 62% today, according to the Bureau of Prisons. About 70% of federal first offenders are serving drug-related sentences, with the numbers standing at 66% for women and 85% for noncitizen offenders.

- Drug-related crime is severely overloading all parts of the criminal justice system.

- Controlling drugs and fighting drug-related crime are among the major costs of government at all levels.

- Federal expenditures for drug control have risen from $1.5 billion in 1981 to more than $14.5 billion in 1996. (Drug-related law enforcement consumes one-half of this budget; treatment, education, crop control, interdiction (interception of drugs), research, and intelligence account for the rest.)

- Drug arrests are up on college campuses, according to a survey conducted by the Chronicle of Higher Education. There were 23% more drug violations reported in 1994 than in 1993, added to increases of 34% in 1993 over the previous year and a 46% increase in 1992 over 1991.

- Loss of time from work and reduced worker productivity due to drug use costs our economy over $60 billion a year.

- In 1993, nearly a half-million hospital emergencies were drug-related.

LEGAL AND ILLEGAL DRUGS

Although alcohol is considered a drug, and tobacco may one day be similarly defined if nicotine is ruled addictive (one cigarette maker has said it is), these are regulated drugs, of dependable quality, and legal for adult use (over 18 for tobacco, over 21 for alcohol). Although alcohol has its own strong links to crime, accidents, and other problems, and overuse of alcohol and tobacco can have serious health consequences, both are socially accepted in American life. We are writing here only of the effects on America of illicit (illegal) drugs.

Frank Schmallenger calls illegal drug use and abuse "a victimless crime with willing participants." This in no way reduces its dangers, and there are in fact victims aplenty. The drug trade's illegal nature coupled with its enormous profit at every distribution level make it hazardous in different ways for everyone involved.

The user is at risk of AIDS/HIV from sharing needles or being sickened by drugs of unknown quality. He or she may turn to high-risk crime to support a costly drug habit.

The street-corner dealer may be gunned-down by a rival or a buyer in a deal gone bad. The undercover detective or FBI agent risks the dangers of detection during a sting. And the uniformed officer is the visible target of anyone in the trade especially during a drug bust. There are no winners.

What Are Illicit Drugs?

Drugs are substances that noticeably affect the body or mind when consumed. Illicit drugs are legitimate drugs not used as intended or psychoactive drugs having no health benefits. There are several illicit drugs in each of these categories: narcotics (opium, morphine, codeine, heroin), depressants (chloral hydrate, barbiturates), anabolic steroids, stimulants (cocaine, amphetamines), and hallucinogens (LSD, mescaline, peyote). Some legitimate drugs prescribed by doctors for health purposes are diverted into illegal channels. Add to this the peddling of "street" drugs at huge profits, and you have the ingredients of a major law enforcement and criminal justice headache.

A Brief Drug History

A century ago, many of today's forbidden drugs were sold legally. Some were the active ingredients in "tonics," "elixirs," or "patent medicines." (Today's soft drink of choice for millions, Coca-Cola, contained cocaine until 1910. Cocaine was considered beneficial by many authorities including Sigmund Freud, the originator of psychoanalysis.) Other drugs, first used as painkillers during the Civil War, stayed on as prescription medicines. (Morphine, for example, had its greatest consumption—and suspected misuse—in 1898.) Opium and its relatives had a strong following among Chinese immigrants before the turn of the century.

Growth of Anti-Drug Legislation

In *Criminal Justice Today*, Frank Schmallenger traced the increasingly strict course of anti-drug legislation in America. In 1875, San Francisco prohibited opium smoking —the nation's first anti-drug legislation. A relatively mild federal law, the Harrison Act (1914), required physicians marketing drugs to register with the government and pay $1.00 a year in taxes. Since then, we have enacted increasingly strict legislation, but illegal drug use has continued to grow. The legislative highlights have included:

- **The Marijuana Tax Act** (1937)—a $100 per ounce fine for possession.

- **The Boggs Act** (1951)—declared heroin not medically useful and made marijuana, heroin, and many other substances illegal.

- **The Comprehensive Drug Abuse Prevention and Control Act** (1970)—formed the basis of present federal enforcement. Its Title II (the Controlled Substances Act) established five schedules (levels) classifying drugs from most to least dangerous and establishing punishments for use, sale, and possession of those on each schedule.

- **The Anti-Drug Abuse Act** (1988)—broadened the scope of federal drug enforcement efforts and increased federal anti-drug funding.

DRUG MARKETING AND CRIME

Illegal drugs move to market just as any "product" does—through a distribution chain. Drugs made from natural substances are grown as crops, harvested, partly or fully processed, and packed. Chemically produced drugs are made in secret, then enter the distribution chain. Drug kingpins ship their output, usually disguised as legitimate cargo. Or they can have couriers or messengers carry it (again disguised) across our borders in secret. Most such drugs come from Asia, Colombia, and Mexico. (According to syndicated columnist Jack Anderson, 70 percent of all illegal drugs entering the U.S. in 1997 came through Mexico, compared to 33 percent eight years before—yet Mexico has been certified as fully cooperating with the United States in battling drug traffic!) Marijuana can be grown in most parts of this country, although much of it is imported. Other domestic drugs include pharmaceuticals diverted from legitimate uses and amphetamines formulated by secret "speed labs" or "meth labs." Many of these drugs are also imported.

Whether drugs are imported or made here, "middlemen" (often members of organized crime families) warehouse the secret shipments, further process drugs (usually reducing their potency as they increase their prices), and send them to big-time dealers. They either sell to street users or resell profitably to street dealers who sell (at a further profit) to customers.

This is a totally cash business, and crooks along the line "launder" their drug money by changing it to other, apparently legitimate valuables —everything from diamonds to racehorses, from stocks and bonds to country houses. Money laundering takes the cooperation of lawyers, investment advisors, and other financial people willing to "look the other way" for a piece of the pie. Countries permitting secret bank accounts, such as Switzerland and the Bahamas, are part of the picture.

Narcoterrorism is another drug-financed activity. Drug traffickers, mostly from South America, finance terrorist groups to buy "protection" for themselves and their drug networks. Both groups benefit. Drug lords underwrite terrorism; terrorists help the drug trade flourish.

Narcoterrorism is only one drug crime connection. Possessing and using drugs are criminal activities. Laundering money is illegal. So is using it to support the drug distribution system. Finally, many drug users commit crimes to support their expensive drug addictions.

DRUG-FIGHTING MEASURES

As described by Schmallenger, these measures include enforcement, seizure, interdiction, forfeiture, and crop control.

Enforcement means invoking the legal penalties for drug possession, use, and distribution (or intention to distribute). These severe penalties do little to dent the impact of drug sales or to reduce drug-related crime. (One expert observed that strictly enforcing anti-drug laws might increase crime by boosting drug prices!)

Seizure involves locating stored drugs, usually through undercover police activity, then staging a "bust" to capture the drugs, equipment, weapons, and cash used in the drug operation. (One California bust netted 20 tons of cocaine, worth $20 billion on the street.) Authorities feel that drug dealers' ability to gather and store large quantities of drugs shows our failure to stop drugs at our borders.

Interdiction is the capture of drugs at our airports, ship terminals, and border crossings. Government forces (U.S. Coast Guard, Border Patrol, and Customs agents) concentrate on airports and harbors. Isolating the drug cargoes disguised within the 430 billion tons of merchandise entering the United States every year is a monumental task. So is finding the drugs carried by any of the 270 million people who cross our boundaries annually. It does not help that we have over 12,000 miles of international borders including desert, forest, and coastline. This scope makes patrolling almost impossible.

Forfeiture is an established anti-drug process. It allows the federal government (and many states and counties) to seize and sell all assets owned by anyone convicted of drug charges. Single forfeitures have been as high as $20 million.

Crop control requires the cooperation of foreign governments to limit or eliminate drug crops. Controls can include subsidies to growers so they grow other crops, or working with foreign governments to put drug controls in place. Since coca and opium are valuable crops in many countries, crop control is not always an option.

EDUCATION AND TREATMENT

These are as much crimefighting methods as making arrests or issuing citations, and law enforcement authorities are at times involved in these essential anti-drug activities. Education, especially teaching schoolchildren, often includes law enforcement departments. In Project DARE (the Drug Abuse Resistance Education program), uniformed police officers counsel schoolchildren about the dangers of drug use. (In a Pennsylvania DARE program, police converted a car seized in a drug raid into the DARE-mobile, a teaching tool for children.)

More than 3,500 school districts and local police teach DARE in 17 sessions for fifth and sixth grades, and nine lessons for junior high grades. Courses run from the consequences of drug use and abuse and resisting peer pressure to decision-making and selecting positive alternatives to alcohol, tobacco, and illegal drugs.

Although Justice Department surveys show DARE to be successful, this and other programs have their critics. In 1996, conservative newspaper columnist Phyllis Schlafly reported that the General Accounting Office had summed up its 1991 report on the $1.1 billion spent by the federal government on drug education for youth: "Impact Unknown." Schlafly contended that most drug education has failed to comply with The Drug-Free Schools and Communities Act, which requires schools to teach that using illegal drugs is wrong. She wrote: "Teaching students that anything is 'wrong' is so [opposed by] public school curriculum writers that they simply ignored the law's mandate." Instead, schools teach what she called "non-directive . . . alternative choices" to illegal drugs. She further wrote: "The illegal diversion of [drug education] funds shows that the educators just weren't interested in addressing the increased use of drugs by teenagers, even when they were given plenty of funds to deal with the problem."

Treatment is costly but essential if we are to contain drug use. In addition to federal funds for drug treatment of federal and state prisoners, there are countless community-funded programs designed to reduce addiction. One that seems to work well is the drug court. Based on a Miami, Florida, program, drug court provides mandatory treatment and repeated drug testing for first-time, nonviolent drug offenders. If someone does not receive court-ordered treatment, or fails a later drug test, he or she can receive stiffer punishments, including prison. Communities nationwide are launching drug courts, fueled by more than $1 billion in federal funding.

Even with generous budgets for drug treatment and education, illegal drugs remain the major law enforcement problem in America. It is interesting to note that, while most but not all federal government departments received modest budget increases for the fiscal year 1998, the Department of Justice (charged with combating drugs, among its many law enforcement duties) received the largest percentage increase of any agency or department: up 20 percent, a rise from $14.5 to $17.4 billion.

CHAPTER 8

State and Federal Drug-Fighting Careers

Almost every careerist whose work we have described in the earlier chapters of this section and the Criminal Justice section plays a part in fighting drugs. Among her responsibilities as America's chief federal law enforcement officer, Attorney General Janet Reno directs the drug-fighting agencies listed in this chapter, as well as those we cannot cover.

Drug-fighting takes place from the street level up. Every police department can promote the community awareness and cooperation needed to work with citizens trying to get drug dealers off the streets. Every police officer can apprehend drug users and low-level dealers. Every crime lab technician may deal with drug-based evidence or work to solve a drug-related crime. Every court officer, from sheriff's deputy to county prosecutor to judge, is involved in drug-related legal cases. Every corrections officer has drug offenders and dealers among his inmates. (In many prisons, the majority of inmates' crimes are drug related.) Even units of the National Guard can make drug sweeps, working with local police as they did in a raid to remove abandoned cars used for drug dealing from the streets of Chester, Pennsylvania.

There are also law enforcement professionals who specialize in drug crimes and criminals. These include the narcotics details: police officers and especially the city, county, and state-level detectives and DEA or FBI agents who conduct drug busts or sting operations—very risky duty. These law enforcement people must know their drug "marketplaces": the dealers, territories, customs, and customers within their jurisdiction.

If they are working undercover, they must act like one of the gang to avoid detection and its consequences. As Jeff Gammage wrote in an article on undercover drug buys for the *Philadelphia Inquirer,* "You're usually alone. You can't wear a bullet-proof vest. Sometimes you can't even take your gun. Your sole lifeline may be a thin radio wire strapped to your body. That lets your colleagues know what's happening, but also can increase your chances of being found out."

Gammage wrote that undercover busts are riskier than ever. Suspects "high on crack and other narcotics" can be paranoid about dealing. The big dollars involved add to risks. And "steep mandatory prison sentences [for those caught dealing] . . . create an added incentive for suspects to try to fight their way out of a bust."

At Bucks County (Pennsylvania) Community College, 100 Pennsylvania police officers learned drug bust combat techniques from a New Jersey SWAT (Special Weapons and Tactics) team. The "Top Gun" program included mock face-offs, with SWAT team members posing as armed felons hiding in parked cars. In another practice, eight armed officers conducted a swift, logical "major drug raid" using techniques to secure and preserve evidence. A goal of the program is to have prosecutors observe real drug raids to make sure the evidence gathered can be used in court. Another purpose of the college program is to develop greater cooperation among drug-fighting law enforcement agencies.

Although all law enforcement professionals may handle drug-related situations, here are careers that target America's illegal drug traffic.

Drug Investigator/Narcotics Agent

According to the VICS (Vocational Information Computer Systems, School District of Philadelphia, Pennsylvania) Reports, these state or federal agents investigate illegal drug activities. They have the power to arrest suspects and seize evidence. They also can audit the records of legitimate drug manufacturers and suppliers. In conducting such audits and investigations, they must decide whether drug possession and distribution are following legal paths. They prepare detailed reports of their activities, and present evidence in court. They are usually qualified in firearms use, and must be requalified regularly. This is dangerous work involving long and irregular hours.

Agents within a state system may work throughout their state. Federal agents may be assigned anywhere in the United States or overseas. Both state and federal careers pay well (see federal examples below), and offer paid vacations, good benefits, and retirement pensions.

Drug agents must have above-average general learning ability and verbal skills, at least average motor coordination, and general good health.

Many states have requirements similar to these for Pennsylvania: four years of experience in drug investigation or in prescription drug manufacture and/or distribution. Year-by-year college training can substitute for experience. (A bachelor's degree in criminal justice or law enforcement would provide the equivalent of four years' job experience.) Federal requirements vary with each government agency (see federal careers that follow), but most require some law enforcement experience or a law or related college degree. Courses to pursue in high school include advanced mathematics, chemistry, English, basics of law (if offered), physical education, psychology, social studies, and sociology.

Job prospects vary by state, but are generally not as good as those in federal drug enforcement. Here, the opportunities are excellent, although acceptance may be difficult. Advancement is based on job performance and recommendations of supervisors.

For information about drug/narcotics agent careers, write:

International Narcotic Enforcement Officers' Association
112 State St., Suite 1200
Albany, NY 12207

ATF AGENT

The Bureau of Alcohol, Tobacco, and Firearms (ATF) is part of the U.S. Treasury Department. According to John W. Warner Jr., author of *Federal Jobs in Law Enforcement*, ATF agents combat illegal traffic in legal drugs (alcohol and tobacco). They also combat terrorist groups, bombers, and organized crime (which may also be involved in illegal drug activity). The ATF enforces federal firearms laws including the licensing of some 247,000 firearms and explosives manufacturers and dealers, and investigating illegal firearms sales, arson-for-profit cases, and major narcotics dealers.

ATF agents must be U.S. citizens, 21 to 35 years old, be in excellent health, with uncorrected eyesight of at least 20/40. Potential agents must pass a thorough background check, a pre-employment drug screening, and a Treasury Enforcement Agent examination. Prior experience should include either all requirements for a college bachelor's (four-year) degree or one year of general criminal justice experience plus two years' specialized criminal investigation. Beginning ATF agents receive eight weeks of intensive law enforcement and investigative training, followed by specialized training in ATF duties. Agents must successfully pass both courses.

Beginning salaries with bachelor's degree range from $19,869 (GS-5) to $24,610 (GS-7). Promotions are usually two grades after one year from GS-5 to GS-7, or GS-7 to GS-9 ($30,106). Geographical assignments may boost starting salaries 16 percent to 30 percent. Benefits are similar to most federal agencies: sick leave, paid vacation, federal holidays, health/life insurance, and a comprehensive retirement plan.

For information, write:

Bureau of Alcohol, Tobacco, and Firearms
U.S. Treasury Department
650 Massachusetts Ave. NW, Room 4170
Washington, DC 20226

DEA AGENT

The Drug Enforcement Administration (DEA) is part of the Department of Justice. At its 1914 start with the passage of the Harrison Act, it was the Narcotics

Division of the Internal Revenue Service. The agency has grown in size and importance with the passage of each subsequent drug enforcement law. (It became the DEA in 1973.) According to Schmallenger's *Criminal Justice Today,* "the DEA is rapidly becoming the largest federal law enforcement agency," reflecting the top priority the government is giving to drug enforcement. The DEA employs more than 4,500 agents and support staff, mostly in 110 United States offices. Some 400 of these agents and staff work overseas.

The DEA is responsible for enforcing all federal drug control laws. Its agents investigate narcotics violators and seize drugs and assets related to drug trafficking. They enforce regulations governing legal manufacture and distribution of drugs, and operate a national narcotics intelligence network. They coordinate anti-drug activities with other law enforcement agencies here and abroad. The agency also researches drug control and exchanges control data with other law enforcement groups.

DEA operates nationally. In enforcing national drug laws, agents and staff specialists gather and present court evidence. DEA work is among the most demanding in law enforcement. DEA agents must be free to travel.

John W. Warner Jr. describes these job requirements in *Federal Jobs in Law Enforcement.* All DEA agents are U.S. citizens. Many are former police officers or have served in the armed forces. DEA agents must be four-year college graduates, have three years of general work experience, and be in good health. They must have excellent communications skills, and pass drug screening tests. Starting salary at GS-5 level is $19,869. To qualify for GS-7 entry-level salary ($24,610 in 1996), they must have one of the following: a 2.9 overall college grade point average, a 3.5 GPA in their major, standing in the upper one-third of their graduating class, membership in a national honorary scholastic society, one year of successful graduate study, or one year of what the DEA calls "progressively responsible investigative experience."

Once special agents win appointments (one will be selected for every 100 applicants), they train for 14 weeks in a DEA program at the FBI Academy in Quantico, Virginia. This course covers the basics of firearms use, self-defense, court processes and the law, investigation methods, criminology, narcotics identifying, and similar subjects. FBI instructors teach the FBI's mission and operating methods. The two federal agencies must work together in controlling drug traffic and its connections with organized crime.

In addition to special agents and field supervisors, the DEA operates state and local task forces that work with local law enforcement agencies in drug investigations. DEA forensic science laboratories support the agency's work and that of the FBI. The DEA also operates an aircraft fleet that uses agent-pilots. It has a financial investigation force trained in accounting, cash flow, and money-laundering.

For more DEA information, write:

Drug Enforcement Administration
Office of Personnel, Recruitment, and Placement
400 Sixth St., SW, Room 2558
Washington, DC 20024

FBI

The Federal Bureau of Investigation (FBI) is another federal agency that fights illegal drugs. Its activities are so widespread and cover so many areas of criminal activity that we have given it a chapter of its own (see chapter 10).

ONDCP

The Office of National Drug Control Policy (ONDCP) is part of the Executive Branch of the federal government. John W. Warner Jr. noted that the Office was created as part of the Anti-Drug Abuse Act of 1988. It mandates and implements national drug control strategies. Its director (nicknamed the "drug czar" by the press) is appointed by the president.

The ONDCP reinforces and helps manage the drug-fighting activities of the ATF, DEA, FBI, U.S. Customs Service, and other federal agencies. It cooperates locally, and is part of every step of the criminal justice process as it relates to illegal drugs, from apprehension to probation, from testing to addict treatment. The Office also undertakes projects in education, community action, drug-free workplaces and schools, international activities, drug interdiction, intelligence, and research. Its staff is largely administrative; those with law enforcement or drug management experience may find career opportunities in ONDCP.

For more information, write:

Office of National Drug Control Policy
Old Executive Office Building
17th St. and Pennsylvania Ave., NW,
Washington, DC 20500

U.S. Coast Guard

Every branch of military service has its law enforcement arm. For example, the U.S. Army has military police and the Criminal Investigation Command. The other services have their equivalents. Any military-based law enforcement experience is a good beginning for related civilian, police, or government careers.

Among our military services, one branch performs a unique role. Unlike the other services, the United States Coast Guard (USCG) is operated by the Department of Transportation, not the Department of Defense. In addition to patrolling America's waterways to promote and enforce boating safety regulations, Coast Guard crews aboard ships and planes work to intercept illegal aliens—and illegal drugs. Coast Guard staffers have full enforcement powers, including search and seizure. In addition to its enlisted and officer crews, the USCG employs special agents and intelligence officers for this all-important work.

Coast Guard recruits attend the Coast Guard Training Center in Cape May, New Jersey. The majority of Coast Guard personnel take advanced training leading to academic degrees.

Sixty percent of Coast Guard officers graduate from the Coast Guard Academy in New London, Connecticut. Acceptance is wholly on merit (the other service academies accept candidates through Congressional appointments). Other Coast Guard officers specializing in port security attend the Port Security School, Coast Guard Reserve Training Center, Yorktown, Virginia. They learn port and harbor security, including related law enforcement. Admission requires either a civilian college degree or a distinguished record as a Coast Guard enlisted person.

For more information, contact:

Coast Guard Recruiting
1-800-424-8883

U.S. CUSTOMS SERVICE

Customs—the collection of fees on imported goods—dates from 1789, and was initiated by Congress and President George Washington. Customs duties are one of our nation's major sources of revenue, and the U.S. Customs Service is responsible for collecting the fees. The Service also controls all merchandise (including tourists' luggage!) entering the United States. This includes all ship cargo and airlines packages coming from overseas into more than 300 U.S. ports of entry. In *Federal Careers in Law Enforcement* (ARCO, 1992), John W. Warner Jr. wrote: "Beginning in the 1960s and continuing to today, Customs officers have fought the illegal influx of opium, heroin, cocaine, hashish, marijuana, amphetamines, and other illegal drugs into the United States." In a reverse move, Customs agents also intercept illegal high-tech exports to foreign countries.

U.S. Customs agents have full law enforcement powers regarding their duties of investigation, assessment of customs duties (fees), and pursuit of illegal activities. Customs job titles include criminal investigator, special agent, pilot, customs inspector, canine enforcement officer, and imports specialist. There are several administrative and support positions as well. Beginning salaries range from $19,869 for customs inspector (federal job level GS-5) or $24,610 for GS-7. Salaries for customs investigator are somewhat higher. Customs officers can advance to GS-12 ($43,658) or to higher grades through competitive examinations. Job and educational requirements are virtually identical to those for DEA agents, described previously.

Prospective Customs agents undergo 14 weeks of basic enforcement training at a U.S. Customs Service Academy. Courses include undercover work, intelligence, surveillance, air and marine law enforcement, among other subjects. Customs agents and specialists generally receive additional academic and job-related training during their careers.

For more information, write:

Office of Human Resources
U.S. Customs Service
1301 Constitution Ave. N.W.
Washington, DC 20229

U.S. Park Police, National Park Service Superintendents, and Staff (Park Rangers)— Local, State, and National

Park superintendents would appear to have the easy life. They live in the outdoors, caring for park visitors who have come to relax and enjoy the scenery. Surely park superintendents (and rangers) have it made? Right? *Wrong*.

Of course there are those pleasures that accompany working outdoors. But there are occasional unruly, even dangerous park visitors. A motorist may not obey the speed limits that parks mandate. What sports car driver is willing to go 15 m.p.h.?

Increasingly, park guards and superintendents are armed for the unexpected. Because parks are often large, leafy, and secluded, they can attract drug dealers. No park officer wants to approach such a group insufficiently prepared. There may be family arguments, alcohol on the premises, and other mischief.

This unattractive picture is the exception. Most visitors to local, state, and national parks are law-abiding citizens who look to the park superintendent or ranger for directions and who obey the particular park's rules. And, too, the majority of park superintendents and rangers are not armed. But they are law enforcers.

At the national level, the U.S. Park Police cover the White House grounds and the federal parks that surround it. Every kind of transportation is used from foot power to helicopter to oversee events such as the National Cherry Blossom Festival and the 4th of July festivities. The Park Police are host to millions of visitors a year who are drawn to the colorful events unique to the Capitol city.

The training program is intense. It begins with twenty-six weeks of indoctrination, followed by five weeks of U.S. Park Police training. The next period of training involves nine weeks in rotating positions, then graduating to full-time park patrolman for the rest of the probationary year. And during their years in park service, National Park Police take courses to hone skills and prepare for greater responsibility.

"Pluses" in the field of park service at all levels:

- working outdoors
- "perks" available such as sick leave, health insurance, etc.
- housing may be offered as part of the package

Negatives include:

- superintendents and rangers may be asked to put in overtime
- work is performed in all kinds of weather
- many assignments are in isolated areas. Rangers and their families must adjust to living far from towns or cities.

The future in this field looks promising. Because of a growing public demand for a safe environment, projections through the year 2005 indicate a 38 percent increase in employment. This is far faster than the national average growth rate. The good news is balanced by the fact that openings are slow to appear. But the fact is that gradually there will be more opportunities in the new century.

The park ranger's salary may begin at $18,700, rising to $41,000 with a possibility for further pay increases with experience.

Park superintendents and rangers, armed or without weapons, are alert to park violations and quick to move in on them. Park visitors can better relax knowing that they are protected and that the land is being aggressively saved for future generations.

Those interested in the U.S. Park Police field should write:

U.S. Park Police
Personnel Office
1100 Ohio Dr., SW
Washington, DC 20242

For those interested in park systems throughout the United States, write to:

National Parks and Conservation Association
1015 31st St., NW
Washington, DC 20007

CHAPTER 10

Careers with the Federal Bureau of Investigation

Who hasn't seen a movie or TV show that depicts the ever-present "G-men"? In today's media, they look virtually unchanged from the ones in the old black-and-white thrillers of the '40s: solemn men in gray suits. The biggest change in how they are depicted is that the most recent versions no longer wear neatly creased gray felt hats.

Stepping out of the world of make-believe into the real FBI, the people who do the jobs are at least as varied as the jobs themselves. Men and women work as special agents and support personnel in areas as diverse as counterterrorism and carpentry.

The real work of the FBI is a world we glimpse through our newspapers almost daily. We have followed their big cases: investigations of organized crime figures and such tragedies as the ill-fated TWA flight 800. We have read about their pursuit of foreign espionage agents and escaped federal prisoners. These are only a part of the great responsibilities the Bureau has in fighting crime. As the primary investigative arm of the United States Department of Justice, it currently has investigative jurisdiction over more than 200 categories of federal crimes, but, like most organizations, it started out working on a much smaller scale.

A QUICK HISTORY

In 1871, "special agent" was an extremely rare title. It was then that Congress granted $50,000 to the newly formed Department of Justice (DOJ) for "detection and prosecution of crimes." For that purpose, the attorney general hired a single investigator.

The workload increased year by year. In 1908, President Theodore Roosevelt's attorney general, Charles J. Bonaparte, established a permanent investigative force. The 13 investigators, 12 examiners, and 9 Secret Service agents, then loosely organized under the attorney general, became special agents of the DOJ. A year later, the attorney general renamed it the Bureau of Investigation.

This bureau looked into many of the big issues of the day—violations of laws involving national banking, bankruptcy, naturalization, antitrust, and land fraud. Then, as the world's history progressed and America faced new concerns, the bureau's responsibilities increased. The White Slave Traffic Act of 1910, the Espionage, Selective Service, and Sabotage acts shortly after our entrance into World War I, and the National Motor Vehicle Theft Act of 1919 added areas of responsibility. Growing to keep pace with these needs, the Bureau consisted of 350 special agents by 1920. The organization added 9 field offices to work more effectively across a large nation.

Four years later, the organization had expanded to 650 employees. The best known FBI man in history, J. Edgar Hoover, became its director. This began a period of expansion and change that lasted nearly four decades. Hoover quickly toughened requirements for the position of special agent. He also created important new divisions, Identification and Laboratory, published the bureau's first manual of rules and regulations, and established a training program for new agents.

The country was in the midst of Prohibition by then, the 13-year period when all production and sale of liquor was illegal. It was an era when big-time gangsters flourished—until nabbed by the "G-men," the government men of the FBI. In the years from 1933 to 1935, they tracked down and captured such gangsters as "Baby Face" Nelson, John Dillinger, "Pretty Boy" Floyd, "Ma" Barker, and the infamous

Weapons and other materials found in the Ocala, Florida, hideout of Fred and "Ma" Barker in January 1935.

(Photo: Federal Bureau of Investigation)

car thieves/bank robbers/murderers Bonnie Parker and Clyde Barrow. Also in 1935, Congress officially added the word "Federal" to the bureau's name.

As tensions in Europe started building and our country eventually geared itself for entry into World War II, the role of the FBI expanded once again. Working closely with the Army and Navy, the bureau took an increasingly important role in cases of sabotage, espionage, and subversion. After the war, the government transferred these responsibilities to a new organization created especially for them: the Central Intelligence Agency (CIA).

In the years that followed, the FBI handled extremely important cases such as the investigation of the murder of President Kennedy, murders of civil rights workers, aircraft highjackings, and the workings of groups implicated in violent social upheaval, such as the Weather Underground.

By the time Hoover died in 1972, the number of personnel in the FBI had reached 20,000. It has continued growing under new directors since that time, constantly addressing and reappraising the rapidly evolving crime scene. The bureau has had to emphasize protecting the country from terrorism and narcotics trafficking. It created a Hostage Rescue Team and gained jurisdiction over terrorist acts against Americans abroad.

As white-collar crime became a bigger and bigger business, the FBI gained additional authority, including expanded wiretapping rights, to combat it. Computer crimes (see section 5), a brave new world in illegal activity, made it necessary to create a new specialized branch, the National Computer Crime Squad.

The FBI is at the forefront of technology; it must be to catch criminals with increasingly sophisticated skills. Get onto the Internet and you will find that the bureau's Web site (http://www.fbi.gov) is complete with a list of the top cases on which it is working, information on dangerous fugitives from justice, and ways for the public to get and give information.

What comes next? Just watch for new trends in crimes. You can bet the FBI is watching, too, and setting up its systems to control them.

THE FBI IN THE HEADLINES

For decades the FBI has played a major part in solving the biggest crimes in our country—and beyond. What follows are just a few of them as reported on their Web site. They provide a good view of the breadth of issues the bureau handles and how it coordinates with other law enforcement agencies.

World Trade Center Bombing: A February 26, 1993, explosion in the World Trade Center's parking garage resulted in six deaths and 1,042 injuries. The blast, caused by a bomb made of about 1,200 pounds of explosives, resulted in a five-story crater with damage of over $500 million. On March 4, 1994, Muhammad Amin Salameh, Nidal Ayyad, Mahmud Abouhalima, and Ahmed Ajaj were convicted for their roles in the bombing. On April 25, 1994, each received a 240-year prison term and a $500,000 fine. Also, money they may receive from interviews or books must be turned over to the families of the six people killed in the bombing.

Salameh's roommate, Ramzi Ahmed Yousef, was also found to be involved in the conspiracy. However, he left this country for Pakistan the day after the bombing on board a Pakistan International Airlines flight. On February 7, 1995, Yousef, a "Top Ten" fugitive, was arrested in Pakistan and was then turned over to the FBI.

Operation Disconnect: Operation Disconnect, currently involving 38 FBI field offices, focuses on identifying and prosecuting illegal telemarketers. Begun in 1993, it is considered to be the most significant federal investigation ever directed at this criminal group. As of November 1995, over 360 people had been charged and about 300 were convicted. Also $7.65 million in property was seized; $6.76 million of that property has been forfeited.

Polar Cap: Polar Cap was a joint investigation into one of the most significant international money-laundering organizations operating in the United States. This group was responsible for laundering an estimated $150 million each year for the Cali and Medellin drug cartels of Colombia, moving millions of dollars through bank accounts in the United States, Austria, Belgium, Colombia, the United Kingdom, Panama, and Switzerland. As of November 1994, 45 individuals had been arrested, and asset seizures totaled over $50 million dollars. Polar Cap was conducted by the FBI Drug Enforcement Administration, Internal Revenue Service, and U.S. Customs Service.

Violence Against Clinics Providing Reproductive Health Services: Following the FBI's investigation, Paul Hill was found responsible for the 1994 anti-abortion–related shooting deaths of Dr. John Britton and James Barrett and for gunshot injuries to Mrs. June Barrett. Hill was convicted on three counts of violating the Freedom of Access to Clinics Entrances Act of 1994. Also, on November 2, 1994, a Florida state jury found him guilty of murder, attempted murder, and firing a gun into an occupied vehicle. Hill was sentenced to die in Florida's electric chair.

Investigation into Beating of Rodney King: On April 17, 1993, after extensive FBI investigation and federal prosecution, a jury convicted Los Angeles police officers Laurence Powell and Stacey Koon of one count, each, of violating Title 18 U.S. Code Section 242 in connection with the beating of Rodney King while he was being arrested. Both officers were sentenced to serve 30 months in federal prison.

Gang Violence: As a result of an FBI investigation, the entire leadership of a violent street gang the "LA Boys" or "Call Boys" headed by Donald "Sly" Green and Darryl "Reese" Johnson, was convicted of racketeering, as well as racketeering and narcotics conspiracy, on March 30, 1994. Green also was found guilty of conducting a continuing criminal enterprise. Before the trial, 26 of 32 defendants pleaded guilty to racketeer influence and corrupt organization (RICO) charges. The most powerful and violent drug-distribution group in western New York was dismantled.

Operation Horsecollar: A task force of FBI agents and New York City police targeted heroin distribution networks in Harlem, which has the highest concentration of heroin addicts in the nation. Investigation resulted in 222 arrests, 167 people convicted, over $8 million seized, 15 organizations dismantled, and 30 groups identified as of November 1994. The operation also has been responsible for a marked decrease in murders in New York and the solution of 40 murders, including the assassination of a New York police officer by a group under investigation.

Ames Espionage Investigation: Aldrich Hazen Ames and Maria Del Rosario Casas Ames were arrested on February 21, 1994, and charged with conspiracy to commit espionage. Ames had been an employee of the Central Intelligence Agency (CIA) for over 31 years. At the time of his arrest, he was assigned to the Directorate of Intelligence Counternarcotics Center. His wife was a university student and had been a paid source for the CIA in Mexico City. Ames was sentenced to life in prison without parole for conspiracy to commit espionage. Mrs. Ames was sentenced to 63 months for conspiracy to commit espionage and 10 concurrent months for income tax evasion.

From these cases we can see that the FBI handles the largest crimes, the ones with potential national repercussions. It has a mission statement that guides its actions:

> The Mission of the FBI is to uphold the law though the investigation of violations of federal criminal law; to protect the United States from foreign intelligence and terrorist activities; to provide leadership and law enforcement assistance to federal, state, local and international agencies; and to perform these responsibilities in a manner that is responsive to the needs of the public and is faithful to the Constitution of the United States.

The areas in which a special agent works are varied. However, in general, the investigative duties are consistent. They are:

- Investigate suspected criminal violations of federal laws to determine if there is sufficient evidence for prosecution.
- Develop and use informants to get leads on information.
- Obtain evidence or establish facts by interviewing, observing, and interrogating suspects.
- Examine records to discover links to be found in the evidence and documents.
- Verify all information to establish accuracy.
- May need to provide surveillance or perform undercover assignments.

- May need to provide findings in clear, logical, and properly documented reports.
- May need to testify before grand juries or serve subpoenas or other official papers.
- May have to carry out a search warrant.

The FBI has the broadest investigative authority of all federal law enforcement agencies. Its emphasis is on long-term, complex investigations, and it is based on a philosophy of maintaining close relations and information sharing with other federal, state, local, and foreign law enforcement and intelligence agencies. Many of its cases involve working in tandem with these other law enforcement agencies.

The FBI divides its investigative programs into seven areas:

- Applicant Matters
- Civil Rights
- Counterterrorism
- Financial Crime
- Foreign Counterintelligence
- Organized Crime/Drugs
- Violent Crimes and Major Offenders

The spectrum of cases in each of these categories is broad, and for some crimes, work must be done in more than one area.

Applicant Matters refers to investigation of the histories and attributes of people applying for sensitive positions in government agencies. This includes candidates for positions in the Department of Energy and the Nuclear Regulatory Commission, the Department of Justice, FBI special agents and support staff, the U.S. Courts, and the White House staff.

The Civil Rights Program investigates allegations of breaches in the rights of Americans as defined by the Constitution and our laws. For example, it handles transgressions of the Equal Opportunity Act and cases of possible discrimination in housing.

The Counterterrorism Program works on cases of domestic terrorism, hostage taking, and overseas homicide or attempted homicide of American citizens. Its work also includes the protection of foreign officials and guests, sabotage, domestic security, attempted or actual bombings, nuclear extortion, and sedition (inciting rebellion against our government). To work effectively, the FBI has jurisdiction in any country where the host government agrees. A major example of cases handled under this program is the investigation of the bombing of Pan Am flight 103 over Lockerbie, Scotland, on December 21, 1988. To conduct this investigation, the FBI worked closely with law enforcement and intelligence agencies of Scotland, Britain, and Germany.

In **The Financial Crime Program,** agents investigate white-collar crimes, non-violent crimes using deceit or concealment to get money, property, or services. Sometimes these criminals aim to avoid payment of money rather than to obtain it or try to create some unfair advantage for the business or individual.

People who commit financial crimes are often quite successful in their fields before they act illegally. They can be leaders in industry and government who have worked for many years to earn the trust of others, only to take advantage of it. Investigations in this program typically cover bank fraud and embezzlement, environmental crimes, fraud against the government, corruption of public officials, health care fraud, and election law violations.

The Foreign Counterintelligence Program is responsible for matters that arise from threats posed by hostile intelligence services and their agents here and by individuals or groups that are sources of international terrorism. Agents in this program work to identify and neutralize these threats. They also provide important information to our country's policy makers on the foreign intelligence activities taking place here.

The Organized Crime/Drug Program deals with drug matters, racketeer influenced and corrupt organizations, labor racketeering, and money laundering. It maintains active investigations in areas in which racketeering most often occurs, such as in gambling and loansharking. Each field office also participates in drug awareness education to help reduce the demand for illegal drugs.

The **Violent Crimes and Major Offenders Program** is involved in an extensive list of crimes. It handles:

- Fugitives wanted as result of FBI investigations
- Escaped federal prisoners (in some cases)
- Probation/parole violation (in some cases)
- Unlawful flight to avoid prosecution
- Crime on Indian reservations
- Theft of government property
- Interstate transportation of stolen motor vehicles
- Interstate transportation of stolen property
- Theft from interstate shipments
- Assaulting, kidnapping, or killing the president, vice president, or a member of Congress
- Bank robbery, burglary, or larceny
- Crime aboard an aircraft
- Kidnapping/extortion
- Sexual exploitation of children
- Tampering with consumer products

Some very large programs straddle two or more of these seven areas. For example, the Bureau has, a program called ANSIR (Awareness of National Security Issues and Response). Its job is to disseminate information concerning national security matters. To this end, ANSIR maintains a National Security Threat List. This details issues which threaten our national security regardless of country of origin. It includes a list of foreign powers posing intelligence threats to us. For obvious reasons, the list is kept strictly classified.

Issues that ANSIR covers include terrorism, espionage, weapons proliferation, economic espionage, the targeting of the national information infrastructure, the targeting of the U.S. government, perception management (spreading of deceptive information to distort public attitudes), and foreign intelligence activities. This wide range of targets is a good example of the crossover of interests between programs. Counterterrorism and counterintelligence, two very crucial and delicate areas, both come into play in this program.

SUPPLYING SUPPORT FOR ALL PROGRAMS

As investigations progress, agents uncover many types of information. This must be analyzed under the strictest and most advanced criteria available. To accomplish this, the FBI maintains several special units, providing all its investigations with reliable and confidential data.

The Laboratory Division examines evidence collected in the course of FBI or Drug Enforcement Agency (DEA) field investigations. It also performs advanced level examinations of evidence for federal, state, or local law enforcement agencies that don't have the facilities or expertise to perform them. The laboratory employs over 600 people, conducting more than 600,000 forensic examinations and two million fingerprint comparisons each year for local, state, and federal law enforcement organizations. Agents in this division sometimes assist in conducting crime-scene searches. They sometimes work undercover, giving technical support in photography, language services, polygraphs ("lie detectors"), and other specialized activities needed to carry out difficult and sensitive investigations.

The Forensic Science Research and Training Center (FSRTC) is an important part of the Laboratory Division. This center trains new agents of the FBI and DEA, the National Academy, and people from federal, state, and local law enforcement agencies in the proper acquisition, handling, and examination of evidence to be used in courts of law. It also provides the FBI Laboratory with forensic science research and quality assurance.

The Identification Division of the FBI is a central bank of fingerprint records. It supplies identification and criminal record services to over 61,000 law enforcement agencies. This division makes it possible for a local police department to contact one national source to determine, for example, whether someone apprehended for burglary has a prior record of burglaries in other states. Before this service was begun, the local police would have to initiate costly searches in all 49 other states to get the full picture of the individual's criminal past.

The National Crime Information Center is another kind of data bank for the criminal justice community. Through it, appropriate agencies can find records of stolen property (such as vehicles and license plates), lists of people with warrants outstanding against them, the criminal histories of people arrested for serious offenses, and the records of some missing people.

The Uniform Crime Reporting Program is the official record keeper for crime in this country. Law enforcement agencies throughout the U.S. send monthly reports on the types and numbers of crimes reported in their jurisdictions. With this data, the FBI is able to assess national crime trends.

ORGANIZATIONAL STRUCTURE OF TODAY'S FBI

We are a big country in a very big world. The bureau has found that only by establishing offices globally can it do its work effectively. The FBI headquarters in Washington, D.C., houses 9 divisions and 4 offices. These give direction and support to 56 field offices located in major cities, in addition to about 400 satellite offices (resident agencies), 4 specialized field installations, and 23 foreign liaison posts.

The director of the FBI, is the head of the entire organization. He is supported by a deputy director. Each of the 9 divisions at the Washington headquarters is led by an assistant director. A deputy assistant director (DAD) supports each assistant director.

Most field offices are headed by a special agent in charge (SAC). Exceptions are the 2 largest field offices, New York City and Washington, D.C., which are managed by assistant directors in charge (ADIC).

The FBI locates satellite offices, called resident agencies, where they are demanded by crime trends. A given field office can have from one to over a dozen resident agencies, each of which is headed by a supervisory senior resident agent.

As of the end of July 1996, the FBI employed 10,529 special agents. It also had 15,398 support personnel who perform professional, administrative, technical, clerical, craft, trade, or maintenance operations. This is a big operation with a big budget. In the 1997 fiscal year, the FBI had a budget of $2,837,610.

SALARIES AND WAGES

Most people in government service, and that includes most FBI white-collar employees, are paid according to the general schedule. Every job title is ranked, and individuals are placed within that ranking depending on their experience. The Bureau pays some individuals, such as those in extremely specialized or competitive categories, according to a special pay-rate system. The highest-ranking personnel receive pay according to a separate executive schedule.

Special agents enter service at the GS 10 level on the chart (see the following page). The 10 steps moving across the chart indicate the pay increases that accrue with time and progress in the position. Agents can advance to grade GS 13 in field

SELECTED FEDERAL WHITE-COLLAR PAY SCHEDULES

Effective January, 1996

GENERAL SCHEDULE	STEPS 1	2	3	4	5	6	7	8	9	10
1	13,132	13,570	14,006	14,442	14,880	15,136	15,566	16,000	16,109	16,425
2	14,764	15,116	15,606	16,019	16,197	16,673	17,149	17,625	18,101	18,577
3	16,111	16,647	17,184	17,720	18,257	18,793	19,330	19,867	20,403	20,940
4	18,085	18,688	19,292	19,895	20,499	21,102	21,705	22,309	22,912	23,515
5	20,233	20,908	21,582	22,257	22,931	23,606	24,280	24,954	25,629	26,303
6	22,554	23,305	24,057	24,809	25,561	26,313	27,065	27,816	28,568	29,320
7	25,061	25,897	26,733	27,568	28,404	29,239	30,075	30,911	31,746	32,582
8	27,755	28,682	29,607	30,533	31,459	32,385	33,310	34,236	35,162	36,088
9	30,658	31,681	32,703	33,725	34,747	35,769	36,792	37,814	38,836	39,858
10	33,762	34,887	36,012	37,137	38,262	39,387	40,513	41,638	42,763	43,888
11	37,094	38,330	39,567	40,803	42,040	43,276	44,512	45,749	46,985	48,222
12	44,458	45,941	47,423	48,906	50,388	51,871	53,353	54,835	56,318	57,800
13	52,867	54,630	56,392	58,154	59,917	61,679	63,442	65,204	66,966	68,729
14	62,473	64,555	66,639	68,721	70,804	72,887	74,969	77,052	79,134	81,217
15	73,485	75,935	78,385	80,834	83,284	85,733	88,183	90,632	93,082	95,531

assignments. Those who move up to supervisory, management, and executive positions are eligible for grades GS 14 and 15. All special agents may qualify for overtime compensation.

BECOMING AN FBI AGENT

Given the very specific and crucially important jobs the FBI does, it is no wonder that it has some tough requirements. In addition, all agents undergo 16 weeks of intensive training at the FBI Academy, at the U.S. Marine Corps base in Quantico, Virginia. However, since particular cases may demand unforeseen skills or knowledge, the director has some leeway in hiring, or, as their Web site page states, "In recognition of these diverse responsibilities, the FBI has traditionally been provided broader discretion in personnel matters than is afforded most other federal agencies." If you have special skills that the FBI considers critical, it may be flexible in some of its requirements.

In general, a candidate for special agent must:

- be a citizen of the United States

- be between the ages of 23 and 37 when entering on duty

- hold a bachelor's degree from an accredited four-year resident program at a college or university

- have three years full-time work experience (Exceptions: law school graduates, or graduates with a degree in accounting or fluency in a foreign language for which the Bureau has a need, may not require the work experience)

Candidates must also be completely available for assignment anywhere in the FBI's headquarters or 56 field offices. The Bureau considers both special agents and support staff available for nonvoluntary rotational transfers until they have acquired 10 years of service in the same office. After that, they will be candidates for voluntary rotation.

Special agents must have uncorrected vision not worse than 20/200 and corrected to 20/20 in one eye and not worse that 20/40 in the other. All candidates must possess valid drivers' licenses.

Early in its history, the bureau discovered the benefits of attracting lawyers and accountants. This accounts for their being eligible without having had three years of work experience. Lawyers are already trained in and appreciate the nuances of our country's laws. This makes them keen investigators of violations, as well as people who are respectful of the rules of collecting evidence so it stands up during court proceedings.

Accountants are especially desirable to the bureau because much of the tracking of crimes depends on understanding financial systems, financial transactions, and their related laws. Since special agents are often called upon to testify as expert witnesses, certified accountants bring with them the knowledge necessary to speak with authority.

The need for special agents with excellent foreign language skills is critical for the handling of cases involving foreign nationals in the U.S. as well as for cases overseas. For this reason, the FBI has waived the work experience requirement for specialists in languages such as Arabic, Chinese, Farsi, Japanese, Korean, and Vietnamese.

A candidate for special agent will go through a demanding application process. He or she will have written tests and an interview. The bureau follows up with an extensive investigation of the person's background, including:

- Checking credit and arrest records

- Interviewing associates

- Contacting personal and business references

- Interviewing past employers and neighbors

- Verifying educational achievements

- Drug testing

- A polygraph examination

- A physical examination (may be required)

The bureau will disqualify from employment anyone who has used marijuana in the last three years or any illegal drug or combination of illegal drugs in the last 10 years. Anyone who has sold any of these drugs is also disqualified.

Once a man or woman has been accepted to become a special agent, he or she begins an intensive period of training at the FBI Academy. No matter what their eventual assignments will be, they receive this basic 16-week, 645-hour cram course in how to be a federal investigator.

The instruction has four main areas of concentration: academics, firearms, physical training/defensive tactics, and practical exercises.

Within these areas, the basic courses cover:

Firearms	Practical Applications
Physical Training/Defensive Tactics	Legal
Forensic Science	Interviewing
Informant Development	Communications
White-Collar Crime	Drug Investigations
Ethics	Organized Crime
Behavioral Science	Computer Skills
Foreign Counterintelligence/Terrorism	

Agent trainees get to use many of their newfound skills during their Practical Applications unit. The FBI has created an urban stage set, a strip of normal-looking stores and offices called the Hogan's Alley Complex. Here, in a realistic

Firearms instruction on the "Combat Course" is part of the 16-week FBI Special Agent Training at Quantico, Virginia.

(Photo: Federal Bureau of Investigation)

setting, students put together all the skills they have gathered—the firearms, physical training, and the use of vehicles and equipment—in simulated crime situations. Actors present the trainees with tough dilemmas, testing their abilities to make appropriate decisions and take proper actions spontaneously.

Hogan's Alley has been an important part of agent training since it opened in 1987. Law enforcement authorities from this country and abroad have taken it as a model for their own training facilities.

Applicants who succeed in their training begin employment with a year of probationary work. On completing that year, they become permanent employees. Their compensation levels start to move up as they become more proficient in their positions and as they advance to positions of greater responsibility. Meanwhile, their educations may be enhanced or updated with further seminars and workshops at the academy.

Although budgetary constraints created a freeze in hiring for a few years, the bureau has entered a new growth phase. In 1996, the FBI hired a record 1,200 new agents. The government has announced a goal of graduating close to 2,000 new agents by 1998.

Many of these new recruits are people signing on for second careers. Encouraged by the announcement of the agency's growth goals, an increasing number of people in other fields are realizing their calling to greater service and greater adventure. A *USA Today* article in March 1996, quoted an assistant training

Students investigate a staged bank robbery as part of their practical training in the FBI's "Hogan's Alley."
(Photos: Federal Bureau of Investigation)

director as saying, "I can't tell you the sense of rejuvenation I feel about what is going on here. There seems to be this hunger out there to give back, to improve the lot of our people. They talk about a higher calling. A lot of them made a lot of money, had big jobs, but they've been there, done that."

More women are now applying to become FBI agents—people like one former naval carrier pilot, a woman fluent in three foreign languages. Deirdre Emmes entered her new career with the FBI at age 36 and found it a place that welcomed and valued her. Compared to her military experience, she found herself more comfortable being a woman in the FBI. The military, she found, was "a little bit rigid and archaic when it came to women. Let's face it," she said, "going on a six-month cruise with 1,000 men is overrated. I've found support here."

FBI PROFESSIONAL SUPPORT PERSONNEL

The bureau needs a veritable army of people who are not agents, people who do the thousands of jobs that make the work of the special agents possible. These non-agents work in professional, administrative, technical, clerical, craft, trade, and maintenance fields throughout the FBI's vast network.

Support positions include:

Budget Analyst	Language Specialist
Intelligence Research Specialist	Writer
Electronics Technician	Computer Programmer
Engineering Technician	Laboratory Technician
Paralegal	Administrative Assistant
Secretary	Typist
Clerk	Electrician
Carpenter	

To apply, a person must be a U.S. citizen with a high school diploma or its equivalent. Some openings require a bachelor's or advanced degree or technical training. Work experience is also required for some positions.

The FBI compensates support personnel according to the same General Schedule as special agents, though in most cases the starting scale is nearer the top of the chart, meaning lower in pay. Entry-level positions may be in the earliest slots on the chart, but can go through GS 9 levels, which translates into about $18,000 at the lowest end (GS 4, Grade 1) to about $40,000 (GS 9, Grade 10).

When a person has special skills, education, or experience, especially experience working in government, and if a vacancy needs filling, the FBI may make exceptions in the starting salary.

CONTACTING THE FBI

All hiring is done through the field offices, and the FBI suggests an interested individual contact the one nearest his or her home. For people with access to the Internet, many of the field offices have home pages with additional information.

FBI Field Offices

(Arranged alphabetically by city)

Federal Bureau of Investigation
Ste. 502, James T. Foley Bldg.
445 Broadway
Albany, NY 12207
(518) 465-7551

Federal Bureau of Investigation
Ste. 300
415 Silver Ave., SW
Albuquerque, NM 87102
(505) 224-2000

Federal Bureau of Investigation
101 E. Sixth Ave.
Anchorage, AK 99501
(907) 258-5322

Federal Bureau of Investigation
Ste. 400
2635 Century Pkwy., NE
Atlanta, GA 30345
(404) 679-9000

Federal Bureau of Investigation
7142 Ambassador Rd.
Baltimore, MD 21244-2754
(410) 265-8080

Federal Bureau of Investigation
Rm. 1400
2121 Eighth Ave. N
Birmingham, AL 35203
(205) 252-7705

Federal Bureau of Investigation
Ste. 600
One Center Plaza
Boston, MA 02108
(617) 742-5533

Federal Bureau of Investigation
One FBI Plaza
Buffalo, NY 14202-2698
(716) 856-7800

Federal Bureau of Investigation
Ste. 900
400 S. Tyron St.
Charlotte, NC 28285
(704) 377-9200

Federal Bureau of Investigation
Rm. 905
E. M. Dirksen Federal Office
Building
219 S. Dearborn St.
Chicago, IL 60604
(312) 431-1333

Federal Bureau of Investigation
Rm. 9023
550 Main St.
Cincinnati, OH 45273-8501
(513) 421-4310

Federal Bureau of Investigation
Rm. 3005
Federal Office Building
1240 E. 9th St.
Cleveland, OH 44199-9912
(216) 522-1400

Federal Bureau of Investigation
Rm. 1357
1835 Assembly St.
Columbia, SC 29201
(803) 254-3011

Federal Bureau of Investigation
Rm. 300
1801 N. Lamar
Dallas, TX 75202
(214) 720-2200

Federal Bureau of Investigation
Federal Office Bldg., Ste. 1823
1961 Stout St., 18th Fl.
Denver, CO 80294
(303) 629-7171

Federal Bureau of Investigation
P. V. McNamara Federal Office
Bldg., 26th Fl.
477 Michigan Ave.
Detroit, MI 48226
(313) 965-2323

Federal Bureau of Investigation
Ste. C-600
700 E. San Antonio Ave.
El Paso, TX 79901-7020
(915) 533-7451

Federal Bureau of Investigation
Rm. 4307
Kalanianaole Federal Office Bldg.
300 Ala Moana Blvd.
Honolulu, HI 96850
(808) 521-1411

Federal Bureau of Investigation
Rm. 200
2500 E. TC Jester
Houston, TX 77008-1300
(713) 868-2266

Federal Bureau of Investigation
Rm. 679
Federal Office Bldg.
575 N. Pennsylvania St.
Indianapolis, IN 46204
(317) 639-3301

Federal Bureau of Investigation
Rm. 1553
Federal Office Bldg.
100 W. Capitol St.
Jackson, MS 39269
(601) 948-5000

Federal Bureau of Investigation
Ste. 200
7820 Arlington Expwy.
Jacksonville, FL 32211
(904) 721-1211

Federal Bureau of Investigation
Rm. 300, U.S. Courthouse
811 Grand Ave.
Kansas City, MO 64106
(816) 221-6100

Federal Bureau of Investigation
Ste. 600
John J. Duncan Federal Office
Bldg.
710 Locust St.
Knoxville, TN 37902
(423) 544-0751

Federal Bureau of Investigation
700 E. Charleston Blvd.
Las Vegas, NV 89101
(702) 385-1281

Federal Bureau of Investigation
Ste. 200
Two Financial Centre
10825 Financial Centre Pkwy.
Little Rock, AR 72211-3552
(501) 221-9100

Federal Bureau of Investigation
Ste. 1700
Federal Office Building
11000 Wilshire Blvd.
Los Angeles, CA 90024
(310) 477-6565

Federal Bureau of Investigation
Rm. 500
600 Martin Luther King Jr. Pl.
Louisville, KY 40202
(502) 583-3941

Federal Bureau of Investigation
Ste. 3000
Eagle Crest Bldg.
225 N. Humphreys Blvd.
Memphis, TN 38120-2107
(901) 747-4300

Federal Bureau of Investigation
16320 NW. Second Ave.
North Miami Beach, FL 33169
(305) 944-9101

Federal Bureau of Investigation
Ste. 600
330 E. Kilbourn Ave.
Milwaukee, WI 53202-6627
(414) 276-4684

Federal Bureau of Investigation
Ste. 1100
111 Washington Ave., S.
Minneapolis, MN 55401
(612) 376-3200

Federal Bureau of Investigation
One St. Louis Centre
One St. Louis St., 3rd Fl.
Mobile, AL 36602
(334) 438-3674

Federal Bureau of Investigation
One Gateway Center, 22nd Fl.
Newark, NJ 07102-9889
(201) 622-5613

Federal Bureau of Investigation
Rm. 535
Federal Office Bldg.
150 Court St.
New Haven, CT 06510
(203) 777-6311

Federal Bureau of Investigation
Ste. 2200
1250 Poydras St.
New Orleans, LA 70113-1829
(504) 522-4671

Federal Bureau of Investigation
26 Federal Plaza, 23rd Fl.
New York, NY 10278
(212) 384-1000

Federal Bureau of Investigation
150 Corporate Blvd.
Norfolk, VA 23502
(804) 455-0100

Federal Bureau of Investigation
Ste. 1600
50 Penn Pl.
Oklahoma City, OK 73118
(405) 842-7471

Federal Bureau of Investigation
10755 Burt St.
Omaha, NE 68114
(402) 493-8688

Federal Bureau of Investigation
8th Fl.
William J. Green Jr. Federal Office
Bldg.
600 Arch St.
Philadelphia, PA 19106
(215) 829-2700

Federal Bureau of Investigation
Ste. 400
201 E. Indianola Ave.
Phoenix, AZ 85012
(602) 279-5511

Federal Bureau of Investigation
Ste. 300
U.S. Post Office Bldg.
700 Grant St.
Pittsburgh, PA 15219
(412) 471-2000

Federal Bureau of Investigation
Ste. 401
Crown Plaza Bldg.
1500 SW. First Ave.
Portland, OR 97201
(503) 224-4181

Federal Bureau of Investigation
111 Greencourt Rd.
Richmond, VA 23228
(804) 261-1044

Federal Bureau of Investigation
4500 Orange Grove Ave.
Sacramento, CA 95841-4205
(916) 481-9110

Federal Bureau of Investigation
Rm. 2704
L. Douglas Abram Federal Bldg.
1520 Market St.
St. Louis, MO 63103
(314) 241-5357

Federal Bureau of Investigation
Ste. 1200
257 Towers Bldg.
257 E. 200 S.
Salt Lake City, UT 84111
(801) 579-1400

Federal Bureau of Investigation
Ste. 200
U.S. Post Office & Courthouse
Bldg.
615 E. Houston St.
San Antonio, TX 78205
(210) 225-6741

Federal Bureau of Investigation
Federal Office Bldg.
9797 Aero Dr.
San Diego, CA 92123-1800
(619) 565-1255

Federal Bureau of Investigation
450 Golden Gate Ave., 13th Floor
San Francisco, CA 94102-9523
(415) 553-7400

Federal Bureau of Investigation
Rm. 526
U.S. Federal Bldg.
150 Carlos Chardon Ave.
Hato Rey
San Juan, PR 00918-1716
(809) 754-6000

Federal Bureau of Investigation
Rm. 710
915 Second Ave.
Seattle, WA 98174-1096
(206) 622-0460

Federal Bureau of Investigation
Ste. 400
400 W. Monroe St.
Springfield, IL 62704
(217) 522-9675

Federal Bureau of Investigation
Rm. 610
Federal Office Bldg.
500 Zack St.
Tampa, FL 33602
(813) 273-4566

Federal Bureau of Investigation
Washington Metropolitan Field
Office
1900 Half St., SW
Washington, DC 20024
(202) 252-7801

SECTION 2

THE CRIMINAL JUSTICE SYSTEM

CHAPTER 11

Criminal Justice and the Courts

WHAT IS CRIMINAL JUSTICE?

Criminal justice is the enforcement of criminal law. It involves fair handling of those accused of a crime. Also important to criminal justice is the understanding of causes of crime and the prevention of future crimes. Criminal justice is based on our society's understanding of right and wrong.

The Constitution of the United States and the Bill of Rights guarantee certain rights to every person, including the presumption of innocence in an alleged crime until guilt is proven beyond a reasonable doubt.

For reasons beyond the scope of this book, many types of crime are on the increase. Areas once assumed to be safe are now less so. At shopping malls and fast food restaurants, criminals have claimed innocent victims who "got in the way" of crimes in progress.

The role of our criminal justice system is to balance the rights of the accused with the rights of society. The criminal justice system, which includes law enforcement, the courts, and corrections, is challenged daily to interpret criminal law.

This section will cover career opportunities in the court and corrections systems. (Law enforcement and all that occurs before an arrest have been covered in earlier chapters.)

Job opportunities in criminal justice are steadily increasing. The growth is due to actual and perceived increases in crime, plus growing public support for the rights of victims. The court system is expanding out of necessity and creating new, more specialized positions. No matter how we view it, the criminal justice system is complex and confusing. Each state runs its independent court system, and there are many differences from state to state. At the city or county level, you will find variety based on community size. Job titles, salary levels, and job prerequisites differ depending on location.

CRIMINAL JUSTICE CAREER PROFILE

Besides the fact that criminal justice is an open, expanding field, why do people pursue careers in this area? Most want to work closely with people. They want to see the justice system function as it was intended: presumption of innocence, fair trial by a jury or judge, and appropriate sentences for those found guilty. They want to prevent crime and protect the public.

Many careerists are looking for action and a fast pace. Although you can find varying degrees of excitement at all levels of criminal justice, the media would have us believe these jobs are nonstop adventure. Those who have worked in the field know that variety and risks are balanced by hours of conventional paperwork and social interaction.

General qualities helpful to criminal justice career-seekers include enjoying people, working well under pressure, being able to make decisions after careful analysis of information, and functioning as part of a team.

Preparation for a career in criminal justice requires a well-rounded program. Jobs call for a high school diploma; most demand two or more years of college. Study includes social work, psychology, political science, and sociology. In addition to "book work," experience in your field of interest is vital. A successful internship is often the tiebreaker for a job when all else is equal.

It is a good idea to know what your career goal is, then determine the best path to get there. This path may vary from state to state or even among communities. Talk to people working in the system. Do an internship or perform volunteer work in your area of interest. Thinking ahead and being prepared are your two best strategies for attaining long-term goals.

THE STRUCTURE OF THE COURTS

You should understand the structure of the American court system before you meet the criminal justice "actors."

When someone is arrested, his or her case moves into the court system. Courts are units of the judicial branch of government. They are authorized to decide controversies and disputes brought before them. Courts settle cases based on statutes (laws) and the state and U.S. constitutions. The courts' goal is to dispense justice fairly and efficiently.

There are more than 15,000 federal and state courts in the United States. Each court has a *jurisdiction* or an area of the law within its authority. Trial courts, appellate courts, and a court of last resort exist at both federal and state levels.

Trial courts rule on issues of fact. They establish a verdict based on evidence and testimony brought to trial. These courts of general jurisdiction can hear all cases, civil and criminal. Civil courts settle wrongs committed by one person against another, while criminal courts handle wrongs related to the rights of **all.**

Appellate ("appeals") courts are the next level. They deal only with the trial court's interpretation and application of the law. They do not debate issues of fact.

Supreme courts consider appeals on issues of fact and interpretation from lower courts. Supreme court decisions are binding on all lower courts.

Limited jurisdiction courts hear minor cases or the beginning parts of more serious cases. Special jurisdiction courts try cases in a limited area such as domestic matters or tax cases.

The majority of courts are at the lowest state level. They are local or district courts. Nearly 70 percent of all their cases are traffic offenses. Less than 2 percent of cases are felonies.

Because the court system is complex and fragmented, attorneys don't always know which court is the "best" court in which to try a given case!

THE CRIMINAL JUSTICE PROCESS— FROM APPEARANCE TO SENTENCING

A local magistrate presides over the first court appearance of anyone arrested. This is called the *initial appearance* or *preliminary hearing*. In this information process, police turn facts on a case over to a prosecutor who presents evidence they believe justifies arrest. The judge or magistrate can decide whether or not the evidence is sufficient to sustain a court case.

A judge who believes there is not enough evidence for trial can release the suspect. If the evidence seems to support the arrest, the next step is *arraignment*. In this procedure, the suspect (defendant) appears before a judge and is formally charged with a crime. He or she must plead guilty or not guilty. At this point, the judge must decide how likely the arrested person is to appear for future court proceedings. If the suspect has a family, a home, and a job, the judge may release the suspect on his or her own recognizance. For others, the judge will set a dollar amount of *bail* and collect the money (usually from a bailiff) before releasing the person for future trial. (The bail amount is based on the type and severity of the crime, and ensures the person's future court appearance.) Suspects considered dangerous are held in jail.

If the suspect pleads guilty, a *plea bargain* may be worked out by the judge, the prosecutor, and the defendant's attorney. This plea bargain sets out the exact sentence for the crime and ends the criminal trial process. The punishment is usually less severe for a conviction established without going to trial. If the plea is not guilty, the case goes to trial.

Very few cases reach the *trial* stage. Of those that do, most are settled at a bench trial before a judge. The judge listens to the evidence on both sides, then decides innocence or guilt. When a case is tried before a jury, a panel of 6 to 18 citizens listens to the evidence and decides on innocence or guilt. With a not guilty verdict, the defendant is released.

Sentencing, usually by a judge, follows a guilty verdict. The judge communicates the sentence and its conditions to the convicted criminal. The sentence can include any combination of fine, prison, and probation. Conditions of the sentence include confinement time and the amount of the fine. After sentencing, the accused may appeal the conviction to a higher court.

After the offender serves an established portion of the sentence, he or she is eligible for *revocation* or *conditional release*. This is probation or parole. When on probation or parole, a former prisoner comes back into the community, but he or she must follow strict conditions. Disobeying these conditions can result in further punishment. Probation and parole are meant to be adjustment periods, preparing the person to rejoin society.

When probation or parole are complete, the parolee is *discharged* and released. That particular case is now out of the criminal justice system.

COURT JOBS

There are various jobs available within the court system. Many local positions have state and federal equivalents with higher pay. In most cases, entry-level jobs can lead to better paying, more prestigious positions. Titles may vary for similar jobs. For example, a judge may be called a magistrate or a justice. Usually magistrates and justices are lower level judges. Their authority is more limited than a judge's.

A district justice has the same responsibilities as a local magistrate. He or she may also act as a justice of the peace, performing marriages and administering oaths. A district justice is appointed or elected to office. The pay scale as a local justice is usually higher near larger cities, but is still relatively low. This position is normally part-time with set court hours. A justice often comes from a law or police background, but this may not be required. According to District Justice David Keightley, community involvement and being well known in his area are more important factors than specific job experience.

Being a district justice is different from being a judge with a jury in a large courtroom. District Justice David Keightley has a magnificent desk, the focal point of a courtroom no larger than a classroom. He is in charge. He, not a jury, makes all decisions. He says some of his decisions will change people's lives forever; others have little or no impact. (He sees many offenders so often, he knows them by name.)

Judge Keightley presides over the district court in Lansdale, Pennsylvania. His full red beard contrasts with his low-key, even voice. But don't let his quiet ways fool you. Judge Keightley is friendly and fair, until someone tries to take advantage of him. Then the fire comes out with commands that tell everyone, "We'll do it **my** way!"

As he listens to the story of a 17 year old with a suspended driver's license, David Keightley fingers a baseball. (He loves to interject his Little League coaching experiences whenever he can!) The offender is wearing baggy pants with a belt that hangs to his hips. Judge Keightley interrupts the boy's confusing story with, "What's the matter with your belt? Did you lose a lot of weight recently? Guess I'm really behind in the style." His sarcasm adds a touch of humor to a serious situation.

What does he like about being a district justice? The unpredictability of it. "Just when you think you've seen it all, something else comes along." He finds that despite the unusual cases, most people are likable. "Sometimes, you can be a criminal and still be a nice guy."

A federal magistrate is appointed for an eight-year term of office by a federal district court judge. He or she has authority to hear petty cases and conduct the beginning stages of felony trials and more serious civil trials. A federal magistrate also has the power to issue warrants. There are more than 400 U.S. magistrates in all. The starting salary for a federal magistrate is about $120,000 a year.

As with other jobs in the court system, there are judges at the state and federal levels. At both, a judge presides over trials by listening to testimony and ensuring that each side follows the rules. If an indigent (poor) defendant cannot afford legal counsel, the judge will appoint an attorney. Judges determine which evidence is admissible and protect the legal rights of each side.

When there is no jury, the judge decides on guilt or innocence. In a jury trial, he or she instructs the jury on the law and how to make a final decision.

State judges are appointed or elected for a specified number of years. Salaries for a state judge range from $56,000 to $100,000 a year. Currently, state judgeships are increasing due to backlogs and the growing number of criminal trials.

Federal judges in the lower courts are appointed or elected to office for a specified term. Their salaries range from $80,000 to $130,000 a year.

Federal justices of the U.S. Supreme Court are appointed by the president of the United States and approved by the U.S. Senate. Each appointment is for life. Positions for U.S. Supreme Court justices open when a justice retires, resigns, or is impeached. The Constitution of the United States requires they be members of the bar. This is indeed the top, the pinnacle of success! Judges at this level make over $170,000 a year.

Today, full-time judges at every level have legal training and courtroom experience. They often gain this experience by starting as local prosecutors or county attorneys. They may then add to their qualifications by working as part-time justices or magistrates.

Criminal Prosecutors

The prosecutor has an important role in the criminal justice process. Prosecutors and their staffs represent the state (the "people") in criminal cases. They must gather and present enough evidence to show probable cause that a defendant has committed a crime. The rights of the offender are carefully guarded; he or she **is innocent** until proven guilty. That burden of proof lies with the prosecutor, and must be beyond a reasonable doubt.

There are over 8,000 state and local prosecution offices across the United States. The increase in crime and backlogs in the court system create plenty of opportunities at this level in the justice system.

Local and federal prosecutors are members of the bar (attorneys). Local prosecutors (also called state's attorneys or district attorneys) run for election for specified terms. This elected position is often seen as a stepping stone for a future political or judicial career. Since prosecutors protect the community by defending *against* crime, a successful prosecutor can gain favor in the public eye.

Prosecutors near larger cities may have assistant prosecutors to help them. Although not a high-paying job, this can be a great way for young attorneys to gain trial experience before moving to a law firm.

At the federal level, prosecutors are called U.S. attorney or deputy U.S. attorney. These officials are appointed by the president of the United States and approved by the Senate. Federal prosecutors handle federal criminal cases. They, like local prosecutors, employ staff assistants. Federal prosecutors are paid well; their salaries range from $89,000 to $123,000 a year.

Defense Attorneys

At the opposite side of the courtroom, defense attorneys represent the interests of defendants. All defense attorneys are members of their local bar associations. There are several ways for a defense attorney to handle a criminal case. The least common is *private retention*. (Relatively few criminal offenders can afford to hire counsel.)

In *Gideon vs. Wainwright* (1963), the U.S. Supreme Court ruled that everyone accused of a crime is entitled to counsel. If a defendant cannot afford a lawyer, the state must provide legal counsel. This ruling created two other types of defense counsel, public defenders and assigned counsel.

The most common form of defense counsel is the public defender. Like the prosecutor's office, the office of the public defender is supported by public funds. Most public defenders are at the county level. Fewer than 25 percent are part of state judiciary.

In many areas, public defenders are elected. The public defender then selects a staff of assistant public defenders, investigators, paralegals, secretaries, and law student interns. The chief public defender usually works full-time, while some of his staff may be part-timers. The criminal caseload in a given area may determine the staff size.

Public defenders perform all the functions of lawyers. They interpret laws, counsel and support their clients, go to trial for their clients, and research and compose legal briefs. They may also take on social work, providing counsel for poorer members of the community who are not criminals but who still need legal aid.

The public defender's office is a good place for young, inexperienced attorneys to begin. They can build their backgrounds in criminal trials before they enter private practice. Experience as a public defender can help those seeking political or judicial careers. Older private practice attorneys looking to lessen their work loads may also work in the public defender's office.

The public defender's office represents more than the criminal population. There are many career opportunities projected for this area.

In communities with lower criminal caseloads, *assigned counsel* replace public defenders. Some jurisdictions list their attorneys. Judges work down the list, assigning each lawyer "equal time" in criminal defense. Other judges use attorneys who volunteer for criminal defense. Volunteers do so part-time; they usually have full-time law practices.

The assigned lawyer is paid a set fee for the case or paid by the hour with a ceiling.

A lawyer in private practice usually earns from $40,000 to $80,000 a year. Public defenders make slightly less to start, and their top earnings are somewhat lower than in private practice. But money and experience are not the only reasons to work in public defense.

Dianne Freestone was appointed the first female assistant public defender of Saratoga County, New York. She was assigned to represent indigent defendants in the justice courts that deal primarily with custody, abuse, and family issues.

From the time she was in eighth grade, Freestone knew she wanted to be a lawyer in the public defense. She saw people who loved and cared for their children, yet lacked education and income. Without a committed attorney, she knew these people would have no one on their side. She chose to stand with them and she found rewards beyond words.

Ms. Freestone says she is not a "barracuda." Instead of being aggressive and competing with men, her advice to any woman choosing to become a lawyer in the criminal justice system is, "Don't give up your femininity; a female attorney should be just that, a female."

She recommends that anyone interested in a career in criminal justice set a goal as early as possible and pick a route to follow. To set a goal, ask yourself what you want out of life. Family? Money? Time? The jobs in criminal justice are varied. Make sure the position you aim for fits your life plans. Know the political orientation of your community. Your connections with the dominant party can determine how quickly you move up in a given community.

Have a diverse background. It's never too early to get involved in outside activities, on campus and in the community. High academics are vital, but your outside involvement sets you apart from the rest.

Choose an internship in your area of interest. This puts your foot in the door and helps you see if this is really the direction you want to take.

Freestone loves what she does. When her husband calls her at work, he wonders just how much **work** actually gets done. "Someone always seems to be laughing," he says. That's how she knows she's in the right position. She can keep a sense of humor and still be rewarded for helping people in need.

Probation and Parole Officers

Probation and parole officers enter a criminal case at the end. Their training and responsibilities are similar.

A probation officer reviews a case before the criminal is sentenced. The officer interviewing the criminal writes a report recommending the type and conditions of sentencing. When the court's sentence includes probation, the probation officer counsels and supervises the probationer. The probation officer works with the offender's family and employer, helping them to understand the terms and conditions of probation. The probation officer makes sure the terms are obeyed, and encourages and guides social adjustments. The offender and probation officer meet regularly. The officer writes progress reports during the probation.

In contrast, the client of a parole officer has been jailed. He or she is being released conditionally, based on the recommendations of a parole board. It is up to the parole officer to help the offender adjust from prison life to the community. Parole conditions are specific and must be obeyed, or the parolee runs the risk of going back to court. The parole officer monitors and evaluates progress.

Probation and parole officers act as social workers and rule enforcers. They must be firm yet fair. Their work is challenging but rewarding. In most cases, these positions require a bachelor's degree in social sciences, human behavior, or criminal justice.

There are probation and parole opportunities at the county, state, and federal levels. Starting salaries are from $20,000 to $25,000 depending on jurisdiction. Because parole officers may supervise more closely, they are usually paid slightly more than probation officers.

Probation and parole officers are usually selected through civil service testing. Contact your local civil service office for eligibility requirements and testing dates.

This is a promising field because of overcrowded correctional institutions and the cost of confinement. With experience or a master's degree, there is room for advancement to district or regional administrator.

ADMINSTRATIVE CAREERS IN THE COURT SYSTEM

There are many administrative positions in the criminal justice system—some within the courtroom setting, others behind the scenes. One of the most visible is the court reporter. This is the person at the front of the courtroom who appeared to be typing during every *Perry Mason* television episode. Indeed, she is a fixture in the American courtroom—a vital link in the judicial process. (This careerist has more often been a woman, but the job is certainly open to anyone qualified.)

The typewriter the court reporter uses is a unique stenotype machine. With this machine, she records verbatim each word said during a trial—all testimony, questions, arguments, and the judge's rulings. Accuracy is vital. What she takes down during the proceeding is later transcribed in manuscript form and becomes the official record of that trial. If a case is appealed to a higher court, that transcript becomes the basis for review of the original trial.

In addition to typing dexterity, a good background in English is important for this position. Since courtroom procedures are often fast paced, the court reporter must be able to work quickly under pressure, often meeting deadlines. He or she must have good hearing and the ability to concentrate for extended periods.

A high school education is necessary, as well as completion of a court reporting course at an accredited technical school or university. After taking this course, he or she can become certified as a registered professional reporter by the National Shorthand Reporters Association (NSRA). Earning this certificate makes the reporter more marketable and increases her chances of later pay increases and advancements.

Although court reporting can be a full-time position, it is often filled by people working part-time. The salary for those who work full-time can be as high as

$40,000 a year (average $30,000 to $35,000). For the number of hours worked, court reporting is considered to be one of the highest-salaried legal careers. Because many court reporters work part-time, the supply of certified court reporters never meets the demand. The Martin School of Business in Philadelphia, Pennsylvania, claims to have 100 percent placement of students graduating from their court reporting program.

This is a good career for someone looking for flexibility and variety, such as working mothers and law students. Although the court reporter's presence is court is predetermined, transcribing can be done at home on an individual's own time. Law students find court reporting to be good background and an excellent way to observe the court system firsthand.

Another option for someone interested in part-time, flexible employment is the position of scopist. A scopist edits what the court reporter has recorded. He or she does not appear in court but acts as an assistant to the court reporters by transforming their transcripts into their final written form. This can be done at home on his or her own time. A full-time scopist can also earn close to $40,000 a year. Like the court reporter, there are never enough scopists to fill the need in the court system.

Another visible position in the courtroom is the bailiff. The history of the bailiff goes back to 13th-century England. Bailiffs were used as night watchmen so the general population could sleep "worry-free." In the event of a fire, robbery, or other crisis, the bailiff would rouse the community and citizens would handle the problem.

The bailiff of today also serves as a "watchman" by keeping order in the court. He or she accompanies the defendants in and out of court and prevents their escape during the trial. The bailiff is in charge of the jury's safety, escorting them to and from the courtroom and remaining in the room with them when they are sequestered. He or she protects the jury from the public and controls the jury's access to the media. The bailiff also announces the judge's entry into the courtroom and calls each witness to the witness stand.

Since the bailiffs are responsible for the security of the court, they must be alert. They must also be appropriately trained in the use of the handguns they carry.

In addition to a high school diploma, the bailiff may be asked to pass a written test and a physical exam. The starting salary for a bailiff is $22,000 a year. Average salaries for seasoned bailiffs are between $25,800 and $30,900 a year.

Bailiffs in federal courtrooms are deputy U.S. marshals. Their responsibilities are the same as other bailiffs, but with federal prisoners, judges, and juries. This job requires a bachelor's degree or three years' experience. In addition to written and physical exams, the deputy U.S. marshal is required to complete several weeks of training. Starting salary for a U.S. marshal in 1995 was $23,938 a year. The average for an experienced U.S. marshal was $29,644. (See chapter 6.)

The court clerk (also called the clerk of court) is often an elected or appointed court officer. Though clearly visible during a trial, court clerks do much "behind the scenes" work before, during, and after a trial. They summons potential jurors and subpoena witnesses for both the prosecution and the defense. Depending on the size of the jurisdiction, they may have assistants. Together they keep a written record of each court case and perform other needed clerical tasks. In some states, court clerks may be empowered to issue warrants.

At a trial, the court clerk "swears in" each person called to the witness stand. The court clerk identifies and marks physical evidence as it is admitted during the proceedings. He or she is also responsible for the security and custody of this evidence.

Most court clerks have a bachelor's degree in business administration. A high school diploma with administrative experience may be acceptable in some smaller jurisdictions.

A court with a full docket will have at least one court clerk and probably several assistant court clerks. Smaller, less busy courts may employ a part-time court clerk. Full-time court clerks make an average of $25,000 to $29,000 a year.

The outlook for court clerks is excellent. They can be the key to a smooth running court system. Though court restructuring is now commonplace, court administration is getting more priority and is "hotter" than ever.

With the backlog in the court system, some newer positions have been created to ease the workload of the key players and reduce the number of delays in the system. Because of current growth and change in the criminal justice field, these careers are all timely.

In the past, courts have survived with judges and court clerks doing all the court administrative work. Pressure to alleviate backlogs and bottlenecks has forced courts to reorganize. Part of this reorganization includes adding a court administrator. The person who fills this position must be well organized; it is his or her job to manage the case flow. He or she does this by analyzing backlogs and recommending solutions. The court administrator works closely with the judges in preparing the court docket (calendar). Efficiency is the primary goal.

The court administrator is also budget conscious, preparing and monitoring the court's operating budget.

In a court with numerous judges, the court administrator provides uniform court management. He or she often supervises a staff of clerks.

The court administrator often gets involved in jury management by determining the number of citizens to call in for the jury pool. He or she also works to reduce the amount of waiting time for jurors who have been selected for a case.

Most court administrators have master's degrees in business administration or court administration. Some have law degrees. Others have bachelor's degrees with previous experience in administration. Court administrator is a good step up for those who have worked as court clerks.

The starting salary for a court administrator is about $28,000 a year. Those with experience make an average of $40,000 a year.

CHAPTER 12

Corrections: The People and the Process

The role of corrections in our society is changing. Administrators in this field are at once excited about the changes that technology and education bring, while frustrated at budget cuts and lack of training dollars.

Gone is the corrections officer of the movies—the corrupt, abusive **male** who hates his job and the prisoners he guards. The corrections officer of today is a dedicated, service-oriented male **or female.** He or she is there because they want to see our corrections system work. They believe that the goal of prisons can be to protect the community from criminals **and** provide these same lawbreakers with skills that can give them hope for a positive future in society.

The frustration comes when reviewing the statistics:

- On any given day there are more than 1.2 million people incarcerated in thousands of jails and hundreds of prisons across the United States.

- There is a total of nearly 4.3 million people in the penal system, one out of every 60 Americans.

- Among all the nations in Western civilization, the United States has the highest rate of imprisonment and imposes the longest prison terms on offenders.

- Incarceration costs the state about $11,302 per inmate each year. Those imprisoned in federal institutions each cost approximately $13,162 per year.

With numbers like these, it is easy to see why most citizens want to sweep corrections under the carpet. And because this area is less visible than law enforcement and the court system, it is easier to ignore or forget.

Members of our communities want to see appropriate sentencing for criminals. Lenient sentencing or community service is taboo; we want our lawbreakers behind bars! Mandatory jail sentences for driving while intoxicated, the "war on drugs," and "three strikes" legislation are filling our prisons and jails to the bursting point.

But our penal system has not always been this way. As a matter of fact, the use of incarceration as punishment for criminal behavior is a relatively new concept.

A QUICK HISTORY

Before 1790, those who broke the law in the colonies were sentenced to punishment that was similar to their offense—"an eye for an eye." It was not uncommon for lawbreakers to suffer physical torture, mutilation, and public humiliation.

The first prison was erected in 1773 in Newgate, Connecticut. It was built by Quakers as a more humane alternative to the torture suffered by early Americans. They believed that time alone to reconsider the crime would lead to repentance and, upon release, life as a reformed citizen. Over the course of the next 200 years, various types of prisons were built—all in response to public attitudes toward crime and punishment. The role of the prison changed; depending on society's viewpoint, it was seen as a place for repentance *or* treatment *or* punishment *or* rehabilitation. At one point (1890 to 1935), prisons were seen as a place that provided cheap labor and goods for the open market.

During the 1960s and '70s inmates were viewed as victims who should not be further punished by removing them from the community. Group homes and work release programs became popular during this time. Parole and probation programs were also developed at this time to assist inmates in their transition from prison back to the community.

A punitive public attitude returned in the 1980s. This point of view is largely responsible for the overcrowding of our prisons and jails that prevails today. From 1984 to 1994, our prison population increased by 250 percent.

We ask the impossible from today's overcrowded corrections system. In *Criminal Justice Today* (Prentice Hall, 1997), Frank Schmalleger has written, "In addition to carrying out sentences, we also ask that (prison) ensure the safety of law-abiding citizens, that it select the best alternative from among the many available for handling a given offender, that it protect those under its charge and that it guarantee fairness in the handling of all with whom it comes into contact."

There are about 1,100 prisons and 3,500 jails in operation across the U.S. These are filled to capacity. Because prisoner numbers are expected to continue rising, more prisons are being built. The area of corrections can no longer be ignored.

PRISONS VERSUS JAILS

The words prison and jail are often used interchangeably by "civilians." There are, however, important differences. Prisons are operated by the federal or state government. Their facilities are large and their inmate numbers are high—often so high they become depersonalized and regimented. Their size and the number of people they house usually makes it possible to separate inmates by sex. They are also able to provide programs and instruction for their many inmates. Prisons house felons sentenced to a year or more of incarceration.

In contrast, jails are run by the county or city. They are small, usually housing fewer than 50 inmates. Many have been convicted of a misdemeanor and are serving sentences of less than a year. Others are awaiting trial and have been denied or unable to post bail. Because of prison overcrowding, jails are frequently used as temporary housing for felons awaiting a vacant spot in a more suitable facility. According to Lawrence F. Travis III, author of *Introduction to Criminal Justice* (Anderson Publishing Co., 1995), nearly 14,000 inmates were in jails in 1986 waiting for permanent placement. Jail buildings are often old and in poor condition. They were never intended for extended use. Programs are not offered because turnover is supposed to be high. Jail employees often perform several job responsibilities—they are seldom trained to provide for the more extensive needs of the more serious criminal.

And who are the inmates that fill our prisons and jails? The "typical" inmate is male, under 30, and without a high school degree. Forty-six percent are convicted of violent crimes, 23 percent property crimes, and 22 percent drug crimes. Although less than 10 percent of the inmate population is female, this is the fastest growing group nationwide.

Prisons may differ in size and architecture, yet the culture remains virtually the same. From the moment a defendant is convicted, he or she enters the regimented society of prison. In response to this humiliation, inmates in every prison have developed subcultures of their own. These "societies" have their own leadership, values, and behavioral patterns that vary little from prison to prison. Inmate subcultures are so powerful, those who chose to remain apart from them are often threatened or physically harmed.

CORRECTIONS OFFICER

At the center of these informal social systems is the corrections officer. He or she keeps things running with a semblance of order; he or she has a personal relationship with each of the inmates under his or her supervision; he or she is vital.

Although there is a dramatic need because of overcrowding and new prison construction, the job of corrections officer is a serious job for strong individuals! Travis calls correctional officers, "the other inmates." Over the course of their careers, many officers spend more time in prison than the majority of inmates they supervise.

Across the nation, there are approximately 352,000 corrections officers. They are employed by the federal, state, and local governments in jails and minimum, medium, and maximum security prisons. Eighty percent are male. Over 60 percent of a correctional institution's staff is composed of corrections officers. Despite the numbers and the importance of this job, the corrections officer has not, until recently, been given the respect he or she deserves. The responsibilities are not only numerous, but stressful. Corrections officers supervise daily activities and work assignments, conduct body and cell searches, and make sure prison rules are followed. They must be alert and security conscious. When they spot trouble, they must think and act quickly. Since they are dealing with aggressive and often violent individuals, corrections officers must be strong enough to protect themselves and the inmates in their care.

Although primarily responsible for maintaining custody, safety, and control, corrections officers are often called on to do informal counseling. They must draw the line between gaining respect and being friendly and empathetic, being careful to be firm but fair. In addition to the "people" side of the job, corrections officers are also responsible for daily reports and paperwork. They must rate their inmates' quality of work, assess their conduct, and record all violations. Because security must be provided around the clock, the corrections officer is expected to work some nights and weekends.

The qualifications for corrections officer vary from state to state. In general, a candidate must be a U.S. citizen, be at least 21 years old, have a high school degree, have no criminal record, and be in good physical condition. With the current emphasis on counseling, some postsecondary education in psychology or criminology is desirable. Passing a civil service exam may also be required. The starting salary range is $17,000 to $20,000, depending on the state and the size of the institution.

A corrections officer at the federal level performs the same functions and must meet similar requirements. The maximum starting age at this level is 35 years old, and the candidate must have three and a half years of relevant work experience or a secondary degree.

A training program lasting from two weeks to several months is given before beginning the job. This training includes self-defense, the use of firearms, and communication skills. There are also ongoing refresher courses provided to help the officers keep current.

The starting salary for corrections officers at the federal level was $23,938 in 1995.

Promotions

Promotions at the state and local levels are generally made from within each individual institution. This is not the case at the federal level where transfer and relocation may be necessary. Corrections officers can further their education to make themselves promotable to the supervisory roles of sergeant, then lieutenant, then captain. With additional training, correctional officers can be eligible for administrative roles or can branch off to become parole officers (see chapter 11).

If interested in employment with the Federal Bureau of Prisons, write for an application to:

National Recruitment Office
320 First St., NW
Washington, DC 20534
(202) 724-3204

The employment outlook for corrections officers will continue to rise with the addition of new prisons to our system. The greatest number of corrections employment opportunities are available at the state level. Since crime and incarceration will probably not disappear, job security is excellent and not based on the condition of the economy.

CHAPTER 13

Other Criminal Justice Jobs

CRIMINOLOGIST

Most people probably **think** they know what a criminologist is, but ask them for a definition and it will probably be incorrect. Although the word criminologist is vague, the job of criminologist is specific. It is a career many people in the criminal justice field would love to have.

A criminologist studies the causes of crime and how our society deals with it. If this sounds monotonous, imagine being assigned a question, then going out into the field to find the answer. Different neighborhoods, social classes, and ethnic groups would have an impact on the answers you receive. Your study would yield unique results even compared to similar studies done as recently as five years ago. It is a fascinating job that includes all kinds of excitement and even danger. It requires a person with varied talents and abilities.

A criminologist is a sociologist. All have bachelor's degrees—most have master's degrees and often a doctorate in criminology, sociology, or psychology.

The job of criminologist offers great variety. Usually research is done in the field. This may include working with police, lawyers, probation officers, judges, corrections officers, and even prisoners. The criminologist studies criminal justice systems and observes neighborhoods. He or she conducts interviews and completes surveys. The data is then examined, organized, and compiled into a report or a book.

Criminologists are vital to our society today. They are the experts who determine why our crime rates are rising. They search for potential solutions. They initiate pilot programs based on their findings and recommendations.

Criminologists can work for a government agency or a private firm. Many also teach part-time in universities.

In addition to a bachelor's degree, the future criminologist should have a clear understanding of how criminal justice agencies work. This can be enhanced by doing a variety of internships. An understanding of computers and statistical methods is also necessary before searching for a criminologist position.

Salaries for this career vary depending on the employing agency. Entry level is usually between $20,000 and $25,000 a year. With experience, salaries can reach $75,000 or above.

For more information write:

The American Society of Criminology
1314 Kinnear Rd.
Columbus, OH 43212

The competition for jobs in criminology is keen. Current budget cuts have decreased government jobs in this field. However, with the rising crime rate and proposed changes in our judicial system, the need for highly educated, experienced criminologists may grow.

POLYGRAPH EXAMINER

Changes in technology have helped create some new criminal justice positions. One of these jobs is polygraph examiner. Although "lie detectors" have been around for several decades, only recently have their findings been allowed as evidence in many courts. You may be surprised to find that polygraph examiners are used in many different settings, not just law enforcement and the court system. Private businesses often hire polygraph examiners to test job applicants. Private investigators even find occasion to hire polygraph examiners. But by far, the largest employer of polygraph examiners are local, state, and federal court systems.

The polygraph is an instrument that measures changes in pulse, blood pressure, and respiration. While connected to a polygraph, the subject is asked carefully prepared questions. Reactions to these questions determine whether or not the subject is telling the truth. Although guilt or innocence cannot be based on this test alone, the polygraph exam can be useful in reaching a verdict, or at least in indicating the possible truthfulness of the person being tested.

The polygraph examiner conducts a four-stage test. Before meeting the subject, he or she collects information by doing some investigative work. Background material about the crime and the examinee is pulled together and reviewed. The second step is a personal interview with the subject. The testing procedure is explained and rapport is sought. The examiner then spends time developing yes or no questions geared to the specific case. The third stage is performing the actual test or series of tests. Usually the examiner breaks the test into sections of about ten questions each. The questions are clear and require little thought. There are no surprise questions and no trick questions. After the test is scored, the final step is a follow-up interview with the subject to discuss the results.

In addition to performing polygraph exams, the examiner is required by law to keep records and reports on each test. He or she may also be asked to serve as a witness in court. When called as a witness, the examiner is asked for objective data results, not opinions.

Those interested in becoming a polygraph examiner must complete their bachelor's degree. An emphasis on criminal investigation is helpful, as is a strong background in human physiology. A six- to nine-week training program is required by most states followed by a six-month internship with an experienced examiner. Almost all states require a polygraph examiner to be licensed; requirements vary from state to state. Examiners must be impartial and have excellent communication skills. One of the challenges of the job is dealing with uncooperative subjects. A polygraph examiner must have a clean history—no criminal background or police record.

Polygraph examiners are paid by the test and by their court appearances. These rates vary from region to region. An examiner can start anywhere from $18,000 to $35,000 a year and advance to $60,000 or more with experience. Polygraph examiners can work for local, state, or federal courts, for police departments, or for the FBI, CIA, or U.S. Secret Service. They may also be employed by security firms or private firms. Others freelance or start their own businesses.

The American Polygraph Association (APA) is a national organization of polygraph examiners. In addition to conducting seminars to keep examiners up-to-date on current changes, this organization also provides information on job openings.

The increase in crime rates and abundance of cases in court has contributed to a demand for polygraph examiners. This need is across the nation in all areas of the system.

There are numerous other jobs that fall into the criminal justice field. These include fingerprint classifier, criminalist, victim services personnel, police sketch artist, court liaison counselor, and pretrial services officer. These positions are available based on the size and jurisdiction of a specific court system. Generally, the larger the jurisdiction, the more varied the court jobs.

CHAPTER 14

The Juvenile Justice System

Today's juvenile offenders make headlines because many are committing violent crimes with deadly weapons. Guns are an increasing element of youthful criminal activity. The surprise is that juvenile crime rates are dropping slightly overall, even as the types of crime are growing more serious.

Frank Smalleger, author of *Criminal Justice Today* (Prentice Hall, 1997), noted that in the early 1990s, 41,000 juveniles across the United States were in custodial care (3,000 were young women). Most were housed in any of a thousand homelike nonsecure facilities, but hard-core young criminals were kept in 70 "secure" institutions. All these underage offenders are called *juvenile delinquents.*

What is a juvenile delinquent? Some have committed only one crime. Others are persistent offenders. They often belong to gangs engaged in criminal activity. Many attach themselves to gangs because they have no significant home or school relationships.

Gangs are not recent happenings. They have walked hand-in-hand with poverty throughout history. Gangs are not haphazard either, but exist in given territories and have strong, if negative, leadership. They offer the gang member a destructive but genuine sense of purpose. Many gangs exist only to deal in drugs. Because drugs do not come cheaply, drug dealing often includes violence. Until communities and the police can offer gang members useful alternatives to their empty and dangerous lives, they will continue to count on the false security of territorial wars, drug dealing, and street crime.

Gangs exist in many communities, but their presence is felt most acutely in the poor neighborhoods of big cities. Here, the semiautomatics and Uzi submachine guns are weapons of choice. Lawrence Travis III, author of *Introduction to Criminal Justice* (Anderson Publishing Co., 1995), cites Los Angeles as the "gang capital" of the United States. Recent statistics show that over 143,000 young people belong to gangs. Most gang members have grown up in family environments that are dysfunctional, dangerous, or both. Thus, these young people often turn to gangs to get **away** from the violence of their homes!

Lower Bucks County, Pennsylvania—hardly a city setting—harbored a teen gang accused of ordering pizzas, then robbing the delivery people at gunpoint. These episodes took place early in 1997. The alleged robbers, who had bail amounts set at $50,000 to $500,000, were tried in Bucks County courts and were convicted. These young people will not be free to traumatize citizens for a long time.

Most juvenile courts do not treat young offenders as adults, although the age to be classified an adult differs among states. This description of the juvenile court system tells how most courts try to rehabilitate young offenders.

FAMILY COURTS

The goal of the family court is to turn a young person away from crime to a productive life. However, this does not always happen. Many specialists in juvenile court procedures are critical of family courts. They do not believe the system is living up to its potential. Never have family courts had the challenges and hardships they face today.

In the early part of the 20th century, delinquents were generally isolated cases that needed a firm hand. Today, younger and younger offenders are influenced by gang pressure, drugs, violence on television, and the potential problems of one-parent homes. It is no wonder that family courts are backlogged and beleaguered by society's expectations of them. On the other hand, many family court officers and support staff try their best to direct the futures of those in their care in positive directions, often in the face of insufficient budgets and other difficult circumstances.

Not all juvenile offenders go through family court. In at least two states —at city and county levels —they are tried as adults. In fact, 2 percent of juveniles nationwide are now tried in adult courts. Juveniles charged with first-degree murder in Delaware, Louisiana, and Nevada move through the adult justice system.

There is also a move in Congress for legislation allowing certain juvenile criminals to be tried as adults. This is to assure that young offenders committing serious crimes would be serving the same prison terms as their adult counterparts. With such laws, juvenile criminals would not be freed within months, possibly to terrorize the streets again.

The juvenile court system includes many careers. These generally parallel those that are part of the adult criminal justice system. The defense lawyer, the prosecutor, the judge, court-appointed psychiatrists, and psychologists are among the many jobs common to both justice systems.

Adjunct careers of juvenile court systems include juvenile counselors, like Miles Thompson of Philadelphia, Pennsylvania. With such support, the young offender might have a chance at a crime-free life.

JUVENILE COUNSELOR

St. Gabriel's Hall in Audubon, Pennsylvania, is 100 years old, and its purpose has changed with the times. First named The Catholic Protectory for Boys, its ornate Italian architecture once sheltered orphaned boys from Catholic parishes in Philadelphia who needed "spiritual and emotional well-being and training in the useful arts." (This meant learning farming or a trade, in a context of sometimes stern discipline.)

Name changes—first to the Philadelphia Protectory for Boys and later to St. Gabriel's Hall—carried philosophical changes with them. In 1911, the flow of orphans changed to "incorrigible boys" being sent to "reform school." School administrators separated these groups with a high wall.

Now, the wall is gone and although the 200 boys at The Hall are not there because they wish to be, attitudes have changed. So has the clientele. "St. Gabe's" now receives most of its residents from the juvenile courts of Philadelphia and neighboring Delaware County. Young men, aged 10 through 18, spend from six to nine months when sent by the county's courts, or up to one year and sometimes longer if adjudicated by Philadelphia. The school is now state accredited and awards a high school diploma to residents completing its courses. Reform school has become treatment center.

Some still come from homes ruled so dysfunctional that the courts send the young men to The Hall as the only place where they might learn. The majority, however, are on probation for a first criminal offense (including drug or alcohol violations or abuse or auto theft) and are sent to St. Gabriel's for violating the "stay-in-school" provision of their parole.

"Nobody is a 'guard' here," said Miles Thompson of the school staff. "We are teachers, child care workers, or counselors. There are no corrections officers in these settings in Pennsylvania. Nevertheless, this is a locked facility ("staff secure" is the term) and the young men are here against their will."

Miles Thompson's official title is HIV-AIDS counselor in the school department. But this dynamic man has varied duties, many learned on the job. He interacts with students as counselor, adviser, and—to some extent—disciplinarian.

"Many of these young men don't understand limits," Thompson said. "They've been on the street, used to doing as they please. They have not learned behavior skills. Many can't cope with a structured setting such as school. (School is stressful.) They see fighting as the solution. In earlier days, punishment by the staff was the key to 'improving' the boys. That's all changed."

Although it is run now as always by the De La Salle Brothers of the Christian School ("Christian Brothers"), today's staff is mostly lay people. The Hall works not in a primarily religious setting but as a contractor to the courts. It is a "wraparound" facility, part psychology clinic, part individual counseling center, part disciplinary institution, part secondary school. It works within a system that relates rewards to behavior, behavior modification (improvement), and academic accomplishment.

"The young men can have monthly visits home," Thompson said. "But these are a privilege, not a right. Young men can lose their home visits if they cross certain boundaries.

"My job—my jobs, I should say—means walking a fine line between firmness and being open, accessible, and honest with the kids. I am not essentially a disciplinarian, but I have to be tough. I have a strong personality, but I try to get my students to see that they can trust me. I do what I say. Being disciplinarian and counselor is a contradictory role," Thompson continued. "It's hard to write a report on a young man for breaking a rule, and then counsel him a day or two later. But when they step over the line, or threaten to, I warn them. Then if they go over, I follow through and do what I said I would."

Unlike many juvenile justice workers, Miles Thompson does not have a degree in law enforcement or child psychology. He has a degree in theater from Hampshire College, Amherst, Massachusetts. During his college years, he worked in Boston creating educational theater with inner-city youngsters. He has acted and directed professionally and came to Philadelphia in the late 1980s to do inner-city teen educational theater among his professional activities.

"I had always been concerned about teens and pregnancy, but in 1988, I started to see the need for AIDS education among teens. I saw HIV infection entering the heterosexual teen population through drug use and sex. I began to work with inner-city Philadelphia youngsters who liked theater. We wrote a play on AIDS that was approved as an education tool by the school district of Philadelphia. We staged it throughout the city. When we turned it into a rap musical, *The Choice Is Yours*, it was wildly successful. Our actors became 'peer educators' and used breakout sessions following the play presentation to talk to other teens about HIV."

With these years of experience in professional theater and teen interaction plus his acquired knowledge of HIV and AIDS, Thompson moved to St. Gabriel's as the school's HIV/AIDS counselor. The next year, he helped found the school's behavior modification cluster. He also assists the dean of student affairs and teaches CPR and first aid to new employees. He is now certified in passive restraint techniques designed to manage youngsters who pose a danger to themselves or others.

"All schools and programs such as ours are seeing more students with psychological damage, and with sexual and physical abuse. We are now seeing crack babies as young teens. They may have a chance, but they're often hyperactive and not learning-oriented. Our whole point today is a more focused approach to behavior, education, and social development. We try to use verbal techniques and psychology to prevent little incidents and slights from escalating into fights between students, or with the staff.

"Things move in little steps. But if I can educate one young man on the risks of HIV, if I can get him to alter his behavior or be aware of his behavior a bit more than he was the day before, I've done my job. If by being there and setting limits—and showing at the same time that I care—I can improve one young man's outlook, I will have succeeded. If nobody does that for him, he won't do it for his children.

Miles Thompson, a counselor at St. Gabriel's Hall, works with young men, ages 13 through 18, who have been committed by the court system. He is shown here performing one of his typical daily duties: teaching AIDS/HIV awareness classes.

(Photo: Joe Morsello)

"Even in a day that's a week of Friday the Thirteenths, I have never said the next morning, 'I don't want to go to work.' I'm dealing with young people who are challenging and difficult but full of promise.

"They teach me about life," Thompson said.

HOME AND SCHOOL OFFICER

While Miles Thompson works with young men incarcerated for their criminal activities or related problems, the home and school officer (a.k.a. truant officer, school attendance officer) works with young people who are not in state institutions and who have certain freedoms. Some truant officers work full-time at tracking down school absentees. These officers may also be "supertutors," encouraging good grades, good attendance, and at the same time administering constant supervision. They keep an eye on their charges by developing personal schedules that will work for the young people and for themselves.

Besides the hand-in-glove relationships aimed at keeping young people on-course, the job requires report writing and visits to the parents' homes and/or their workplaces. Energy is important, too. The standing and walking required by constant supervision can be as exhausting as the mental challenge of helping young people become productive members of society.

The home and school officer is a challenging job by any title. The word "dull" is not written into the contract!

School district of Philadelphia salaries for home and school officers are typical of the northeastern United States. Those with bachelor's degrees earn from $28,000 to $43,600 a year, depending on experience and tenure. Those with master's degrees earn $29,000 to $51,000; the individual with a doctorate can expect $29,000 to $54,000. Degrees should be in education, psychology, sociology, or social work.

By 1997, officials in Pennsylvania were asking the federal government to continue funding school-based juvenile probation programs, but with a minimum of red tape. Governor Tom Ridge, U.S. Congressman James Greenwood, and Stephen White, a member of the Bucks County Juvenile Detention Center, believe some of the programs are very successful. White said, "The philosophy of school-based probation is not punishment. The philosophy is to make the school work for that kid." This is the goal of the entire juvenile justice system—to turn the child away from crime.

CHAPTER 15

The Future of Criminal Justice Training

What do you do if you work in a criminal justice position and your supervisor informs you that you must get a degree in criminal justice to be considered for a promotion? Or you've been working at a criminal justice job for years, only to be told you must complete a degree to keep your job?

There are effective degree completion programs all across the country, but none as accommodating as the accelerated degree completion program at Chestnut Hill College in Philadelphia, Pennsylvania. This program is geared to people who work full-time and have a family, but who must earn a degree for one reason or another.

Many enter the program with a less than positive attitude. They are told by the system that they need a degree—one more thing to consume time they don't have. It doesn't take them long, however, to discover that Chestnut Hill College is different.

Chestnut Hill College has its roots as a Catholic girls' college. This background has an impact on their criminal justice accelerated program. The mission of the college is to infuse values in the courses they offer. They believe the criminal justice system needs reform and their program will train people for this necessary change. The college is also seen as an institution that empowers women in careers that have been traditionally male-dominated. Many courses are geared to women, children, and family. All of the accelerated programs are offered to both men and women.

Dr. Kathleen Rex Anderson, associate dean and director at Chestnut Hill College Accelerated, was instrumental in planning and implementing the accelerated programs at the college. There are seven accelerated degrees available. These were purchased from Allentown College in 1996. From 1992 to 1996, the Chestnut Hill program was a satellite of Allentown.

Once students start classes at Chestnut Hill College, they find that courses help them in their current jobs. The classroom environment is interactive, allowing them to discuss work-related issues. Students are able to apply what they learn immediately.

Since most classes are offered in the classroom rather than as independent study, the faculty must meet three requirements:

1. They must have professional experience in criminal justice.

2. They must have academic credentials necessary for teaching.

3. They must have a commitment to adult learning and an understanding of where their students are in life.

Ms. Sara Kitchen Benn, division chair of social sciences, is just one of the many dedicated faculty members at Chestnut Hill College. With a background in law, Ms. Benn is the ideal professor for courses geared largely to women.

Courses are scheduled to enable students to finish their degrees as quickly as possible. Each course is 8 weeks long, rather than the traditional 15-week semesters. There are six 8-week "semesters" per year; students can enter at the start of any of these semesters.

Another unique feature of the accelerated program is that students may "step out" when life gets overwhelming and classes do not fit in. The student can relax, knowing that Chestnut Hill College will welcome him back when he or she decides to "step in" again. There is no pressure to complete the degree within a certain time. Degree completion time varies considerably. In addition to working at their own pace, most students come in with some previously earned credits. Dr. Anderson says this encouragement and understanding contributes to the high retention of students in this program.

The campus is conducive to the commuting student. It is located in a safe, peaceful neighborhood that is easily accessible by car or public transportation. Services are offered to make their lives less hectic. The dining hall operates continuously, so students can get a healthy meal anytime. A fitness center and pool are also available for their use.

Chestnut Hill College also offers internship opportunities for the few students who do not have job experience. A part-time master's degree program is also available for those who want to go even further with their education.

Chestnut Hill's unique accelerated program makes it possible for criminal justice professionals to see how their jobs fit in with the whole system. It lets them move on in their careers while giving them a greater understanding of the big picture.

SECTION 3

PRIVATE SECURITY

CHAPTER 16

Private Security: Cutting-Edge Careers

Private security is predicted to be one of the top employment fields for the next several years. As an industry, private security is forecast to increase at 10 percent or more a year, far faster than American industry as a whole. In fact, employment of guards is expected to grow 34 percent between 1990 (when there were approximately 883,000 guards employed in the United States) and 2005. This is much faster than the average for all occupations through the year 2005. *George* magazine (February 1997) listed security guard as #9 among the top 10 jobs destined for growth over the next 10 years. With additional training and new responsibilities, the security **guard** of yesterday is the security **officer** of today and tomorrow. This book will use the latter term exclusively.

The positive outlook for private security is most prominent in the area of surveillance equipment and its use. The design of increasingly sophisticated monitoring, detection, and reporting systems has created a new job area, design engineering. Electrical, electronics, and computer engineers work full-time to forestall criminal activity. This, in turn, creates a demand for security officers trained to use advanced equipment.

Many security officers work in the private sector. They are meeting demands that police departments cannot always fulfill, cannot afford to do, or which fall outside the tax-supported public sector. Private security firms are training officers to perform duties ranging from monitoring crowds at stadiums to patrolling plants, offices, and recreational areas.

African-Americans will be gratified to find these careers welcoming them. *Ebony* magazine reports that law enforcement is high on the list of inviting careers. Joseph M. Wright, Executive Director of the National Organization of Black Law Enforcement Executives, says that jobs in every facet of law enforcement will increase at about 5 percent annually. (As we mentioned, private security, with about double this growth, offers even better starting opportunities.)

The image of the private security "guard" has improved with every decade. The textbook, *Private Security Trends, 1970–2000 Hallcrest Report II* (Butterworth-Heinemann, 1990), points out that in the 1970s, the typical "guard" was barely paid minimum wage, often had limited schooling (a ninth-grade education was considered adequate for hiring), and lacked job training.

Times have changed. Today's security officers, from mall protector to security manager, are younger, better educated, better trained, and more ambitious. However, the field is also excellent for mid-life career-changers and for those facing enforced retirement who wish to perform a worthwhile service and earn extra income.

Some private security officers are armed; most are not. Officers in the public sector—assisting or replacing law enforcement officers, for instance—are more likely to be armed. And the Pinkerton, Brinks, or Wackenhut armored car officers who pick up great sums of money are armed to the teeth. Their cargoes are so valuable that they take specific positions in the trucks and as they enter and leave buildings. This ensures safe delivery or pickup of valuables.

The need for security is magnified with each terrorist attack, car theft, and shoplifting incident. Police departments cannot keep up with these security demands. This is why private security is growing at an unprecedented rate.

A pervasive fear of crime has turned homes into fortresses and schools into metal detector checkpoints. Sports and screen stars live in constant fear of attack. Monica Seles was a world-class tennis champion before being knifed by a deranged spectator. Battling depression and pain to emerge victorious again, she is now heavily guarded as she travels from one tennis open to another.

In business and industry, crime-based losses are estimated at $100 billion a year! And the total cost of crime in America comes to $450 billion a year, according to a Justice Department report. This has, in turn, created a private security force of over a million people who earn collectively over $6.5 billion a year. Part of the growth is due to the need for night work as well as day jobs. Making security a 24-hour job swells its numbers.

Private security staffs work in a growing number of areas. They are involved in airport security, university security, and subway, tunnel, and harbor surveillance. Security forces patrol office buildings, hospitals, museums, and government property,

In short, there is hardly an area in one's life that is not affected. Visibly, we see security people in malls and stores. Invisibly, we are watched by hidden cameras in banks, office buildings and stores, on bridges, and elsewhere.

Many private security people work to strengthen the public sector. They may be hired by government agencies to protect diplomats and patrol court houses. They are even hired to guard lives and homes when a neighborhood feels insecure with public law enforcement alone.

In *Private Security Trends 1970–2000, Hallcrest Report II* (Butterworth-Heinemann, 1990), William Cunningham and his coauthors tell the story of Starrett City, a Brooklyn, New York, neighborhood of 20,000 residents. This geographical area felt a need for its own private security system some time before other towns, boroughs, neighborhoods, and businesses began looking into hiring their own security people.

The results of a survey conducted by Pennsylvania State University on this added security are riveting. The study personalizes the fears the Starrett City residents had before they hired their own protectors. The survey is summarized in a chart captioned "Respondents' Opinions of Life Without Private Security." Over 89 percent agreed that their community would not be safe without added forces, and 83.5 percent believed that Starrett City would be unsafe without this help. An impressive 89.9 percent believed that more people would be robbed, while 73.8 percent said that no one would wish to go out at night. More than one-half said they would have to move if they lost this personalized security. These are impressive figures in favor of additional neighborhood protection. The responses also reflect the sad state of some neighborhoods.

If you study the background of the Starrett City private security force, 83 percent of the personnel were high school graduates, and some have additional college background. Because the Starrett City force is proprietary (the employees own the company), its members are more career-oriented, more devoted to a cause of which they are a part.

The private security officers you see in malls are the ones most familiar to the public. But these officers are everywhere. They patrol vast areas, often interacting by radio or intercom, or via computer. Officers who protect a corporate building may also have other duties such as receiving packages and registering visitors.

The private security "system" can range from a single officer patrolling a used car lot at night to a human and technological network that tracks the comings and goings of nearly everyone in the Empire State Building.

Officers may check building visitors in high-security areas for weapons, explosives, or unlawful materials (drugs or contraband). They must make sure nothing is stolen when equipment or supplies are delivered or removed. They note fires, prowlers, and any unlawful activity or presence. In a sense, the officer is a paramilitary person, often impressively groomed and always ready to respond to any incident or mishap.

Laboratories, government buildings, and many corporations have vital information that must be protected. The safety of computer codes and defense secrets is essential; private security officers are taught the logistics of keeping these secrets secure. (These officers often have high-level security clearances.)

On the lighter side, officers at libraries and museums enjoy interacting with visitors as they protect property. Golf club security staff members may travel the course on golf carts to ensure that those who play have paid their fees. Or they may guide players as gently as a shepherd, to see that they maintain a pace of play that keeps the rhythm of the whole course in sync.

Officers use scooters, bicycles, electric carts, patrol cars, and foot power to perform their duties. Some have trained canine companions. Or, if they are building-bound, they are assigned to stations with banks of TV screens that monitor the activities of the authorized—and the unwelcome—in many areas of the building. This includes roofs, fire escapes or inside stairs, and entrances and exits. The task is to make places safe from any individual who is determined to get data, plant bombs, or commit other misdeeds.

Many officers control all the systems to help make a building safe. They check the sprinkler systems, thermostats, and alarm systems. But sometimes these check-points do not work. Recently, robbers struck Pennsbury Mansion, the magnificent, pre-Revolutionary home of William Penn near Philadelphia, Pennsylvania. They took priceless items, including William Penn's pewter plates. The historic property's complex alarm system didn't work. When thieves took the heirlooms, the Mansion's security alarms never rang. Fortunately, the robbers found the goods too "hot" to sell and dumped them in the nearby Delaware River. The treasures were found 10 days after the theft. The robbers were dredged up, too, thanks to an over-heard conversation.

Despite occasional dramas such as this, powerful security systems are meeting the problems of crime in revolutionary ways. At no time in the past have crimi-nals been faced with so many systems and so many trained officers, all designed to catch them in the act. The gap between the public's perception of crime and its actuality is closing.

Security people can work unusual hours. However, they are often able to plan their work to accommodate their home lives. Work hours can encompass the usual eight-hour shift, or they may rotate to balance daytime, weekend or holiday duties with fellow officers.

Working the night shift (usually 10:00 p.m. to 6:00 a.m. or midnight to 8:00 a.m.) may make it possible for an officer to help at home. Day officers tend to be those with posts at private sector or government buildings, or who patrol malls and museums. Night people often protect construction sites, truck terminals, and sim-ilar facilities, perhaps with guard dogs, and nearly always using radio to contact a base within the structure.

Not all security officers would feel that times are better. Some are as relatively undervalued as they were in the 1970s. And since the "guard business" is still so competitive, many security companies perceive that, in order to get the job, they must bid low. The result of these bidding wars is low wages and benefits. Today, more security companies are resisting the low-wage compromises, but part of the wage problem is that today's times are lean and mean. Downsizing (a euphemism for firings) and employer unconcern are part of the economic package for some officers.

Calvin Dash, a private security officer at the Philadelphia Museum of Art, is a victim of the 1990s. While he protects paintings worth millions, his pay is only $7.25 an hour, after a 15-cent-an-hour increase within the last year. The low salary Dash earns has forced him to take a second job as a protective officer in a private building. The two jobs, running back-to-back, give him one hour a day to himself!

Steve Lopez, a cause-oriented columnist for the *Philadelphia Inquirer*, focused on Dash's problems in print. Because he challenged his security company, Dash may lose his museum job. He and several other officers are forcing the museum and its security company to look at the inequities in their work.

Besides the low pay, Dash must deal with hassles such as morning call-ins, in which he arrives at the museum only to be sent home. The excuse is that there is not enough work that day. For their efforts, officers who are turned back at the door receive a paltry one-half hour's pay. All this because the economy is "tight," according to the security company, as reported by Lopez.

Calvin Dash is a fine person. He is ambitious, a voracious reader who would like to teach economics and labor history. But because of economic conditions that allow security companies to tighten the belt, Lopez said Dash can't get ahead. In his column, the reporter noted several examples of apparent harassment directed against Dash.

In dealing with the idea that this was happening in a temple of art, a place of beauty, columnist Lopez wrote: "There's something obscene, in fact, about paying security [people minimal] wages to watch over multimillion-dollar treasures, and then suggesting that they ought to consider themselves lucky [to be there]."

Calvin Dash moved to do something about his predicament. He went to the Local 36 of the Service Employees' International Union. The union organizer, Denys Everingham, said that SEIU is expanding because many service-sector employees feel abused. At the union's urging, Philadelphia's deputy mayor, Gerald Murphy, promised to investigate the situation at the city-owned museum.

Steve Lopez noted: "It's all Calvin Dash—an employee of the '90s—asks. That, and some respect and consideration."

Thus, while the image of the private security officer has improved considerably, there are still groups that receive unfair treatment. And if the early 2000s mirror the 1990s, all security people must stand up and be counted.

However, they have a bright future. Robert Fischer and Gion Green, authors of *Introduction to Security*, fifth edition (Butterworth-Heinemann, 1992), put the future of private security in succinct and dramatic perspective: "For every product manufactured, someone is waiting to make an illegal profit by stealing or through manipulation of processes and records. For every security device installed, someone is determined to find a method to defeat it."

What greater justification is needed for the entire field of private security?

CHAPTER 17

Entering Private Security: What to Expect When You're Screened and Trained for the Job

SCREENING

A private security firm and a corporate security department have one thing in common: They want to be certain that you are a good candidate for security work. Screening is essential, whether your work will be *proprietary* (working with a corporation as an employee) or *contractual* (working for a mall, hospital, or other security-needy institution as the employee of a security firm).

This is equally true whether you are a high school graduate or even a retiree set on becoming an entry-level security officer or a careerist going for a bachelor's degree in security management followed by corporate employment.

The screening process includes criminal and financial background checks, psychological testing, past employment verification, integrity and drug tests, and perhaps a polygraph (lie-detector) examination. The more sensitive your potential employment, the more detailed the screening process will be.

Companies hiring those who score well on background tests enjoy a payoff in "reduced losses, better people and lower turnover," according to Fischer and Green, authors of *Introduction to Security*, fifth edition (Butterworth-Heinemann, 1992).

Employers may have problems determining your potential reliability as an officer or manager because of certain privacy acts. There are laws that can prevent unusual or intrusive probing into your background. On the other hand, a would-be employer has many ways of determining your career potential. Because the opportunities for in-house crime are so great (90 percent of employee crime is not prosecuted), an employer must be able to measure your strengths.

Certain factors are "bell-ringers" for employers. Fischer and Green define these red flags: personality test results that show an inability to work well with others; an unstable job record, with "memory loss"—missing or questionable elements.

With humor and good sense, Fischer and Green write: "the 'grasshopper' [type] does not make a good candidate." Salary reductions along your job route, unexplained gaps in employment, or the inability to supply past employers' names and addresses would count against you. And if you have severe credit card or other debts, you're not the best person to be given financial responsibilities.

The polygraph test is generally off-limits for prospective employees. As a job candidate, you are covered by the Employee Polygraph Protection Act of 1988, but there are exceptions. Companies hiring private security officers to handle currency, *commodities* (tradable or redeemable securities), and privileged (secret) information are allowed to give you a polygraph test. Also, pharmaceutical companies and others who manufacture or distribute drugs or other controlled substances can check your honesty as a future employee with a lie-detector test. Certain government security positions also require polygraphs.

A valid polygraph test is generally administered by a qualified examiner. (Except in Illinois, where polygraph results are inadmissible, polygraph examiners are part of the criminal justice system since they are often used to gather evidence for criminal cases.) However, polygraph tests aren't foolproof. Your condition on a given day—tired, stressed, or worried—can affect testing. (A controversial big-city mayor once took a much-publicized polygraph test—and flunked, with disastrous political consequences!)

Another test that private security employers rely on is the PSI or Personal Security Inventory. This test is designed to measure your honesty and integrity through subtle questioning. How you answer questions about tricky situations provides clues to your reliability. As with polygraph tests, the PSI can mislead. But they both show a degree of consistency that can make you a desirable or risky choice.

Drug testing is not as restricted as the polygraph. The federal government realizes that workplaces should be drug-free, so the law permits urine analysis and blood sampling to detect drugs. Fischer and Green also mention a hair test for the presence of drugs. A strand of hair "maintains a 90-day record of materials ingested by the body." In the face of this remarkable test, candidates with shaved heads—a trait that could be viewed negatively in the "establishment" world of private security—would have another strike against them: appearing to avoid the hair test!

TRAINING

If you have passed the drug tests, background checks, and other screenings, your next step may or may not be a training course. Those in private security feel that training hours for certification as a security officer are far too few. In fact, in 19 states, no training is necessary, although all security officers must be certified. The Private Security Task Force recommends at least 8 hours of "preassignment training," at least 32 hours of additional training, and on-the-job supervision/training.

Some states, such as Pennsylvania, require training in the use of firearms, blackjacks/clubs/batons, and other lethal weapons. There are 24 schools certified for such training under Pennsylvania Act #235; other state requirements may differ.

A comprehensive security officer training school covers a myriad of areas. These include subjects as diverse as public relations and first aid, drug control and communications skills, and crisis management and public interaction. You must also be comfortable with alarm systems and the operation of electronic security devices.

Primarily, security officers learn how to protect people, goods, and property— even nuclear power plants. Such officers have incredible responsibilities because they guard our present and our future. These officers may have several months of training before being assigned to duty. Even then, they work additional months under strict supervision before going it alone.

There are further "basics" in the ideal officer training program. Fischer and Green describe such a program as including company orientation, training in corporate policies, the operation of each department, self-discipline, and package and vehicle research (alertness for drugs and bombs). In short, you would be molded into the ideal security officer—ever alert, with exemplary demeanor.

While security education continues to grow—witness the four-year security management majors offered by many of today's colleges and universities—security training often remains woefully insufficient. While private officer staffs continue to grow at more than two-to-one over public police forces with a 12 percent increase in demand each year, Fischer and Green note that training does not keep pace. Public police officers receive at least 320 hours of basic training; private security officers' training is minimal, even nonexistent!

SHOULD SECURITY OFFICERS BE ARMED?

If a police officer comes tearing through a high-security building to make a burglary arrest, one can assume that officer is armed—and needs to be. If a private security officer goes in search of a thief caught in the act by surveillance cameras, you can fairly well assume the private officer won't have a weapon. Yet both the police officer and the security officer are at equal risk (will a jumpy burglar pull a gun?).

Because private security forces are taking on more public law enforcement duties, it is time to rethink the question of arming these security officers.

Bill Clark, author of "A Call to Arms" (*Security Management* magazine, October 1995), noted that gun use has grown. "There are approximately 200 million handguns in use today." (That is one for every adult and most of our children.) This proliferation, coupled with an ever-growing focus on violence, begs for the arming of private security officers. Since the police may lack manpower for emergency situations, private security must fill in the gaps.

Armored car officers carry guns because, of all job areas, collecting and transporting vast amounts of money is the most risky. Although the movie industry has often used armored car holdups as entertainment, the truth is that being an armored car officer is an unromantic, highly dangerous job.

Not all security officers need guns (*Private Security Trends, 1970–2000, Hallcrest Report II* [Butterworth-Heinemann, 1992] reports that 10 percent of the security force is armed and that this number is dropping.) But private officers in vulnerable, volatile positions have the right to defend themselves. In the process, they may save an innocent bystander's life.

Training for armed security officers is a must. States across the nation have definite rules regarding the armed security officer. The minimal training previously accepted for a guard carrying a gun has been altered to require the same weapons training given a law enforcement officer. This includes a specified number of hours in range and classroom instruction.

Private security officers emerge from this training as professionals, capable of protecting themselves and securing the areas under guard. They also have new respect for lethal weapons.

LIABILITY

If you are seeking a job in either private security or law enforcement, you should recognize that you (and your employer) can be held liable for supposedly improper actions. Although examples are rare, police officers and the departments for whom they work can be sued for alleged misconduct. The reasons for bringing suit range across the law enforcement landscape and can include civil rights violations, excessive use of force, bribery, and corruption. (The rare cases should always be balanced by the selflessness and dedication of the overwhelming majority of law enforcement officers.)

Private security companies, on the other hand, are more frequently the targets of lawsuits. To protect themselves, corporations with their own security forces, or security firms that provide corporate services, carry high-limit liability insurance.

Many cases have gone to court where a security officer has allegedly failed to do his or her duty. Victims have the legal right to sue security companies and individual officers. The victim of a rape that might have been prevented had a security officer not been inattentive can file suit for negligence, but to win, must prove that negligence existed. In a real case, a security company whose officer stole $400,000 worth of gold was sued by the manufacturing company that suffered the loss. (It is an officer's duty to protect cash, gold, diamonds, or other valuables—not to steal them!)

In 1996, a tragic example of alleged security officer negligence was the fire that caused the death of 23 rare primates at the Philadelphia Zoo. This was the worst fire disaster in American zoo history. The zoo claimed that two security officers, with 19 years of experience, failed to notice the fire in its early stages because they were not at their assigned stations. Instead of patrolling near the primate house, the two were allegedly in another building making phone calls. When they did smell smoke, they assumed it was from a railyard adjoining the zoo, a past source of fire odors. The officers, a man and a woman, were dismissed despite their protests. It remains to be seen if lawsuits will be filed either way—the officers for wrongful dismissal, or the zoo for damages resulting from alleged negligence.

In many negligence cases, private security companies have hired incompetent individuals as officers or have failed to train their staffs properly. Thorough background checks are a necessity. It is the duty of a private security company to hire competent people, train them fully so they become qualified, pay them decently, and monitor their activities.

There is a way of protecting against possible financial liability. Firms and people in positions of financial responsibility are often *bonded*. Bonding is ensuring that those in positions of trust are responsible for their actions. For a fee, usually based on the dollar amount of the coverage, bonding (surety) companies provide protection against financial loss. If the bonded person or organization violates its position of trust, the surety company pays back the amount lost or stolen.

To be bonded, a person must pass a background check that should reveal any questionable past activity.

The bottom line: Consider your background before you plan to enter the private security field. And if you are accepted, train fully and serve honorably in an honorable profession.

CHAPTER 18

The Many Jobs for Private
Security Officers and Managers

The security officer field contains a varied job menu. There is no such thing as a security officer "type" because they work in so many areas. The officer on duty in a museum is not the same as the trained-to-stay-cool security force hired by a company to protect its assets during a bitter strike. The armored car officer who makes sure your money and ours gets to its destination is not the officer who prowls an airport looking for terrorist bombs.

Yes, of course there is the prototype guard—erect and all spit-and-polish down to the triple-creased shirt-back, a figure of authority and reassurance.

But people coming out of high school, college, or other occupations to enter the security industry have a wide choice of duties within the profession. And as world politics and everyday life become more complex, new avenues will spring up for the private security person.

Robert J. Fischer and Gion Green, authors of *Introduction to Security* (Butterworth-Heinemann, 1992) note that former FBI agents are attracted to the private security field. In turn, security forces of all kinds are making good use of former or retired FBI agents' expertise.

Another bright note is the outlook for women and minorities in private security. Nearly 10 percent of private security officers are black women, and security opportunities have doubled every 15 years for women in general. If women are now serving in every area from bodyguards to security managers, who can say how fully they will be sharing the field with men in the near future?

Let's examine:

- Airport officers
- Armored car officers
- Assets protection officers at a strike scene

- Bank officers

- Bodyguards

- Campus and corporate security

- Consultants

- Mall officers/security detectives

- Private investigators

- Private security/alarm systems

- Public-sector private security

- Security managers

- Related security jobs

AIRPORT OFFICERS

For years, security workers at airports have scanned carry-on baggage and the passengers who own it. Check-in baggage on international flights goes through metal detectors. Today, the rise in domestic and international terrorism makes airport officers more essential than ever. Because terrorists will stop at nothing to achieve their goals, an airport with hundreds of daily flights and thousands of passengers can be a prime target for the destructive acts of political extremists.

Airport officer positions begin at entry level (baggage and passenger screeners, cargo security) and range to top-level security opportunities. (The latter are often occupied by former FBI agents.)

This salary range applies to most uniformed officers such as those on duty at airports, in armored cars, banks, school campuses and corporate offices, malls, etc.: $7.50 an hour at entry level to $25.00 an hour, and up. The higher earnings depend on factors such as whether or not the officer is qualified to carry weapons and seniority (with employee officers earning slightly more than their contractual counterparts). Training in sophisticated surveillance equipment and procedures will also increase income.

ARMORED CAR OFFICERS

In 1990, there were more than 107,000 private security companies, with over $51 billion in yearly revenues. (These numbers may be even larger today.) Armored car companies are among the major security businesses and account for a good portion of the industry's earnings.

The *armored car* (really a truck) has long been a symbol of authority and financial protection. Somehow, its boxy, brightly colored body with perhaps a well-known company name and its tiny bulletproof glass window slits are at once forbidding and reassuring. And the stories of armored car holdups are as colorful as the trucks themselves.

Despite the obvious security built into the armored car, some robberies have been successful. Armored car officers carry guns to protect their lives and their cargoes. In 1990, $10.8 million was stolen from Armored Motor Service of America. Some years earlier, a Philadelphia longshoreman, Joey Coyle, became a folk hero when he grabbed several bags of money that had bounced from the accidentally opened rear door of a moving armored truck. He left a cash trail the police could easily follow. (A film chronicled his escapades, including his capture as he tried to flee to Mexico with loot in his cowboy boots!) He was brought to trial, of which a *Philadelphia Inquirer* reporter wrote: "The jury . . . bought his plea that all the money made him temporarily goofy. The jury not only acquitted him; it cheered him."

Armored car companies have expanded their activities. Although their principal task is still protecting currency, the advent of new banking systems and procedures has widened their scope. Armored car drivers often collect customer deposits from automated teller machines and parking meters. They will also accompany merchants carrying cash in high crime areas and use advanced equipment to protect property. Or they may be guarding high-profile government sites rather than money.

One armored carrier, Wackenhut, began as early as 1983 to go far beyond money protection. The company gives polygraph (lie-detector) tests and investigates cases of arson and fraud. The company has developed "Big Brother" equipment, including a handprint screening device that makes sure the person entering a nuclear site or similarly restricted area is entering legally. This system has replaced identification cards that just may not belong to the people flashing them! Wackenhut can also boast a device that will survey the contents of a closed car trunk. The "contents" can include people hiding in these cramped spaces to avoid detection.

ASSETS PROTECTION

Another security field involves the protection of corporate assets and property by private security staffs during employee strikes. Assets protection is purchased by a strike-affected company before the event, since local law enforcement can do little to protect the private property owned by the corporation and being jeopardized by strikers. (See chapter 20, "Cargo Theft and Strike Control/Assets Management.")

BANK OFFICERS

Bank officers are generally found in the larger city banks where there is a steady and heavy flow of customers. When not checking their electronic cameras for suspicious activities, they may be directing customers to various sections of the bank, and adding to customers' comfort levels. Large banks with millions of dollars at stake consider security a priority.

The future for entry-level bank officers is uncertain. Closed-circuit TV systems are fast becoming the "eyes" of the banking industry. Even now, the small local bank or branch may not have a security manager; these duties are often delegated to one of the bank's senior managers. And officers are a thing of the past in most banks' branch offices.

BODYGUARDS

A bodyguard is traditionally thought of as a muscleman, strong in physique, with not too much "upstairs." But Robert Fischer and Gion Green, authors of *Introduction to Private Security* (Butterworth-Heinemann, 1992), report a new stereotype straight out of television. "Television makes it look like bodyguards have to be 6' 3" with blond hair, blue eyes and a California tan." Fischer and Green feel that this is a one-dimensional view. Intelligence, patience, and an eye for detail are much more realistic attributes. Women are now considered highly desirable as bodyguards.

Even the term "bodyguard" is seldom used in the security industry. The more apt term is executive protection agent. A highly trained agent is one who blends with his or her "protectee" and keeps the protectee safe and on schedule through extensive planning and "advance" work. The ideal candidate is a retired or former U.S. Secret Service agent.

The rest of *Introduction to Private Security*'s bodyguard/protection agent profile indicates that it is essential to know safe weapons-handling, self-defense and wrestling, and such cutting-edge skills as a knowledge of alarm systems and closed-circuit TV. The modern protection agent must be prepared to protect anyone from corporate executive to diplomat or ambassador. We would add that, if the agent is also an executive or diplomatic chauffeur, a performance-school course in protective driving is a must. (Such instruction is taught at the Bob Bondurant School of High Performance Driving in Tucson, Arizona.)

Schools for executive protection agents are proliferating in answer to violence and terrorism here and abroad. Their instruction prepares these private security officers to offer constant protection. Thus they must fit into the protected person's leisure time activities as well as his or her working life. What may seem the ideal job can actually cause burnout, the writers of *Introduction to Private Security* claim. The position may demand constant travel as well as singular devotion to duty.

The salaries ($25,000 to $30,000 a year) are generous, and most jobs include additional allowances for clothing, meals, hotel rooms, credit cards, and other amenities that add appeal. Because many protection agents have the elite background of law enforcement or military service, chances are the job spells excitement, while the rigorous schedule is something they have long ago taken in stride.

CAMPUS AND CORPORATE SECURITY FORCES

College campuses were once domains of study, leisure, and a sense of security. Today, robberies, rapes, and even murders are committed on these once safe grounds. There may only be occasional crimes, but even one incident on a campus will have parents of resident and commuting students on edge until summer vacation postpones the problem or graduation ends it.

Besides major campus crime, security officers will also keep busy observing postexam, postgame, and even postparty partying! College students can get rowdy, especially in groups. Containing this natural enthusiasm can often challenge campus security forces.

It might surprise you to learn that there are many types of campus security jobs available. *Introduction to Private Security* states that "line officers, field supervisors, shift commanders, a coordinator of line operations . . . a director and training officer" are among the job titles. And as campuses—many the size of mini-cities—continue to remain accessible to the public, the security prospects remain good.

Corporate campuses, too, require equally detailed and dedicated security forces. The corporate environment may be somewhat more sedate than the college campus, but the need for security, and the forces that provide it, are virtually identical to those used to monitor the halls of ivy.

CONSULTANTS

Many firms need help in choosing the proper surveillance equipment for their particular needs and in selecting the right security staff, from officers to managers. This is not generally a job for those in law enforcement. It takes a very special person with far-reaching security skills to assess the needs of a particular company.

Many such people could add "doctor" to their names, since they have advanced degrees. They are often paid what can only be viewed as fantastic amounts. *Introduction to Private Security* authors Fischer and Green note that some consultants are able to " . . . bill over $200,000 annually." Equally good news is that security consulting is expanding rapidly and will continue to do so over the next decade.

Consultants are totally independent, giving them an autonomy not available to people who are part of a corporate executive structure. The bright future for leading-edge specialists is not surprising as the corporate world needs to be ever more productive, ever safer.

Besides advising corporate clients on security staff size and the nature of protective equipment, private security consultants provide expert solutions to specific security problems affecting a given company. Guarding against terrorist activities has been a major concern. Private companies as well as governments can be targeted for attack. A forward-thinking consultant, armed with the latest security knowledge, can be a tremendous corporate asset.

MALL OFFICERS/SECURITY DETECTIVES

Keeping mall merchandise secure and protecting shoppers are responsibilities shared by individual store owners who employ uniformed and undercover security detectives, and by the mall security force. Mall officers may protect by the visibility of uniforms, badges, and two-way radios. In some malls, the maintenance people are radio-linked to the security system, their visible radios serving as a caution to would-be troublemakers. Sometimes, mall officers "hide" by dressing as shoppers. But a mall officer generally resembles a law enforcement officer—spit-and-polish. From Smokey Bear hat to crisp shirt and well-shined shoes or boots, he or she is a presence to be respected. While such an officer may be your basic security person, professionalism and bearing show that climbing the career ladder is probably the goal.

The mall security officer—black, white, male, female—is not a "roamer." He has specific jobs to do and areas to cover. She is often linked to police officers circling the mall in well-marked police cars. A radio call can alert law enforcement (or four-wheeled mall security) that someone is fleeing with stolen merchandise. At night, mall security may accompany departing shoppers to their cars, and at all times, clearly marked mall security jeeps and vans patrol the parking areas to deter auto thefts. A second shift may work in a mall with extended shopping hours. And a security manager with an assistant or two controls the minute-to-minute doings of the security troops.

Security may be provided by the mall management or under contract to a company that specializes in mall security. Mr. David Stevens, security manager of the Plymouth Meeting Mall near Philadelphia, Pennsylvania, reports that his firm, The Rouse Company, owns 85 malls and shopping/tourist complexes nationwide. These include the glamorous Baltimore Inner Harbor and the 300-store Underground Mall in Atlanta, Georgia. Naturally, security plays a tremendous role in The Rouse Company's day-to-day activities.

Mall officers can expect anything, even stampeding Santas! One December 23rd, nine ho-ho-ho-ing Santas visited the Oxford Valley Mall in Lower Bucks County, Pennsylvania. These costumed 20-something men had made several stops at area clubs, and thus came by their red noses naturally.

Mall customers enjoyed their jolly presence until one of the Santas embellished "Merry Christmas" with a few unmentionable words.

Police Officer Peter Feeney, who was inside the mall, took exception to the raucous holidayers. The mall's security officers escorted all nine Santas out the door. As they breathed the crisp, fresh air of Christmastime, Officer Feeney bestowed holiday gifts of his own: $372 summonses to each Santa for disorderly conduct.

Fast-forward to spring. Nine unchastened ex-Santas appeared before District Justice John Kelly. A 29-year-old spokes-Santa (a bookkeeper in his day job) told the judge it wasn't fair to haul them all in for the mis-lip of one. The others nodded. Besides, the advocate said, there was no way to prove which of the cheery mouths uttered the words that are not in Santa's vocabulary.

Justice Kelly agreed, and the young men went free—perhaps to find coal for their own stockings for next Christmas. (But imagine all the disillusioned four-year-olds left in their wake!)

Security detectives working for retail stores, hotels, airlines, and similar outlets perform duties as varied as uncovering theft of services and investigating fraud.

Starting salaries for those with police or college background are approximately $20,000.

In 1993, the City of Philadelphia reported these yearly salary ranges for several classes of municipal security personnel; similar salaries today would be somewhat higher:

Facility Guard I	$17,590–$17,966
Facility Guard II	$24,197–$26,405
Library Guard Supervisor	$24,846–$27,140
Municipal Guard	$22,757–$24,764

PRIVATE INVESTIGATORS

(SEE ALSO CHAPTER 5)

Private investigation falls under no particular employment "umbrella" of this book; it is neither solely law enforcement nor criminal justice, not private security as such nor cyberspace crime detection. However, private investigation can be an important part of all the above.

Books have been written on investigative disciplines. These range from complex and expensive operations such as tracing assets over several continents or determining the extent (and sources) of Asian software counterfeiting to mundane activities such as determining the validity of a workers compensation claim.

The authors of *Private Security Trends, 1970–2000, Hallcrest Report II* point out the many roles of a private investigator. These duties can coincide with and vary from the police department or federal investigators or others working in public law enforcement.

While the law enforcement investigator may be dealing with the headline crime that splashes across daily papers, the private investigator is usually hired long-term by law firms, private security organizations, and insurance companies. As *Private Security Trends* notes (with tongue in cheek), the private investigator or PI bears little resemblance to the high-profile private eye on television shows.

For one thing, most investigative work is done with computers. Yes, there is still a lot of "gumshoe" work, but the investigators (and investigative firms) with staying power are those that carve out a niche such as K&R (kidnap and ransom) or who build databases of bad guys (counterfeiters, gray marketeers, fraud artists, and so on).

PIs can work as "solo fliers" or for large security firms, some of which are branching out from simply providing officers for routine security duties. All investigative firms use "stringers" who specialize in certain work. (For instance, there may be only one or two pros who really know how to find assets in Argentine banks.) In describing the private investigator's roles, *Private Security Trends* reports that PIs do "background investigations including credit checks on personnel applicants," and look into company theft in virtually any business, including private security! They search for stolen goods, perform undercover drug work, and seek evidence for use in criminal trials.

Do not assume that solo flier PIs handle only the low-end jobs such as divorce cases and workers comp. There are retired FBI, CIA, and Secret Service investigators who earn $125 an hour and up, handling major international cases. (In fact, there are only a handful of large (over $7 million a year) investigative firms. Thousands of PIs make reasonable livings by billing their time at $35 to $75 an hour.

The jobs of the PI in private security have a narrower focus than the wide-sweeping investigations apt to be conducted by an independent private investigator. The PI working in private security may investigate for his own firm or work for others. This work includes checking the backgrounds and the daily activities of employees. A background check can save a lot of misery later. People involved with drugs or who have criminal records (petty or otherwise) are the ones who can cause trouble in a company. Pilfering of equipment or poor performance are often made easier by inadequate surveillance.

Private investigators can trace missing persons, gather information for law firms in civil court cases, and conduct investigative work in divorce proceedings. In *Introduction to Security*, Fifth Edition (Butterworth-Heinemann, 1992), the authors write that salaries for private detectives are good, and outlook, excellent. To balance the scale, "Long days and seven-day work weeks are the norm when a PI is on the case."

Private investigators often cooperate with public law enforcement officials. They can work undercover, assuming a fictitious identity to investigate people who do not suspect their true profession.

Naturally, a PI must know the law, know how to uncover needed information, and be articulate. The *Introduction to Security* authors suggest that a membership in the National Association of Legal Investigators is helpful and informative.

Private investigators earn from approximately $17,000 for a self-employed PI who investigates domestic disputes for attorneys, to as much as $110,000 a year for those in managerial positions in industry.

PRIVATE SECURITY JOBS WITH ALARM SERVICES

Many homes have welcome flags waving by their front doors—a big sunflower, an Easter bunny, pumpkins and goblins, or sails in the sunshine. Equally prevalent are security alarm signs spiked to the suburban lawns or affixed to the town house gates; thus, the welcome flags have a caveat: They do not invite burglars into the home.

Private Security Trends, 1970–2000, Hallcrest Report II notes that the alarm service is a swiftly growing industry in our crime-conscious society. This comprehensive industry employs many thousands of private security workers. It employs people in four groups: sales staff; system installers; those who relay triggered alarms to company personnel or local police; and finally, "alarm respondents," private security officers who hasten to the affected home or office if the system does not involve police response. Alarm respondents or investigators with electronic and/or police science experience may have starting salaries of about $25,000 a year.

Anthony J. Minio of Ambler, Pennsylvania, is working toward a secure future. He is building his own security company, one home and business at a time.

Minio has always lived in Ambler, a borough near Philadelphia with a mix of small-town businesses and suburban homeowners. He is the chief of the volunteer Wissahickon Fire Company and an electrician by profession. His security firm is an outgrowth of his electrical contracting business.

"When home security began to take hold in this area, I was asked by a large security company to service the systems they installed, a job that fit right in with my experience as an electrician. As I did this, some people in our town asked me if I could install security systems for them.

"I figured if I was servicing systems for someone else, I could specify and install them myself. That's how it began. The fact that almost everybody in town knows me, either through my electrical business or the fire company, didn't hurt! Now I design and install systems for both businesses and residents.

"One reason people buy from me is that they know me—lots of my security customers give me their house keys when they go away on vacation. Also, I personally service every system I put in. If a big company installs your security system and it needs repair, you usually don't get anyone you know, and you rarely get the same person twice. If one of my systems needs fixing, the customer knows he's getting service from just one guy—the boss!"

PUBLIC-SECTOR PRIVATE SECURITY

Most private security forces are just that—officers and supervisors who work for malls, corporations, banks, and other places that need protection. But for several reasons private security officers are working in the public sector, in areas once reserved for law enforcement people. One reason for the jump over is that townships, counties, and towns are finding they do not have money enough to maintain traditional police departments. These communities find it is more efficient to replace or augment police officers with private security officers. However, this activity is not without controversy.

Security job seekers should learn what those in the field already know: the limits of authority of private security forces, and their potential for liability and lawsuits.

According to Milo Geyelin, reporting in The Wall Street Journal, private security officers "generally . . . have no more than a citizen's power to arrest and . . . no authority whatsoever to question, detain or search [someone] without risking a lawsuit."

As agents of the state, police officers cannot be sued in the normal performance of their duties unless they exceed their authority or abuse their power; however, private security officers, especially when augmenting or replacing police, may be "sued for simple mistakes," according to Geyelin. On-the-job behavior of private security forces is controlled by state liability laws that limit improper conduct, not by the constitutional restraints that apply to police forces (see "Liability" in chapter 17).

A second public-sector activity has been the creation of explosive-proof surveillance systems for the military. Private security forces may also protect government property and workers. Such security forces cannot make arrests but can move in when a situation looks suspicious. Many government-employed officers monitor surveillance systems; others may patrol buildings and grounds. Whatever they are doing, the task is designed to protect government interests and property—and indirectly, to protect you, the American citizen.

SECURITY MANAGERS

According to *Introduction to Security* by Robert J. Fischer and Gion Green (Butterworth-Heinemann, 1992), students wishing to work in the security industry should take academic courses in security, computer science, electronics, business management, law, police science, personnel, and information management. All security people need to know the basics of communications, management, and law. How much students learn about loss prevention, fire protection, and computer security, or any of the above subjects, would depend on the specific career areas they wish to enter.

The security manager of a corporation, or of a firm that offers contract guard services, is considered an important executive. He or she has tremendous responsibility to protect lives and property. In return, many perks are part of the employment package: excellent salary (equivalent to a chief of police in a medium-sized jurisdiction), full benefits, and an important role within the company structure. The security manager may rise through the ranks in the security arena. A bachelor's degree in criminal justice or security management is a virtual essential; a graduate degree can be even more of a door-opener. People with military or law enforcement backgrounds often claim top security positions.

Vance International, a prestigious private security company, is staffed by the cream of security managers. The firm's founder and president, Chuck Vance, was a special agent in the U.S. Secret Service through four presidential administrations. Vice-president of operations, Larry Sheaff, was the deputy director of the Secret Service. Harvey Prior, another official, was the chief of police for the Uniformed Division of the Secret Service. The company staff also includes managers from the FBI, Scotland Yard, major metropolitan police departments, and the U.S. military. The high salaries garnered by these directors reflect the sensitive and commanding role of the security manager. He or she has policy-making authority in this challenging field.

As its name implies, this is an international firm. It began in 1984 by offering executive protection for royal families, foreign diplomats, and heads of state who come to this country. It still performs these duties, plus asset protection, uniformed protection, investigations, security training, and countersurveillance (the "sweeping" of supposedly secure areas to unearth spying devices and thus protect clients' business interests).

The authors of *Introduction to Security*, fifth edition (Butterworth-Heinemann, 1992) quote Saul Astor, president of Manage-ment Safeguards, on the glowing future for executives in private security. "The rise in staff has been meteoric, and there is no leveling off in sight. Security organizations are paying exceptional salaries to qualified young comers," according to Astor.

A security manager's job is to supervise an officer force, to help determine protection policies for his or her employer, to manage all aspects of security personnel (working hours, pay and benefits, grievance management, promotion, hiring and firing, etc.), and to maintain given security levels within established budgets. Their duties may be to protect company property and employees, to operate protective surveillance, or manage loss prevention ("sticky-fingered" employees or store customers).

Security managers at the upper level often have powers equal to law enforcement officers. They may carry weapons and use sophisticated communications and detection equipment. This peak of the private security mountain is tremendously rewarding to those with the skills and experience to monitor the darker side of life.

Security managers with college degrees in their specialty can start at the $26,000 to $30,000 mark depending on company size. Loss prevention specialists and managers, whose duties can range from reducing retail store shoplifting to investigating international piracy of intellectual property, can earn from $20,000 to over $100,000 a year. The chief of security for a worldwide Fortune 500 corporation may earn a high salary commensurate with great responsibility.

RELATED SECURITY JOBS

Private security officers and supervisors work in an ever-increasing number of complexes open to the public. These include but are not limited to retail establishments, health care facilities, casinos, and hotels. And, although it is behind the scenes, computer security is a particularly important job area.

The authors of *Introduction to Security* note that retail companies (department and discount stores) will simply not stay in business without security forces. Shoplifting is so prevalent and so disastrous to a store's bottom line that all sorts of private security people are part of the profit picture. (This is true despite the growth in and improvement of electronic theft detection devices attached to merchandise; these devices help reduce but do not eliminate retail theft.) Jobs exist, from the entry-level blue-jacketed officer to the undercover investigator, from the credit investigator to the top-of-the-ladder security manager.

Fischer and Green report that it's fine to have a college degree in security management, but many stores are willing to train resourceful, alert young people and mid-life career changers. The latter is good news for those facing forced retirement and looking for something meaningful to do.

Security in health-care facilities is an equally robust job field. Security officers and other types of hospital guards are in growing demand. Likewise, hotel security offers many career opportunities. The hospitality industry, plagued with problems ranging from thefts from supposedly secure hotel rooms to more serious charges, is polishing its image and needs security people to turn the perception of protection into reality. The growing number of casinos need to protect assets and customers, often 24 hours a day.

Computer security is the most fascinating, least understood, most advanced career area in this book. We have devoted section 5 to the exciting opportunities in this field.

CHAPTER 19
•••••••••••••••

Terrorism and Private Security Officers

Unlike natural disasters—earthquakes, floods, and tornadoes—terrorism is a planned disaster, created to produce the greatest possible devastation. In the United States, terrorism now includes every activity from assassinations to the destruction of the Oklahoma City Federal Building.

Until the World Trade Center bombing, terrorism was seen as something that happened in other countries. The FBI and CIA helped protect overseas offices of American companies that were targets of terrorists. Now, America itself is under fire. Terrorists' devastation in this country has become so great that, in desperation to avoid further acts of terrorism, corporations, airport authorities—even the federal government—have had to call upon private security resources. (Result of this activity: more openings for security people.)

Increased domestic terrorism has fueled a lively debate between the proponents of unrestricted civil liberties and those favoring sufficient federal control to ensure public safety. Then, too, there is discussion as to whether more physical barriers are an answer to terrorism rather than a stepping-up of intelligence-based technology. (In either case, the objective is to stop fanatics long before they detonate their ideas.)

Recognizing that no one is safe, we now examine two of the country's most devastating terrorist acts, the short-circuiting of a third, and the role of private security in the aftermath of all these events.

In 1993, a terrorist group plotted to demolish New York's towering World Trade Center. The 10 radical Muslims damaged an underground parking area with stunning accuracy and shocking power using a bomb fabricated in someone's garage! If one could say that anything was lucky about this tragedy, it was that this *jihad* did not get to carry out its master objective. They had planned to set off five bombs within 10 minutes of the World Trade Center bombing, blowing up the United Nations Building, the George Washington Bridge, the Lincoln and Holland tunnels, and an FBI building. The group had also planned to assassinate Egypt's president, Hosni Mubarak.

Originally it was thought that the tragic Oklahoma City bombing was the work of Middle Eastern terrorists. But soon, evidence pointed to two right-wing, pseudo-military terrorists. The primary goal of such people is to destroy the United States government. In this instance, they failed to do that, but their pernicious act left all of America unnerved.

The death toll from the bombing neared 200, with hundreds of others injured. The bombers used either a timer or a remote control device to detonate one-half ton of explosives.

In *A Force Upon the Plain; the American Militia and the Politics of Hate* (Simon & Schuster, 1996), the author, Kenneth Stern, pointed out the government's heretofore indifferent attitude toward terrorism in America. He restated the recurrent warnings by the American Jewish Committee to do something—warnings that were dismissed as inconsequential just nine days before the Oklahoma City blast. "The proverbial barn door had been left gaping," Stephanie Saul wrote in a review of Stern's book.

In his 1996 book, Stern wrote that militia groups are a genuine threat to America. Composed of the democracy-soured, such hate groups preach racism and insurrection. (Example: The government destroyed the Branch Davidian sect at Waco; therefore, we, in turn, will bomb the Oklahoma City Federal Building.) Such right-wing extremists are a menace. However, they are protected by the very rights they would undermine.

America's most deeply held beliefs of the constitutional right to assemble, to express diverse unpopular opinions, and to carry arms makes it immensely difficult to establish a policy of interference with any extremist groups.

Terrorists are fighting a war that prosecutors in the World Trade Center bombing trial called "A wave of urban terrorism." The destructive goals of extremist groups are wide ranging, although all reflect right-wing philosophies—a holy war against the United States. For instance, the Muslim terrorists wanted America to stop supporting Israel and Egypt and vowed to punish the enemies of Islamic fundamentalism.

The trial for those who carried out this unprecedented attack was based on a Civil War charge of "seditious conspiracy." It took place two years after the event in a courtroom bristling with protective measures, including concrete barriers and bomb-sniffing dogs. The defendants were given maximum sentences except for those who pleaded guilty in exchange for plea bargains. Innocent lives were lost; this murderous group deserved their punishment, and more.

The Order, a right-wing hate group, had equally destructive plans. Good detective work prevented group members from blowing up railway and telephone lines and poisoning water supplies. "Basically," said a spokesperson for The Order, "we wanted to bring down the [federal] government. There wasn't a question in our minds that we couldn't do it."

Not all their schemes were foiled. They robbed armored cars and distributed the money among several hate groups. And they had no qualms about murder, assassinating talk-show host Alan Berg, among others.

To make our country safe from deranged but highly calculating groups, American and international, the nation has greatly increased both public law enforcement and private security. After the trial of the Muslim extremists, security measures were tightened at airports and on security-sensitive streets. At airports, automobiles left unattended at curbside were quickly towed away; all vans and any cars with tinted windows were restricted to remote parking areas; airline passengers had to show picture IDs at flight check-in.

In Washington, President Clinton acknowledged that Pennsylvania Avenue bordering The White House could be dangerous for the country's Number One citizen. On the previously "friendly" street where tourists could happily poke their noses through the fence and enjoy the sight of blooming beds of flowers, people can still walk, but vehicles can no longer pass by The White House.

Hot on the heels of the World Trade Center tragedy, U.S. Secretary of Transportation Federico Pena ordered a variety of security measures. Some were to protect Pope John Paul II during his visit to the United States. Security was also tightened during the United Nations' 50th anniversary when world leaders gathered in New York.

A private security company, Surveillance Systems, Inc., was chosen to help protect John Paul II on the historic February 1996 papal visit. The company, headed by Paul J. Fischer, won a $50,000 New Jersey State contract to upgrade the security system at Giants Stadium, site of one papal Mass. The company had earlier obtained a $100,000 contract from the U.S. Department of Defense to install the security system at the stadium for the 1994 World Cup soccer games.

Giants Stadium's already sophisticated security system was decidedly improved for the pope, to include surveillance cameras that automatically focused when moving in on a target. If security people need to check "section 321" of the stadium, three cameras zoom in to provide a detailed close-up of what is happening in that area.

Pope John Paul's visit could conceivably have become another terrorist horror. Paul Fischer and his company were there with the systems and the expertise to see that this would not happen.

The recent bombings in America led to increased public and private security. (Private forces often take over when police protection is insufficient or greater safeguards need to be installed.) Security was boosted around many federal buildings. In Denver, guards patrolled day-care centers operated for federal court employees. Nearby parking meters were covered with red "no parking" hoods to thwart the planting of time bombs in parked cars.

In Washington, the Gutenberg Bible was removed from its glass case in the Library of Congress and locked in a basement vault. As expected, the World Trade Center rapidly acquired a siege mentality image when the building was surrounded by 6,000-pound concrete barriers. Security cameras mounted high on the towers now pinpoint trouble from on high. Three hundred fifty private security officers patrol the many hallways and concourses, checking on anything suspicious.

Private security guards will be much in demand because American citizens prefer added protection to the restrictions on freedom inherent in antiterrorist legislation.

There has been a question of limiting antiterrorism measures to structural changes and sturdier construction. This could prevent the progressive collapse that occurred when the entire front of the Oklahoma City Federal Building was destroyed, leaving the floors to sink on one another. But the FBI believes that greater intelligence activity—wiretapping, placing informants within domestic extremist groups—is more effective than physical forms of security.

"If you want to counter terrorism, 80 percent is a matter of getting good intelligence," said L. Paul Bremer, who headed the Reagan administration's counterterrorism office.

To improve communications between public law enforcement and private security, the FBI has a new program, DECA-fax. DECA-fax is shorthand for Department of Espionage Counterintelligence and Counterterrorism Awareness. A mouthful, yes, but the FBI has found the fax-based organization to be an effective law enforcement tool. The program allows domestic corporations to learn where all sorts of dangers lie.

DECA-fax was begun in the New York City area by FBI Supervisory Special Agent Larry V. Watson. He found that many corporations wanted instantaneous information on terrorist alerts, industrial espionage tricks, profiles, and pictures of known terrorists—any information that could protect them.

Now, private security companies and corporate forces nationwide subscribe to the service. It uses laptop computers with fax auto-dialers. Security people who sign up for the free program are entered into the computer database. DECA-fax agents having information about any terrorist activity will then auto-dial the data to all the fax numbers supplied by subscriber companies.

DECA-fax was an immediate success. It is really a "neighborhood watch," said Watson. The information that DECA-fax transmits to corporate security forces will vary. In New York, for instance, one of the first DECA-faxes was a notice stating that the FBI will pay awards up to $500,000 for information about suspected espionage activities.

In different parts of the country, anniversaries may be important—not "happy anniversary" celebrations but tragic anniversaries: dates that mark such events as the Branch Davidian fire, the Ruby Ridge standoff, or the World Trade Center bombing. Such anniversaries tend to bring terrorists and hate groups out of the woodwork. These are times when federal, regional, and corporate security forces need to be on extra alert.

CHAPTER 20

Cargo Theft and Strike Control/ Assets Management

These are two security areas that offer a variety of careers. The first involves law enforcement and private security; the second is a private security specialty.

CARGO SECURITY: LAW ENFORCEMENT AND PRIVATE SECURITY INTERACT

Although public enforcement teams may pursue cargo thieves, private security is an important part of the picture. Transportation companies—often called carriers—protect their cargoes with security managers who supervise private officers using traditional detection methods and the newest surveillance equipment.

Cargo theft is serious. In an article written for *Security Management* magazine, "Cargo Security Goes the Distance," (October, 1995) Roger W. Moore and Jeff Gerloff stated, "In New Jersey, the dollar value in goods stolen from a single tractor-trailer rig totaled more than all combined bank robberies [in that state] for 1994."

Roger W. Moore knows whereof he speaks. His perceptive comments are based on his experiences as manager of corporate security for Roadway Express, Inc., of Akron, Ohio. Coauthor Jon Gerloff is Roadway's western division manager of corporate security.

Cargo theft has been going on for years, in ever-growing volume. Ocean shippers, railroads, and trucking companies are bedeviled by hit-and-run thieves. The pilferers are hard to catch because goods in transit are especially vulnerable to theft. In *Introduction to Security* Fifth Edition, (Butterworth-Henemann, 1992), Robert J. Fischer and Gion Green point out the big business of cargo theft: $13.3 billion in direct losses every year, with the average theft totaling $75,000 worth of goods. These figures date from 1990; the numbers are higher today.

However, two trade associations have developed interesting deterrent systems. The Western States Cargo Theft Association (WSCTA) and the New Jersey State

Police's Cargo Theft and Robbery Unit are steadily making it more difficult for cargo thieves to raid warehouses, grab loot from loading docks, or ransack freight cars left in rail yards overnight.

The Western States Cargo Theft Association initially consisted of security managers from private industry. Later, it added law enforcement personnel. (The private security managers involved naturally earn higher salaries than the support staff does.) In 1990, the Los Angeles County Sheriff's Department launched the Cargo Criminal Apprehension Team (CAT). CAT is formidable and multi-jurisdictional. It includes law enforcement staff from the Los Angeles Sheriff's Department, the California Highway Patrol, the FBI, Los Angeles Post Office, and the Vernon, California, Police Department.

In this hardball game, CAT brings to bat every high-tech trick and undercover device at their disposal, including sting operations and electronic surveillance.

The CATs get most of their operating money from the cargo carriers and their insurance companies. This support allows them to train investigators, pay informants for their information, and provide "flash money"—the dollars needed to buy stolen property during undercover operations. Moore and Gerloff write that this step is "a prelude to search and seizure."

An informant may not be a savory person, but he or she is a necessary part of law enforcement. An informant accepts money in return for telling police just what fellow criminals are doing, or planning.

An example of the cargo CAT's successes was intercepting thieves who had stolen a truckload of shrink-wrapped, top-shelf liquor for a quick trip south of the border. With the help of an informant and flash money, the cargo CATs were ready with a search warrant. Catching the thieves on the spot, they recovered $228,000 worth of the $230,000 truckload.

During 1994, these intrepid crimefighters recovered merchandise worth $95.6 million and made 652 arrests. This record should have cargo thieves thinking twice about what Moore and Gerloff call "assaults against commercial truckers."

Just who are these cargo thieves? They come in three varieties, the random criminal, the professional, and the insider. Teenagers who need drug money, for instance, are often nabbed because they strike at random and are not very good thieves. Professional criminals, on the other hand, are cunning and knowledge-able. Moore and Gerloff note that "they know exactly what they want when they strike, and . . . where to get it." Finally, there is the employee-thief within the cargo organization. Fischer and Green do not even mention outsiders as a threat to the industry, targeting instead those who, theoretically, work for the good of the company. The authors do note, however, that outsiders may work with insiders who know the "who, what, where and when" of goods in transit. These dishonest employees expect payoffs from the thieves for their information.

First, we will address the professional cargo thieves who are on the outside. They know the schedules of the transporters they target. They are also specific about what they want. Loading docks, freight yards, and truck stops are all vulnerable because these cargo marksmen have great targeting abilities. They perfect their art by observation and a knowledge of how cargo moves. (Thieves can make off with entire trucks as well as their cargoes.)

According to Fischer and Green, the leading pilferer is the cargo industry employee. And his greatest ally is confusion. Many people have access to a cargo facility, whether it is a ship terminal, freight yard, or truck loading dock: warehouse workers, stevedores and longshoremen, forklift truck operators, drivers, dispatchers. The work pace is constant. The dishonest employees take advantage of the beehive of activity (unlike worker bees, who stick to business!). Movement—the essence of the cargo industry—allows for clandestine activity.

Transportation companies must be on the alert. This fact underlies the importance of the private security forces they employ. These cargo protectors attack the problem of theft from several angles. Cargo—boxed, palletted, shrink-wrapped, or in rolls—demands super security. Transportation and shipping companies need well-trained security managers. They also need stellar security systems just as other large organizations do. Security officers are all-important, but, as the old Yellow Pages slogan put it, "Let your fingers do the walking." An electronic security system can "walk" almost every inch of a building complex inside and out. Closed-circuit television and other monitors can spot illegal movement and capture it on film.

These amazing CCTV "baby-sitters" are only the beginning of a security system's capabilities. Cutting-edge technology now allows illicit movement to be tracked from 11,000 miles above Earth. As Moore and Gerloff point out, "Satellite tracking systems are perhaps the most sophisticated tools in the transportation industry today." These sci-fi devices can locate a particular truck in any part of the world. The satellite can report on a truck's speed, direction, and even if it is in an area where it does not belong.

When the satellite zeroes in on trouble, the information is relayed to a control center, which notifies the carrier's dispatcher. The dispatcher, in turn, reports what's wrong to police in the area where the truck may be operating illegally. All this technical legerdemain can happen in less than 45 seconds!

Cargo theft is one more example of the interesting and varied ways private security is used for corporate protection. There is "improved communication between law enforcement, private security, and corporate management," write Moore and Gerloff. Pilferers will think twice about pursuing shrink-wrapped (and other) cargoes, knowing they can be legally "shrink-wrapped" themselves!

Opportunities in cargo-related security appear strong, since the problem of theft is constant. Salaries are on a par with similar jobs in security management and loss prevention (see chapter 20).

STRIKE CONTROL AND PRIVATE SECURITY

Vance International, a Virginia-based private security firm, is multifaceted—you name it, they protect it. They are one of the country's most versatile security companies, with services ranging from uniformed guards to international investigations, from education and training for future security officers to the protection of diplomats.

Chuck Vance, the firm's president and chief executive officer, recently appeared on TV's *48 Hours* and has been interviewed many times on *Larry King Live* and other shows as an across-the-board security expert. (His background: Secret Service through four presidential administrations.) Every company principal has a dramatic law enforcement background such as ex-FBI or senior officer in the Washington, D.C., precinct that protects Capitol Hill, for instance.

The firm is far smaller than a Pinkerton's or Wackenhut, according to William Little, vice-president of marketing for Vance International. "The difference is our service mix—it's dramatic," he said. "We are the Rolls-Royce, not the General Motors, of security. If you want superior service, come to us."

One of these services is Vance's subsidiary, Asset Protection Team, Inc. (APT), a strike control force that in its dozen years of operation has protected the assets of over 400 firms during labor disputes, companies such as Caterpillar, Bridgestone/Firestone, Detroit News, and McDonnell Douglas.

A corporation facing a strike can contract with Vance International for protective services before the strike deadline. Specially trained members of the Vance Asset Protection Team then guard buildings, plant sites, cars and trucks, and other company assets, protecting against any destructive actions taken by those on strike. At the same time, the team keeps the strikers from doing irreparable harm to their futures as employees.

Since strikes occur on private property, public law enforcement staffs can offer little or no help to a company faced with an acrimonious labor dispute. (Only if the general public is put in danger can police take even limited action.) Thus local police are glad to have Vance forces on the scene. Often, only the presence of a force such as the Asset Protection Team keeps the lid on a strike and makes the difference between a smoothly settled dispute and a prolonged, bloody confrontation.

The Vance Asset Protection Team consists of men and women with military or law enforcement backgrounds. They serve two purposes on the strike scene. Equipped with video and still cameras, they can document any strikers' actions taken against corporate property or nonstriking individuals. Also, they see that the strikers do not do so much damage that they cause a permanent break with their employers.

Little explains the documentary effort this way: "Because of our cameras, the message to strikers is, 'You are no longer anonymous. We can see who is throwing rocks, slashing tires, vandalizing the buildings, or assaulting working employees, and when you do it.'"

The Team's reward for such vigilance can range from verbal abuse to barrages of well-aimed rocks. But Asset Protection Team members are trained and tested, schooled to stay cool in the face of confrontation. They know that potential trouble is part of their territory, and managing it calmly is their job. (The majority of strikes, although noisy and contentious, provoke relatively little violence.)

Little points out that, although strike control forces are invariably hired by management, "We see both views at the same time. Our aim is to make sure strikers behave well enough so they have a company 'home' to go back to when the strike is over. At the same time, we are protecting the employers from tremendous physical damage and financial loss."

CHAPTER 21

Security Systems and the Jobs They Create

We use ever-more-amazing systems to protect people, products, intellectual property, and military secrets. According to Paul J. Fischer, president of Surveillance Systems, Pottstown, Pennsylvania, these systems are replacing people in private security jobs. "But the systems makers are employing people, so there are opportunities for experienced security workers. They can change careers by building on their security experience. With further training, they can design, construct, market or install systems like those that cost them their jobs!" (*Private Security Trends, 1970–2000, The Hallcrest Report II*, Butterworth-Heinemann, 1990) bears out Fischer's claim. The electronic security segment is growing at 11 percent a year, compared to a 7 percent growth rate for the entire private security industry.)

This career area is expanding because of what Fischer called the perceptions and realities of crime. The perception is that crime is all-pervasive. The reality is that as America becomes more urbanized, neighborhoods become more prone to crime as they become more densely populated.

"If you have a town of 500 people, there might be one bad guy, and nobody worries much. But if you have 5,000 people packed into one city neighborhood, you'll have 10 bad apples. Same percentage—but because the city folks live close together, their perception is that criminals are everywhere.

"Security has been and is the necessary evil. Everyone wants it but no one wants the inconvenience. However, most people will sacrifice inconvenience for safety. You want to know you're safe wherever you are."

One goal of security technologists is to maintain or improve safety margins while reducing inconvenience.

ACCESS CONTROLS

Access controls are among the fastest-growing and most innovative security systems. They protect buildings and factories by limiting entry to authorized people through nearly foolproof screening. In an interview, Fischer described some of these advanced access control systems.

"All sorts of commercial and industrial businesses use access controls," Fischer said. "Prices are dropping and system efficiency is going up. Card-based access control is great for places such as casinos. Here, many employees need lots of access but security has to be tight. Card readers do away with one employee having to carry a huge ring of keys to unlock different doors. Instead, he or she uses one card. It opens any door for which that employee has clearance. Each locked door has a card reader and three lights, like a traffic signal. If the person is not authorized to enter, the light flashes red. If the system is doubtful—that is, if the card is not authorized or it did not read right the first time—the light is yellow, and the user tries the card again. If the person is cleared, the light flashes green and the door unlocks."

Access control systems include:

- **Biometric readers**—These were used at the 1996 Olympic Games to admit qualified athletes, coaches, and other participants. Biometric ID is growing in industry as well. Each qualified person gets an ID card containing his or her photo, name, and a "smart" radio frequency (RF) microchip. The smart chip has been encoded with the geometry of the user's hand. To pass through an electronic entrance, the user places the card in a slot and his hand in a hand geometry reader. The door opens only if the user's hand geometry matches that on the card.

  Other sophisticated biometric readers use the retina of the eye (one chance of a repeat in 94 billion people, according to Paul Fischer), fingerprints, and voice recognition. A DNA access control system would be foolproof. Such a system is experimental, but it has one problem: It requires a separate DNA sample for each access—not practical.

- **Card readers**—A magnetic strip on each card contains digits that call up questions on file in a host computer. The system admits or denies the person presenting the card, based on answers that only the approved cardholder could give.

- **Integrated readers**—These devices grant or deny access to the person presenting a magnetic card by bringing up a video file of the person, filming a video on the spot, and computer-matching the two to verify his or her identity.

- **Time control systems**—These combine card readers with time recorders. With the system, each employee uses a reader card to log in and out of work. The card identifies each person and automatically prepares his or her paycheck, based on working hours recorded, computerized salary or hourly rate information, tax withholding, etc. Such a system can be programmed to restrict employee overtime. A supervisor must override the automated system to authorize overtime.

"The future of access control is broadening," Fischer said. "The cost-benefit ratio is improving, making many forms of access control more affordable.

"For example, airlines and travel agents could encode flight tickets with data that would match that on a host computer at the airport. This would immediately okay that ticket-holder for his or her flight while improving airport security."

CCTV

Closed-circuit television (CCTV) is one of Surveillance Systems' specialties. Advances are strong here, too, Fischer said. "Cameras that view a scene, zoom in on the details, and record everything are now the standard. The advances include microcamera technology. This lets security managers hide tiny cameras in everything from wall clocks to electric toasters.

"We have designed and installed 'smart' camera systems. These respond to action. If there's trouble at a spectator event, the operator touches 'section 24B' on a keypad. The cameras zoom in and automatically focus on that one segment of people. You can break a stadium, factory floor, or office building into preprogrammed grids. The operator touches codes on a keypad, and the cameras move into place and start running.

"There are also smart camera systems with automated integration. They respond to motion detectors, door openers, automatic timers, and smoke detectors. They transmit pictures to videotape and real-time TV screens."

The firm has designed and installed explosion-proof CCTV systems to monitor hazardous areas such as explosive storage. Cameras can observe and record in biochemical and radioactive areas, spots too dangerous for human observers. Doctors often use CCTV for medical training. Students can see surgeons operate "up close" without being in an amphitheater or near the patient. CCTV monitors intensive care units. And nurses at their stations can view individual hospital patients in their beds.

"There is a natural crossover between private security technology and police department applications," Fischer said. (See chapter 2.) "For example, police are using video surveillance at traffic lights and for speeding violations. Video systems can light a suspected car, videotape its license plate, record it going through a red light, or calculate and record its speed on film—even print and mail a violation to the driver! Some of these systems include signs telling drivers they are being videotaped. They work!

"Police often put time-date video cameras in patrol cars to use for recording traffic stops. And police use video systems on highways to monitor traffic flow. The benefit is in using electric message signs to reroute drivers around accidents or delays. This is leading to the day when we have traffic control by computer. Such a system would use satellites to send accident reports and 911 calls to emergency crews and relay travel data to motorists. You'd have an in-car computer that would download and display instructions for avoiding a problem ahead."

OTHER ELECTRONIC APPLICATIONS

Of his company, Paul Fischer said: "We custom-design to meet needs for which there is nothing out there. We will design and manufacture an original electronic or computer-based system because there are so many developing applications. These deal with security, but we also address assembly line problems, customer service, quality control, and manufacturing efficiency. Customers say, 'If I could do this (whatever it is) with monitoring, I would,'—and we try to make such things happen.

"We had a manufacturer of large toys who had trouble with small bags of parts being left out of product boxes. These packages varied in individual weight so you couldn't use a scale to detect missing bags in lighter-weight boxes. So we devised a monitor using electronic article surveillance (EAS). We applied encoded microchips to each bag and used a radio frequency (RF) sensor on the line. The sensor easily detected boxes without parts bags before the boxes were sealed."

EAS originated as a loss prevention system. It uses microchips encoded with "triggers" buried in merchandise tags (or even in product packages). These set off RF alarms at store exits if shoplifters try to leave with merchandise. (Clerks deactivate the triggers at check-out when customers buy.) The cost-per-package is now so low that even little-ticket items such as twin-packs of flashlight batteries can be protected by microchips.

An offshoot of this technology, IDEAS, embeds complete property information into almost any physical asset from a laptop computer to a cellular phone—in short, any movable item that a company wants to protect. The microchip records what the item is, who is responsible for it, and whether it may legally be removed. If someone does take a tagged item, the system can note when it was taken and from where.

"Schools have interesting security problems," Paul Fischer noted. "Protecting property and monitoring grounds are suburban school priorities. Safety—detecting drugs and weapons—is the main concern of inner-city schools. In either case, school boards hesitate to make schools too prison-like. Parents can get upset if you install metal detectors or CCTV monitors—but such security measures may be justifiable, given the nature of a particular school. It's hard for the security consultants who advise school principals—and school administrators—to know where to draw the line.

"There's no question that security has a place in schools. Too often, computers get trashed or stolen, among other things that happen. School boards have to protect their expensive property just as businesses do—and that calls for sensors, cameras, alarm systems—whatever it takes."

Fischer and his scientific crew know all about this. The company has installed many school security systems including complete computer protection for Philadelphia's Drexel University.

OPPORTUNITIES AND EARNINGS

The two principal job areas in security systems are sales and marketing and design engineering.

Sales Engineers: There are few custom designers who also manufacture systems, such as Paul Fischer's company. Most security experts who help design systems know what it takes to sell them on their performance. "Typical security engineers are salespeople, too," Fischer said. "They may be ex-security or loss prevention workers who learn how the security system they are selling works. That way, they can propose it to a client. If you have basic security knowledge and good people skills, you'll do very well once you learn the engineering essentials."

How well is "very well"? Engineering-minded security system salespeople can earn from $25,000 to $100,000 a year. Earnings are largely in commissions. (These will vary by company.) Those selling low-end security systems will earn on the volume of product they sell. An engineer-salesperson installing a $250,000 system need not sell many in a year to do well! A sales-only type without either a background in engineering or security operations can expect to earn less—from $9,000 a year up, depending on experience and skills learned on the job.

"The changeover makes sense," Fischer said. "Where I used to work, they had 12 store detectives, or loss prevention specialists. Now there are three, because of budget problems. But any of the nine no longer working can become qualified to design, sell and install security equipment. It's not too broad a reach from store detective to technical consultant or assistant automated loss prevention specialist. This means that people can either get new jobs in sales, or stay where they are by learning all they can about the automated systems that are coming in to replace them."

Design Engineer: These are highly technical people with electrical/electronic engineering skills, creativity, and problem-solving abilities. These independent people are not always good with the public, nor are interpersonal skills part of their wizardry. Design engineers of this type usually earn salaries averaging $36,000 to $40,000 a year. Highly skilled engineers and the leaders of engineering teams (especially those who can be part of sales presentations!) may earn up to $95,000 depending on the nature, complexity, and innovations of the systems they are designing.

As for Paul Fischer, his career path is unusual for one so young (he is 26). He began his company part-time when he was a senior in technical school, studying security and investigation. To learn to handle customers and increase his security knowledge, he took a retail security job after high school. Within six months he had been promoted to assistant loss prevention manager and later moved to loss prevention manager for the corporate offices of his security firm. During these fast-paced years, Paul, a natural at inventing technological applications, founded his company in 1988 to build large custom monitoring systems. The firm incorporated in 1993 and has expanded steadily. "I learned how security systems worked in my loss prevention jobs—but retail security is tough. I figured if I was going to make that much effort, I might as well work for myself!

"We keep trying to make better and better large, custom surveillance and security systems. I will always be learning because there will always be new challenges. Criminals are sharp competitors!"

Although it has been said that crime doesn't pay, fighting canny criminals has its rewards. Surveillance Systems, Inc., Paul Fischer's small but aggressive and inventive company, has had its first million-dollar sales year.

(The authors wish to acknowledge the contributions to this chapter made by Paul J. Fischer, president, Surveillance Systems, Inc.)

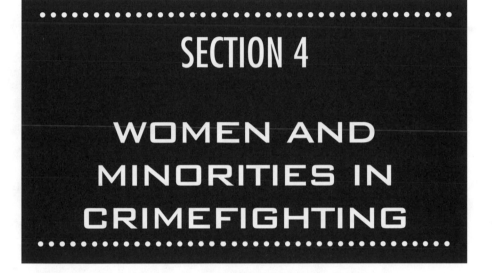

SECTION 4

WOMEN AND
MINORITIES IN
CRIMEFIGHTING

Women in Crimefighting: Looking for and Finding Jobs in Law Enforcement and Other Areas of Crimefighting

Thirty years ago, working as support staff was the only role for women in this field. Twenty years ago, women started moving out from behind their desks and onto the front lines, but were on a separate, more "protected" track than their male counterparts. In the last decade, women have finally begun claiming their places as effective agents for law enforcement.

Several generations of women have paved the way for today's new recruits, and now more and more women are deciding that the time is right to join up. Law enforcement, in all its forms, is ready for them. This message comes from Attorney General Janet Reno, who holds the top law enforcement position in the country. The message also comes from women like Helena Ashby, chief of detectives for the Los Angeles County Sheriff's Department (the nation's third largest police agency). And it comes from people like Captain Jeanette Dooley of the 14th police district in Philadelphia, a city in which over 1,100 out of 6,300 sworn police personnel are women.

Captain Dooley oversees one of Philadelphia's most respected police districts. Her district stands out in a city that has recently experienced some corruption within its ranks. Dooley believes that good training and a solid set of ethics will help a police officer stay on the right track. And "the more encouragement and support they receive, the more excellent they become," she said in an interview in the latter part of 1995 with the *Chestnut Hill Local*, a Philadelphia-based newspaper.

Dooley is tough as well as compassionate. While she is "willing to bet money on the honesty of the men and women of the 14th police district," she still conducts locker searches for any signs of questionable behavior.

Captain Dooley offers encouragement and support to her officers on a daily basis. She told the *Chestnut Hill Local* that if a hostage situation arises, she is right on the scene with her officers to contain it.

Dooley remembered a confrontation that sounds like something from a grade "B" movie. The groom was arrested in the middle of a wedding service that took place within her precinct. She promptly requested a meeting with all the clergy in her district to ask if the situation was handled well. The clergy felt that the officers conducted themselves properly in an uncomfortable situation. The feedback was tremendously encouraging for her and her officers.

Dooley wants feedback from the **entire** 14 district community. A positive reaction from the residents is a form of support for the districts' officers. A community that welcomes and respects its officers automatically raises their spirits and encourages high standards of behavior.

At the end of her interview with the *Chestnut Hill Local*, Dooley made a comment that should inspire both those interested in a career in a police department and those who know the police force from the outside. "Remember a personal experience you had with a police officer." For many this could be a simple request for directions courteously answered, for others it may have been a life-saving experience. Police officers **want** to help.

Since the publication of the article, Captain Dooley has been promoted to commanding officer of civil affairs for the Philadelphia Police Department. In this role, she oversees the control of strikes, protests, and civil conflicts. Captain Dooley's officers may stand guard at events ranging from the orderly strike of the Philadelphia Orchestra's musicians to an inflammatory confrontation in front of the Israeli Embassy to protest Middle East unrest.

While many women are now interested in police work, others have been drawn to the profession of the private investigator. Home computers and increasing savvy make women ideal for the often time-consuming but rewarding effort of tracking down criminals, missing persons, deadbeat fathers, and others.

African-Americans will be gratified to find many law enforcement career areas welcoming them. *Ebony* magazine reports that law enforcement is one of the most viable careers for blacks. Joseph M. Wright, executive director of the National Organization of Black Law Enforcement Executives, says that jobs in every facet of the field will increase at about 5 percent annually.

African-Americans are now being actively recruited at the federal, state, and local levels. Law enforcement agencies are finding that minorities have a broadening effect on the field, particularly in urban areas where they are working with largely black or Latino communities.

Thus, minorities (including women) find law enforcement jobs in large cities like Los Angeles, Chicago, Detroit, Atlanta, Miami, and Philadelphia. In fact, some of these city police departments are headed by African-Americans. Stan Embry is an African-American in the Los Angeles Police Department. Embry has risen through the ranks to lieutenant. Some 17 years ago, when he joined LAPD, he encountered racism and its insidious effect. Today, Embry finds this attitude

Captain Jeanette Dooley, former commander of the Philadelphia police 14th district, is now head of the department's civil affairs unit.

(Photo: Philadelphia Police Department)

less prevalent. With the changes, the Los Angeles Police Department is making a concerted effort to hire African-Americans. The youngest training officer of

probationers (new recruits) is black. The LAPD is seeking to reverse the negative image created by a few officers.

Lieutenant Embry, in charge of vice operations in the San Fernando Valley, has not stopped climbing the law enforcement ladder. His rise to the top appears almost inevitable because of his distinguished record. This includes courageous behavior in the mid-'90s Northridge earthquake. Directing police from a command post on a street corner, he rallied them to action despite electrical transformers exploding over his head.

Federal law enforcement agencies are now actively seeking women and minorities. Of the 10,000 FBI agents, nearly 1,000 are women; 500 African-American males and 80 African-American females are part of the FBI investigating team.

Realizing that these figures are still a meager showing, the FBI (and the Secret Service) are developing programs to attract interested candidates. The FBI is also trying to erase an unpleasant record of female harassment. A mid-'90s report by newscaster Dan Rather pointed out the need to change the behavior and attitude of this powerful organization. In a world that has always been dominated by men, the Federal Bureau of Investigation must look at women as a **positive** resource.

Law enforcement agencies in general realize that women and minorities may need an extra hand when they enter recruit training or begin their actual stint in a police department or private security field. For women and minorities who need extra help in their police or private security training, there is the Crime Prevention Assistant program. This program bolsters an existing one, giving an extra hand in physical and psychological instruction.

The International Organization of Black Security Executives (a "partner" to the National Organization of Black Executives) informs African-Americans about opportunities in private security. Colleges and universities present programs to give the black students a step up in the career ladder.

African-American policemen often have support at the local level. The Montgomery County, Pennsylvania, police have a Black Law Enforcement Association, which encourages blacks to enter the field and offers incentives to keep them there.

The President's Commission on Law Enforcement and the National Advisory Commission on Criminal Justice Standards have become allies for the potential female law enforcement officer. Traditionally, women officers were relegated to dealing with youth offenders or confined to desk jobs. These commissions want to get women into mainstream patrol and investigation duties.

Despite greater opportunities for women in law enforcement, many are made aware of that shadowy area where they are compared to men and criticized by them. Many women are fighting to emerge from this stereotype and assert their equality.

On this image problem, Jeanine Pirro, district attorney of New York's Westchester County, says, "The problem for me was I had to act like a man . . . I had to try a case like a man. But in communing with a jury, I could be a woman . . . I would be compassionate with them."

District Attorney Pirro recalled a "double-standard" moment. "I had a chief of police who came in to see me and said, 'I don't want to talk to you, I want to talk to a D.A.' I said, 'I **am** a D.A.' He snapped back 'Look, lady, what do you think this is, *Charlie's Angels?*' I want to talk to a **man.**"

Despite such incidents, women are reaching heights undreamed of a decade ago. U.S. Attorney General Janet Reno has stayed for a second term with President Clinton. She has captured America's respect for admitting major errors like the Branch Davidian compound fire. She has made positive moves including reinforcing police presence on our streets across the country.

An African-American woman, Helene Ashby, is the high-ranking Chief of Detectives for the Los Angeles County Sheriff's Department. "There may be sexism and racism in the department," Ashby commented. "However, I've never been treated badly. I came in at a time when things were changing."

Ashby's professional experience includes being a rookie deputy at the Sybil Brand Women's Institute in East Los Angeles. She rose in the ranks to captain during her stay there. "Women," she says now, in a police department still noted for conflict, "have access to all jobs."

Her parents were an unusual pair. Her father toured with the Duke Ellington band, so she grew up attending his gigs. Her mother stayed home instilling a strong work ethic in her children. Perhaps her father's nomadic life helped Ashby gain a sense of independence, while her mother at home gave her stability.

She married Verne Ashby, a successful businessman, and proceeded along an impressive educational route to her present position. This included a master's degree in public administration from Harvard University's Kennedy School of Government and a three-month course at the FBI's National Academy in Quantico, Virginia.

Helene Ashby did not consider her race an obstacle. With her drive, she probably never had time to ponder the problem.

While Sandra Day O'Connor shines on the Supreme Court, another Sandra— Sandra Schultz Newman—has distinguished herself as the first woman justice of the Supreme Court of Pennsylvania.

Judge Newman does not necessarily like the formality of being a judge. "Call me Sandy," she says, comfortable with her nickname. But this invitation applies only outside the courthouse. Judges and justices expect and deserve their titles.

"As judges, we have our faults and we have our good points," Justice Newman said. In short, the judge is human.

In campaigning for Pennsylvania Supreme Court justice, she ran on her record, which included a term as a judge of the Pennsylvania Commonwealth Court. She said that while serving on this court, she had written scholarly opinions. "I think they show intellectual thought combined with sensitivity."

Judge Newman, like Helene Ashby of the LAPD, did not achieve the honored role of justice of the Pennsylvania Supreme Court without the drive needed for such an endeavor. Her father was a Philadelphia grocer who set high standards for her. He expected her to work hard, thus setting in action the single-mindedness that would help her gain her coveted office.

Judge Sandra Schultz Newman is the first woman elected to the Supreme Court of Pennsylvania.
(Photo: Standard Photo Service)

How does she fare on a court over 200 years old that had never "seated" a woman? Very well, she thinks. And not for very complex reasons. She feels, as a woman, that she will help bring a greater sensitivity to court cases.

Has Judge Newman ever felt discrimination in her field? In response to this well-worn question she cited an incident on her first day when she was assistant prosecutor in the D.A.'s office in Montgomery County, Pennsylvania. As she approached her new desk, she noted with pleasure a leafy, colorful plant perched on the corner. How nice to be welcomed this way! Giving the plant a closer look, she realized that it was marijuana from the evidence room!

"I was the only female in the office and they were testing me." Judge Newman laughed heartily at the joke, and her reaction guaranteed her a place in the "club."

While Judge Newman is no longer harboring a marijuana plant—unless it's evidence in a court case—she may have more and more female judicial company because of "celebrity" Marcia Clark.

Marcia Clark, prosecuting lawyer in the O. J. Simpson case, is considering hosting a television series called *Lady Law*. Women judges would figure prominently in the show, along with female police officers and district attorneys. The present black female police chief of Atlanta, Georgia, Beverly Harvard, is a step in the right direction and a likely Clark model. Clark was inspired to do the series "after young women came up to me and said that they never thought about law enforcement as a career until they saw me [in the Simpson case] on TV."

Katherine Spillar, a former cochairwoman of the Police Commission's Women's Advisory Council, would approve of Clark's television show premise. Spillar is concerned with the dearth of women in crimefighting.

Female representation in LAPD, Spillar feels, is not moving at nearly the rate women activists would like. Spillar says the target of making the department 43 percent female will not be achieved until 2022. This angers her and other activists.

Spillar looks at the situation in practical terms as well as a problem of discrimination. "The failure to bolster the ranks of female officers in the LAPD is costing taxpayers millions," she notes. Why would this be so? "Women de-escalate potentially violent situations. They have greater sensitivity than men in many ways." A male police officer often acts in an aggressive way that can precipitate expensive lawsuits. As a result, there is a marked increase in citizens' complaints about police behavior—some of it justified, some due to notions of "political correctness." In this high-voltage atmosphere, the cautious but reasoned actions of a female police officer may prove far more effective—and in the end, far less costly—to this beleaguered police department.

Janet Reno, Lieutenant Embry, Judge Newman, and Katherine Spillar do admit that law enforcement opportunities for women and minorities have improved light years over the decades. The 21st century should see an even greater acceleration of crimefighting jobs for **all** American citizens.

SECTION 5

CYBERSPACE CRIME

CHAPTER 23

The What, Where, and How of Cyberspace Crime

Before we can talk about cyberspace crime, and who detects and prevents it, we have to ask some basic questions: What is cyberspace and how do we get there?

Although the word is used in business, in the press, and in general speech, it's still so new a concept that it hasn't made its way into most dictionaries.

The word was born in science fiction, coined by author William Gibson in his 1982 book *Neuromancer*. It was borrowed from *cybernetics*, which is the study of the way in which information is moved about and controlled, whether it's in machines or the brain. To the sci-fi fan, cyberspace was the concept of the place where electronic information of any sort exists when traveling from one computer to another.

Cyberspace is a "virtual" space, a place that seems real but exists only as long as the power is turned on. It is lodged in computer memory and travels through networks, telecommunications equipment, and digital media. It gets bounced off communications satellites, and it runs through phone lines and through cable TV lines when people interact with the programming.

The number of people entering cyberspace has skyrocketed since the advent of user-friendly systems. Today, an estimated 40 million people are on-line worldwide, with the number growing literally every hour. An estimated 200 million e-mail (electronic mail) messages zip across our planet every day, and that is growing rapidly, too.

A QUICK HISTORY

Computers were originally developed to calculate, to perform computations that were more complicated and time-consuming than simple adding machines could handle. An English mathematician, Charles Babbage, invented the first of such machines in 1839. It worked from instructions fed in as a coded message on punch cards. The code was the critical piece that would make more complicated computers possible.

The concept and the device itself grew until it reached the size of ENIAC (Electronic Numerical Integrator And Computer), unveiled at the University of Pennsylvania in 1946. Developed for the army during World War II, this room full of equipment weighed 30 tons and sat on 1,800 square feet of space. ENIAC could calculate ballistic trajectory, considering wind speed, ambient temperature, and the angle at which the weapon was fired, in just 30 seconds. ENIAC was the first truly digital general purpose electronic computer, using numbers and letters in the form of a system of electronic impulses. It was impressive, and people knew that such capabilities could have an important impact in any field where problems needed solving.

Only a handful of people were able to make ENIAC work, and there was only one computer. There was not any need for communication between units since there were none other than the one at this university. With the invention of the transistor came the ability to do away with bulky vacuum tubes, and computers started to be miniaturized. IBM (International Business Machines) introduced its first fully transistorized model in 1959, and computers started to hit the mass market, becoming somewhat more user-friendly. With a fair amount of training, people in universities and businesses around the world started setting up databases, not just using computers for solving problems but for storing information of all kinds: words, numbers, then eventually graphs, photos—all kinds of graphics.

The next revolution happened with the introduction of the silicon microchip, a tiny card that could hold thousands of miniature computer circuits. This made personal computers possible. In 1977, the small and affordable Apple II computer entered the market and changed the computer industry, helping computers spread from universities and industries to homes.

However, that alone did not make up cyberspace. Working within one's own computer is not cyberspace, even if it's loaded with 3-D images and surround-sound stereo. Once the computer got linked to the telephone, allowing computers to "talk" to each other, to transfer data to each other, cyberspace was born. Terminals at sites other than a central unit could now have access to software and other data stored by that central unit. This was the first use of computer networks.

These networks soon developed lives of their own, becoming the conduits for the truly vast array of information that is now on-line. Through networks we can gain access, often completely anonymously, to electronic mail, bulletin boards, message services, conferencing services.

INSTANT ACCESS—FOR CRIMINALS, TOO

Without the vital link of computer networks, most corporations and organizations in the country today would not function effectively. But this network has opened up what has been called the new Wild West. Behind the screen of distant or untraceable locations, cyber-crooks are like the masked gunmen of Dodge City. Don't let the cowboy comparison fool you, though. This is not just a crime that is made in America. The whole world is experiencing a quantum leap in the spreading of information. As the *International Review of Criminal Policy—United Nations Manual on Prevention and Control of Computer-related Crime* (1994) states, this comes as a mixed blessing:

> *The burgeoning of the world of information technologies has, however, a negative side: It has opened the door to antisocial and criminal behavior in ways that would never have previously been possible. Computer systems offer some new and highly sophisticated opportunities for law breaking, and they create the potential to commit traditional types of crime in nontraditional ways. In addition to suffering the economic consequences of computer crime, society relies on computerized systems for almost everything in life, from air, train, and bus traffic control to medical service coordination and national security. Even a small glitch in the operation of these systems can put human lives in danger. Society's dependence on computer systems, therefore, has a profound human dimension. . . . The consequences of computer crime may have serious economic costs as well as serious costs in terms of human security.*

Today we are very aware of the problem of computer crime, and it may seem as though it's a recent addition to society. Actually, if we go back to the first use of a computer-like system, we find computer-like crime. Back in 1801, a French textile manufacturer, Joseph Jacquard created a device run by a forerunner of the computer punch card. The holes in the card were instructions to Jacquard's weaving machine, making complex patterns extremely easy to produce. Naturally, the mill's weavers were outraged, seeing their livelihoods threatened by a machine. Rather than confronting their boss, they sabotaged the system. And so the first computer crime was recorded—almost 300 years ago.

As systems developed, those with criminal intent kept pace, changing to meet available technological loopholes just as generations of insects evolve to resist each new pesticide. The crimes keep escalating, though the exact number is hard to pin down. A 1987 American Bar Association survey found that of 300 corporations and government agencies, 72 claimed to have been the victim of computer-related crime in the preceding 12-month period, with losses ranging from $145 million to $730 million. Just four years later, another survey of 3,000 organizations in Canada, Europe, and the United States revealed that 72 percent had had computer-security breaches in the preceding 12-month period. Of those, 43 percent reported that the incidents involved criminal offenses. Interestingly, in this same survey, 8 percent of the respondents were uncertain whether or not they had sustained a computer security incident.

This last item can be especially disturbing to people doing business in any field in which data is stored in computers. Computer crime is often "invisible"; that is, it is hard to locate because of the quantity of data and the speed at which it moves. Often the people responsible for investigating the problems are over their heads in the complex environment of computers where a typical operating system will have from 200,000 to 25 million individual instructions. These systems are rarely fully understood by anyone, not even by their own designers. Since investigators are so often not able to locate the problems, many choose to write off the losses. And often they do not acknowledge any damage since they can't pinpoint its source.

Much of the publicity about computer abuse and break-ins has centered on societal misfits working out of their basements. "Hackers" are able to figure out how to get through the network of telephone and computer lines into files that are intended to be closed to outsiders. These may be files such as accounts in financial institutions, files containing sensitive government information, or files with important data that any institution needs to protect in order to carry on its work.

More than these malicious outsiders, malicious insiders or former employees actually pose the greatest threat. Various reports place the blame on insiders for between 73 percent and 90 percent of corporate computer crime.

Again, the complexity of the system creates its own mask. Often, those supervising the EDP (electronic data processing) staff know less about their systems than the people they are supervising. This gives the EDP person fairly free rein. Add to this the fact that EDP people are often encouraged to use the computers after hours, when other people are not on them. They are pretty much on their own and on their honor. These factors create a situation that an employer can eventually find out of control.

Types of Computer Crimes

Wherever computers are in use, there is a potential computer crime somewhere close by. The crimes are so numerous that in 1996 corporate America spent $6 billion to safeguard its networks. This is not just an American phenomenon, however; it's worldwide. The problem is so global, in fact, that it is an important area of study for the United Nations. Their *International Review of Criminal Policy— United Nations Manual on the Prevention and Control of Computer-related Crime* (1994) outlines the most common types of computer crimes.

In computer operations, every step is susceptible to criminal activity, the report points out. Input operations, data processing, output operations, and communications have all been targets.

FRAUD BY COMPUTER MANIPULATION

The kind of assets that are most often attacked through computer crimes are intangible assets, such as money on deposit or hours of work, which are often represented as data in computer programs. As a means of simplifying business transactions, more and more deposits of funds are handled as electronic data entries, rather than as the physical transfer of dollar bills. This means that the transactions are becoming increasingly vulnerable.

All manner of information on individuals and businesses lies within computer files. In addition to personal and financial information, there is credit-card data. The criminal community has made quite a business of selling this information to counterfeiters who make up false credit cards and travel documents.

In a sense, these criminals have taken a safe and easy road; they can make major gains, inflicting severe losses on their victims, without ever setting foot on their premises. Unfortunately, these crimes do not require a great deal of sophistication on the part of the perpetrators. Often called "data diddling," it can be done by any person who can gain access to the input stage of data processing—and it is very difficult to detect or track down.

Once cyber-criminals gain some real technical skills, they can go on to even more devastating schemes by changing the commands within programs. This is called program manipulation.

The Trojan horse is an example of such manipulation. It is named for the mythological wooden horse in which Greek forces hid to gain entrance to the city of Troy. Once within the city walls, the Greeks poured out of the giant structure and laid siege to the city. In the same way, today's Trojan horse can gain entry to a computer system and release its damaging message once inside. That message is typically a set of computer instructions that get the system to perform an illegal function, such as making an unauthorized deposit, at the same time that it performs a legal one. An extra twist is that the Trojan horse often will be programmed to self-destruct after a particular amount of time, so that there is no evidence of the illegal instruction.

The Salami Technique is another colorfully named form of computer manipulation. Following the approach of sneaky sausage eaters who shave off many thin slices of salami so that the loss is barely noticeable, specialists in this form of computer fraud take advantage of processes that automatically repeat in some systems. An additional, illegal instruction is linked to the normal one, saying, for instance, that with each transaction $100 is to be removed and transferred to a separate account. When this amount is shaved off large sums, it doesn't raise the suspicions of anyone working with the accounts. Over the course of a day, however, taking thin slices from different transactions could add up to an amount worthy of a charge of grand larceny.

COMPUTER FORGERY

Anyone who has seen the latest graphic and printing capabilities of computers can agree that telling an original document from a copy is sometimes nearly impossible. Laser printers and laser copiers make the copying, alteration, or complete forging of documents much faster and better than was ever possible in the past. Business documents are often created that can imply ownership of items or funds not belonging to the criminal.

Forged documents can allow an unauthorized person to gain access to files, materials, and buildings. Again, this is the kind of trickery that used to be seen only by watching *Mission Impossible*, but now is available in most large offices.

DAMAGING COMPUTER DATA OR PROGRAMS

The threat of a computer *virus* can just about immobilize anyone who works in cyberspace. It is a criminal form of sabotage, a separate program that, in its worst form, lodges in a system much like a disease. Viruses are miniprograms that can attach themselves to regular programs and then reproduce to infect all programs in a system, eating up or altering data as they spread. Criminal use of a virus, or its cousins, *worms* or *logic bombs*, is aimed at stopping or hindering normal functioning of a system. It can be the work of a competing company, trying to ensure its own advantage. This form of sabotage has also been used for stealing bits of data (*bitnapping*) and getting attention for terrorist groups.

Some viruses are harmless; others are devastating. Often they carry with them irreversible destruction of data. Europe experienced its first major attack in 1990, when the medical research community faced a ransom demand. The perpetrators wanted money paid to them for the "cure." The result was that a vast amount of medical data was destroyed.

A worm is a program that also changes or destroys data, but it is somewhat less threatening because it cannot keep making copies of itself and spreading.

A time bomb or logic bomb is a virus that is set to ignite or activate on a particular date, with extortion part of the scheme leading up to that date. If a ransom is paid, the criminals will reveal the location in the computer system of the intruding program.

The same programs can be considerably less harmful. Several years ago, a Philadelphia company was alarmed by a warning about a Yankee Doodle virus. They backed up all their files and tried desperately to contact virus-busting experts before the dreaded July 4th deadline, at which time the program was apparently set to activate itself. The experts only had time to leave a "Not to Worry" phone message. When the day came, people nervously logged on to their system. At exactly four o'clock, the virus came to life with a tinny sounding version of "Yankee Doodle." The company agreed with its expert advice that a serious debugging was not worthwhile, even though the serenade became a daily feature of their workday.

UNAUTHORIZED ACCESS TO COMPUTER SYSTEMS AND SERVICE

The desire to gain unauthorized access to computer systems can be prompted by several motives, from simple curiosity, as in the case of many hackers, to computer sabotage or espionage. Intentional and unjustified access by a person not authorized by the owners or operators of a system may often constitute criminal behavior. Unauthorized access creates the opportunity to cause damage to data, system crashes, or obstacles to legitimate system users.

Perpetrators know several ways of breaking into systems, preying on their vulnerabilities. They find loopholes in system security or procedures. Hackers often electronically impersonate legitimate users of a system by capturing their passwords. They can be current employees not authorized to have access to certain files, former employees, or people completely outside the company or organization. They can often gain access from any compatible computer system, even if it is halfway 'round the world.

Some organizations plan and execute break-ins just to show the victims how vulnerable their systems are. WheelGroup, a San Antonio security firm, conducted just such an intrusion on the computer system of a Fortune 500 firm after an executive of WheelGroup told *Fortune* magazine in a 1997 article, "It's really very easy to do. If it's a big network, it may take us an evening. Otherwise, it may take two hours." These hackers were truly professional, with some elegant previous work on their resumes. One of them proudly talked of a recent case in which he got into the payroll system of a large pharmaceutical firm in less than an hour. "We could have given anyone a bonus," he said. "Within two hours we cracked 30 percent of their passwords. They were shocked."

The methods these professionals used are so widely known by the criminal element that no secrets were divulged in the step-by-step log of the break-in, which appears in the February 3, 1997, issue of *Fortune*. It's merely as if they told muggers that people tend to keep their money in their wallets.

An international criminal hacker can use electronic bulletin boards to communicate information about incidents of break-ins and the methods used. Take the case of an attempted Canadian break-in. Details of that incident were found on suspects in an unrelated case in England. They had retrieved the data from a bulletin board in Germany. This makes clear the downside of the rapid spread of information and the ease of access computers afford. Not only do cybercops have the huge task of trying to track down glitches in a single program or system, but they have to be ready to look around the world for trails.

Creators of up-to-date communications systems keep building in security measures, but those who are intent on intruding are only a step behind them. Portable cellular phones and beepers are lifesavers (sometimes quite literally) to many busy people. Whether for business or personal use, they have become indispensable. The criminal community has caught on here, too, by duplicating the microchip technology and developing the skills to pick access codes out of thin air. They can then pick up the true owners' messages and make calls on their numbers without ever being billed.

Voice mail and call-forwarding are computer systems. They are also vulnerable to break-ins, through which important messages can be stolen, redirected, deleted, and generally proven to be anything but private and secure.

PIRATING

Are there still pirates? Maybe not the famous bandana-wearing followers of the skull-and-crossbones who used to terrorize the high seas, but pirates are still out there. Now, of course, their tools and techniques are more sophisticated. Their booty is often computer programs, which they reproduce and sell as if they were products of the original developers and producers. This causes substantial economic losses to the legitimate owners, who find their sales mysteriously tumbling while their product's use is rising. Worldwide, losses have been staggering, and they are growing each year.

Through communications networks, the downloading of programs without payment to owners is commonplace. Not all countries agree that this should be considered a criminal offense. In fact, some jurisdictions find pirating quite lucrative.

CHAPTER 25

Recent Cases in Cyberspace Crime: Looking at Some Real Examples of High-Tech Capers

Once the power of the world of computers was a small circle of technical experts, but now it can include anyone who can read and write. To get an idea of our society's needs for protection, let's take a quick look at some of the big cyberspace capers of the recent past.

SOFTWARE PIRACY

In 1994, a Florida State University systems administrator, Ray Curci, noticed that an extraordinary number of people were logging on to a rarely used computer in the system. Most were from abroad, and once they logged in, any record of them seemed to vanish. Realizing that he was dealing with hackers, Curci located their quarry, a data bank with no identifiable name in which lay a huge collection of software programs. The name of the game was pirating, unauthorized copying of programs. The trove included test versions of Windows 95 (which at that time had not yet been released) and OS/2 (the new IBM operating system still being developed), plus an array of games and word processing programs. The hacker-in-chief had supplied systems to help others break passwords and cover up their electronic tracks. Curci quickly scrambled the stolen programs, making them unusable. Even as he did so, more hackers rushed to download before their supply became off-limits.

The situation was so serious that Microsoft, one of the software companies whose goods were being lifted, offered a $10,000 bounty for information leading to the arrest and conviction of perpetrators. Another company, DeScribe, whose new word processing program was among the pirated items, offered a $20,000 reward.

In a 1995 case, a 20-year-old student at MIT was indicted for conspiracy to commit wire fraud. Working over the Internet, he allegedly permitted the distribution of over $1 million worth of copyrighted software.

Later that year, Richard Kenadek, whose bulletin board (a Web page where anyone with Internet access can post a message) was named "Davy Jones Locker," was indicted for allowing pirated programs to be traded there.

These were not isolated cases. In 1993, software theft on the Internet totaled about $2 billion. The Software Publishers Association (SPA) estimates a large portion of the total figure of $7.4 billion that the industry lost was through all forms of piracy.

The next year, when software producers earned $8 billion from business application sales, they lost an estimated $8.1 billion in revenue due to piracy. The SPA estimated that there were 1,600 bulletin boards carrying bootleg software at that time. The additional theft occurs when organizations use pirated programs or pirate their own to create enough copies for the many individual computers they own.

By 1995, worldwide piracy losses had grown to $13.1 billion, according to a survey of the Business Software Alliance and the Software Publishers Association. Vietnam, El Salvador, China, Oman, and Russia led the world in levels of the crime committed.

The SPA is well aware of the difficulty of preventing or tracing such easy-to-commit crimes. Software presents a unique theft problem because it is so easy to duplicate and because the copy functions identically to the original. Unlike other products such as audio- and videotapes, there is no degeneration in quality from copy to copy. And the copying process is effortless. A program that reflects years of hard work and millions of dollars of development takes only a few seconds to copy. The cost, too, is negligible; a product that may cost anywhere from $20 to $20,000 can be copied by any PC (personal computer) user for no more than the cost of a few blank diskettes, and hard disk users avoid even that minimal cost.

BREAKING AND ENTERING

Software isn't all that can be stolen. For example, CompuServe, one of the large on-line information services, found itself in a class action suit brought by 140 music publishers, outraged that many of their copyrighted popular songs were being downloaded free by the company's subscribers.

Going back into what may appear like ancient history in this fast-paced environment, we can look at the 1978 case of Stanley Mark Rifkin, a story told in *Introduction to Security* Fifth Edition (Butterworth-Heinemann, 1992) by Robert J. Fischer and Gion Green. Rifkin was a computer consultant to the Security Pacific National Bank of California. He entered the bank's electronic funds transfer room under the pretext of conducting an audit of wire transfer operations. He used the time to record the secret authorization codes for transferring funds. He then used the codes to transfer over $10 million to a bank in New York, and then transferred these funds to a Swiss bank account.

In a more recent case, a group of hackers operating from Majorca, Spain, stole 140,000 telephone credit-card numbers. They used American and European bulletin boards to sell them. A total of $140 million in long-distance calls resulted—some of it used for buying on-line time to download pirated software. The huge loss had to be absorbed by our long-distance telephone carriers. Such costs inevitably trickle down to the consumers.

A star in the rogues gallery of cybercrime is Kevin Mitnick, the man who may have been the inspiration for the movie *War Games*.

Mitnick allegedly penetrated the North American Air Defense Command when he was in his teens, starting a long career of hacking. He broke into dozens of corporate, university, and personal computers over the Internet. By working his way into the telephone system, the most far-ranging computer system in the world, Mitnick was able to create unbillable phone numbers, have call-forward calls transferred to unauthorized numbers, interrupt service, and tap lines virtually anywhere. He was arrested in 1988 for stealing a computer code from Digital Equipment Corporation, turned in by a friend who had come to view him as "a menace to society."

Once his term was up, Mitnick didn't stay away from his computer addiction for long. Soon up to his old ways on-line, he tempted fate by making a Christmas Day attack on the system of Tsutomu Shimomura, one of the world's leading computer security experts. Shimomura was able to track the hacker back to his terminal in North Carolina and lead the FBI there.

In interviews with Jonathan Littman, author of the book *The Fugitive Game* (Little Brown & Co., 1996), Mitnick revealed that he felt the animosity he has aroused is unwarranted. "I don't consider the acts I'm accused of being heinous," he said. "Things that I'm accused of [copying the source code for cellular phone service, wiretapping FBI agents, and attempting to social engineer, or con, Department of Motor Vehicle officials . . . I'm just saying, if they were true or not, I don't think it's public enemy number one material."

"I'm the type who's a master safecracker," Mitnick stated. "I'd read your will, your diary, put it back, not take the money, shut the safe, and do it so you never knew I was there. I'd do it because it's neat, because it's a challenge. I love the game."

Many young hackers agree; they're in it for the thrill of simply being able to do it. However, this supposed nonmercenary approach to hacking is not shared by all those who take part. John Lee, one of the founders of a hacker group called "Masters of Deception" seemed to brag that he could "commit a crime with five keystrokes" on the computer. He said he could change credit records and bank balances; get free limousines, airplane flights, hotel rooms, and meals "without anyone getting billed," change utility and rent rates; distribute computer software programs free to all on the Internet; and easily obtain insider trader information.

The profit motive was certainly also strong for a group tracked down in August 1995. Using a computer in St. Petersburg, Russia, a group had worked for over a year to illegally transfer $10 million from accounts of Citibank in New York. With a bank that spokeswoman Amy Banks reported moves half a trillion dollars a day

(Cartoon courtesy of Copley News Services)

through its payment system, the series of three-digit withdrawals was hard to find until spotted by corporate customers. Deposits were made in banks around the world, from Israel to California before the main perpetrator, a 34-year-old Russian, was nabbed in London. Most of the cash was recovered, and the bank made sure none of its depositors lost any money through the fraud.

Outsiders pose only part of the threat. According to Ira Winkler of the National Computer Security Association, their threat is relatively small. "Hackers are generally amateurish," he says. Referring to a survey by Ernst & Young, a consulting firm working in this field, he reports that 80 percent of attacks on computer systems come from inside an organization, made by disgruntled employees or individuals planted inside by a rival.

One recent insider case was that of an engineer at MCI. In 1994, he was charged with selling 60,000 calling card numbers. While he made $3 to $5 for each sale, the company sustained over $50 million in illegal long-distance charges.

MASTERS OF WORMS AND VIRUSES

For the mere sport of creating havoc, some people introduce a small alien bit of electronic data into a system (see chapter 24 for identification of different types of worms and viruses). An example was the case of Robert Morris, as described by Deborah G. Johnson, author of the book *Computer Ethics* (Prentice Hall, 1993).

"Around 6 p.m. EST on Wednesday, November 1, 1988, a computer 'worm' was discovered in a system in Pennsylvania," Johnson wrote. "Soon the worm was spreading itself across the Internet, which connects many research and university systems. By 10 p.m. the worm had managed to infect the Bay Area Research Network (BARnet), which is one of the fastest and most sophisticated in the nation."

Johnson goes on to describe how the worm exploded quickly throughout the Internet. Teams of computer wizards combined forces to stop the threat.

The worm used three means of attack. First, it simply cracked various passwords by force. Then it invaded the core of UNIX, a program widely used in the network, gaining access to a main function known as 'sendmail' and adjusting its commands. Its final job was to overstack data into a status report function. Disguised as a legitimate command, the worm did all its work without attracting notice. And when it was done, when infection of one site was complete, the worm replicated itself. The newly born worm went into a new system, causing operational difficulties. Operators began to notice a slowdown.

Eventually, a Cornell University computer science graduate science student named Robert T. Morris Jr., was found to be the infector. Within 48 hours, the worm had been isolated, and notices had gone out explaining how to destroy the pest. The systems involved suffered no permanent damage, but were proven extremely vulnerable. Their passwords were acquired fairly easily, and the systems came to a virtual standstill.

As punishment for his prank, Morris was suspended from Cornell by a university board of inquiry for irresponsible acts. He also went to trial in January 1990 at the federal court in Syracuse, New York, where he was charged with violating the Federal Computer Fraud and Abuse Act of 1986. The Morris case was unprecedented in United States courts; it was the first to test the 1986 act.

During the trial, Morris revealed that once the worm was set loose he realized he had made a mistake and tried to stop it. Nevertheless, the court found him guilty. He was placed on three years' probation, fined $10,000, and ordered to perform 400 hours of community service. He could have been jailed up to five years and fined $250,000.

Opinions were divided about the seriousness of Morris's crime and the appropriate punishment for it. Some people held that since no actual damage was done, Morris's act merely served as a way of alerting systems managers to their computers' weak points. For such a lapse of judgment, some people felt community service was more reasonable than time in prison. Others felt that a jail sentence would be the only way to dissuade legions of copycats.

As we discuss later, many firms now perform this sort of break-in-as-systems-troubleshooting for a fee, but they do it under controlled circumstances and with the cooperation of the company being "attacked." It **is** helpful to the client, showing them shortcomings in their defenses. This is how legitimate business is learning to piggyback on the breakthroughs made by the crooks.

CHAPTER 26

Jobs in Fighting Computer Crime

The computer industry, as quick moving and as technologically advanced as it is, is still in its infancy. The jobs cover a wide range of titles, and the details of what the same title holder does often vary a great deal from one organization to another.

What are these titles? They tend not to sound much like detective or police titles. They are more often computer-linked names, such as systems administrator, information security manager, technical analyst, or technical administrator.

Large businesses have individuals who are in charge of information security. In many small and mid-size corporations, however, most people with this responsibility are part-time according to David Bernstein, editor of the magazine *Infosecurity News*. Businesses, ever mindful of the need to keep their employee ranks down, find their current staff who are already in information systems and who already know how to secure their own data. People who had been doing computer programming, he says, are "thrust into information security as part of their general duties."

On the other hand, Bernstein also points to important trends he has seen over the last five years. First, a growing number of people are choosing to specialize in information security, realizing that it is an important field and that it is separate from other areas of life with computers. Secondly, a slowly growing number of universities are adding computer security studies to their computer science programs. They see that this is a need that is becoming bigger and more critical to organizations of all sorts. Now is the time to get in on it.

Rather than locking in specific responsibilities for job titles when the actual responsibilities change so much, we are going to look at the kinds of organizations that work in different areas of information security and in fighting information crimes, looking at the job descriptions as they fit into real organizations.

In some cases, the specific training and qualifications are essential to doing the jobs. In others, you will see that the field is wide open to anyone who loves technology and is willing and able to take the time to build work experience based on that. Some other positions evolve directly from law enforcement backgrounds, with technological wizardry being the last piece that is added on.

FEDERAL BUREAU OF INVESTIGATION
NATIONAL COMPUTER CRIME SQUAD (NCCS)

In existence since 1992, the NCCS is charged with investigating violations of the Federal Computer Fraud and Abuse Act of 1986. These crimes include intrusions into government, financial, most medical, and federal interest computers (meaning two or more computers, located in different states, which are involved in a criminal offense). This also extends to computers working from other countries and includes more than just the high-tech versions of theft, more than hackers and criminals; it includes terrorism or foreign intelligence.

"Computer crimes are a daily problem," said Randy Prillaman, FBI deputy assistant director in a 1996 interview on the radio program *FBI, This Week*. "What we've done is we established what we refer to as the Computer Investigations Threat Assessment Center," or CITAC. The FBI performs in two roles in investigating computer crimes. One part is criminal investigation. The other is the side involved with protecting the national information infrastructure. This may be threatened by criminals who wish to meddle with the system that makes it possible to place phone calls or send e-mail messages.

The FBI does not get involved with run-of-the-mill computer crime cases. It concentrates on cases that are on a national scale, like major investigations of financial fraud and drugs. Breaking into a corporate computer system may be a matter for local jurisdictions, but when someone intrudes into a federal computer network, it is a federal violation and that makes the bureau spring into action.

Ken Geide (pronounced Guy-dee) is the FBI's section chief of CITAC. Formed in 1992, it has been made a part of each of 56 FBI field offices. It supplies support to three regional computer crime squads, in New York, Washington, and San Francisco. The bureau, Geide said, expects to expand the number of regional computer crime squads.

"This is a growth industry," he reported in our interview. "In terms of priorities, it's one of the highest in both areas: criminal offenses and national security. Recruiting for CITAC is crucial."

Being a wing of the FBI, the people at the top of the work pyramid are special agents who, like all agents, have undergone a rigorous 16-week training period. Geide called these investigators "the core element of CITAC teams."

According to Geide, many special agents in CITAC have advanced degrees in information science or computer science or have backgrounds in information systems in the corporate world. "Agents must know information systems and computer systems," he said, "but much of the skill of an investigator comes through investigations. There is a convergence of technical discipline with training and on-the-job experience."

The FBI is establishing a standard, fixed curriculum of continuing education for investigators and staff in CITAC, Geide pointed out.

The pay scale for special agents is outlined in the General Schedule. The starting point is at grade 10, and it goes up to grade 13.

FBI employees in this area have plenty of room for job growth. "As with other government service," Geide said, "an employee rises through the levels. It's geared to responsibility: As agents become more competent, they can then compete for supervisor at the field level for management of teams."

A full cast of FBI employees works along with the special agent investigators. Non-agent FBI personnel, like members of CART (Computer Analysis Response Teams), support the investigators with their forensic capabilities. They also assist in securing cyber evidence. These people know computer systems and languages.

People at FBI headquarters in Washington, D.C., also give support to the CITAC field offices. Intelligence operations specialists have expertise in specialized areas, such as computer systems and political or geopolitical issues. Intelligence research specialists supply important information on the technicalities of policies and issues.

Non-agent positions start at the low end of the GS scale and cap off at grade 15 for technical specialists and managers.

FBI NATIONAL COMPUTER CRIME SQUAD

RICHARD RESS

Richard Ress has been a supervisory special agent for two years. He oversees the National Computer Crime Squad of the Washington, D.C., field office. In our interview, he explained what he does and how he came to be in the position.

With an accounting degree and experience on Wall Street, Ress came to the FBI in 1982. He had limited formal education in computer science at that time, but aware of the rapid changes that continually take place in the field he noted, "Even if I'd had a master's back in the '80s, it would be useless today."

The bureau placed him in the Economic Crimes Unit, in the White Collar Crimes section at headquarters. As program manager, he administered programs on bankruptcy fraud, marketing fraud, international money laundering, telemarketing fraud, and computer crime. He has seen a full spectrum of kinds of wrongdoing and considers that this adds to his appreciation of the complexity of computer crime.

"To give you an overview," he began, "what is transpiring in the real world right now is a lot of crime. That crime, which traditionally occurred in the real world, is now starting to occur in cyberworlds, on the Internet and

continues

other closed networks. Some of it's pretty easy to understand: kiddie porn, fraud by wire cases that might have involved phone calls and letters through the mail before, but now involve e-mail. Drug dealers are on the 'Net. You name it."

The mission of Ress's squad is specific and does not deal with most of these crimes. "We look only at cases that effect the viability and integrity of the national information infrastructure. This encompasses a number of different areas. It covers the public network (the phone companies, long distance and local, and all data service providers), all government agency networks (including the Department of Defense, all the military sites and networks, and major corporate hubs and networks, such as Boeing, which has the largest private network in the world). It covers the Internet, all the university sites. Years ago, these used to be separated networks; they were not interconnected, so that you could not access Boeing's computer system from at home with a modem."

All that has changed with the extraordinary advances of technology. Now, what Ress referred to as a "cloud" exists, in which vast numbers of computer sites are interconnected. "This basically means anyone involved in that superstructure is vulnerable because they can be accessed from thousands of points around the globe," Ress warned.

"Information security is only as strong as the weakest link in the chain," he continued. "That sometimes can be extremely weak. There are people out there, generally referred to as hackers and crackers, who are causing great, extensive damage in terms of shutting these systems down, stealing from the networks, altering data (like changing billing and accounting information) on those networks."

Intrusions on systems come from both inside and outside an organization. "Beyond the hackers, who we look upon as the noisemakers, there are levels of industrial espionage," Ress stated. "There are insiders who are downsized out of a company, let's say, and for revenge they go back in because their security access has not been deleted. They crash the system, or they steal information and give it to their current boss."

The mission or the FBI squad is primarily in the area of network intrusions. It is high-tech, highly sophisticated crime that occurs strictly in a cyberworld. The computer itself is either the victim or the tool to commit the crime.

"Computer crime is a new crime," Ress pointed out. "Ten years ago it was practically unheard of and today it has exploded. It is literally a very new area for law enforcement, a new area for the justice system which works to find applicable laws, it's new for security personnel who have the task of protecting their networks."

The job is clearly not an easy one or one for which there are established, tried-and-true methods. "It's really a complicated nut to crack," he admitted, "and right now the FBI is pretty much at the cutting edge, although it's sometimes rather blunt. We're up at the front doing the best we can. Countries around the world are looking to us for training, for examples, for direction and guidance. We work a lot of cases with law enforcement around the world. We have to because these intrusions are either transmitted through other countries or are emanating from other countries. We have hackers in the U.S. who are attacking systems in other countries. We deal frequently with Scotland Yard, with the Australian Federal Police, the Royal Canadian Mounted Police, the police in Germany, Hong Kong, Italy and Sweden. We have broad jurisdiction."

Aside from fighting crime, the bureau often finds itself in a teaching or coaching role with less technologically-advanced countries. "The FBI has worked in law enforcement around the world for years," Ress said, "but what's happening with the computer crime is that there are only four or five countries that really have their acts together and are in a position to detect the crimes and then be able to refer them to a competent agency to prosecute them. We happen to be one of those five. The other countries don't have the expertise, don't have the laws on the books, don't have good police infrastructures. In some former Eastern bloc countries they're still trying to figure out how to get people into jail for street crimes, forget about computer crimes."

At the bureau, Ress has administrative oversight for the entire squad. This covers all matters, from personnel issues to interaction with the front office on administrative, technical, and investigative matters. He is the go-between for the investigators and the front office executive management and is also responsible for all the investigations on the squad in terms of oversight: granting approval for certain techniques and reviewing all the reports and paperwork coming in, going out, and going to our files. Ress is responsible for liaison with the Department of Justice at a management level and for establishing and maintaining contacts with other law enforcement agencies, both in the U.S. and abroad. He also coordinates with all companies, from the AT&Ts to the occasional mom-and-pop victims of computer crimes that crop up.

"About 150 or 200 cases go through the office in a year, derived from 400 to 500 complaints," Ress estimated. "My job doesn't have a typical day. To cover all the things involved I need about two weeks—it's phone calls, e-mails, it's person to person contacts, it's committee meetings and going to conferences.

"The most challenging part of this job," he continued, "is trying to do what's never been done before. Our primary mission is to find the bad guy and put him in jail. That's difficult in the real world. In the cyberworld, you don't have a lot of the traditional investigative techniques like fingerprints, handwriting exemplars, eyewitnesses, boxes of evidence to go through. You compare this to a bank robbery, where you may have a getaway car or dyed money. None of that exists yet in cybercrime."

This is a line of work that beckons to the adventurous spirit, to people who can create solutions. "We are literally 'the wild cyberwest,'" Ress said. "It's an open field. Our biggest challenge is trying to do today better than what we did yesterday when we are the only example to compare ourselves to. There's no one to look up to.

continues

"The cases are very complicated," he said. "We need to understand the flow of information, but sometimes you have to do that without documentation. You take guesses sometimes, you serve 20 subpoenas and hope that something comes back with the information you need. You get out and talk to a lot of people. You're constructing a big puzzle with very small pieces.

"The hardware and software knowledge that our agents here need is evolving at the rate of an evolution every four months. By the time you get a good grasp of it, there's a new product on the market. I guarantee you that every time the bad guys are the ones who figure out how to exploit it."

Ress sees few comparisons between computer crime and street crime. "Computer crimes don't occur at a normal rate of time," he noted. "In a bank robbery, the alarm goes off and you know it's either occurring or has just occurred. Maybe you can get there in 10 or 15 minutes and have a chance of picking up the trail. In 10 or 15 minutes, a computer crime can occur, stop, be deleted, erased, never to be found again. That will probably occur in about three seconds flat. So response time is impossible to match. It's occurring literally at the speed of light, 186,000 miles per second. You can communicate with a computer in Hong Kong, on the other side of the world, in about ⁴/₁₀ of a second. There's no way you're going to chase that with a car with a blue light.

"That's an extreme challenge. When a victim calls you and says, 'We're under attack,' by the end of the conversation they can tell you, 'Never mind. It's gone.'"

Ress doesn't work alone. He credits his squad—10 extremely talented people working with him. He sees himself as a facilitator, a coordinator. "You turn 10 good agents loose and you don't manage them; you keep up after them. My job is to keep them in check and give them what they need, whether that's approval, equipment, names, phone numbers. You just feed them that kind of stuff and they just keep going."

In relation to the kind of training needed to do this work, and the kind of personality, Ress gave some surprising answers.

"There is some basic computer training agents go through which remains relevant: data communication protocols, which is the way data moves over networks, really hasn't changed for 15, 20 years. We received some formal training in that. Probably the best training, though, and the cheapest, is the on-the-job training. You learn an awful lot investigating these cases, weaving through the evidence, talking to the victims, talking to other companies that we solicit to help us understand.

"When I came into this position, they were looking for someone with varied criminal experience in the bureau, someone from headquarters who knew the big picture, who had program management oversight of the computer crime program, who had experience in undercover operations both from the management standpoint and from street experience. They wanted someone who 'thinks in unparochial ways,' someone who would be able to do what you may not find in the manual.

"The agent of the 21st century is going to need to be a visionary. I don't see myself like that, but I'm not afraid to cut across the grain either. In an outfit that's very much based in tradition and law and oversight, cutting across the grain isn't necessarily the safest route to take. I think they were looking for someone who could do it, but not in a cowboy fashion. I could ask a question and get an answer. I knew my way around the phone directory and up and down the halls. That's what the job has turned out to be. That's why I'm on the phone while the agents are on computers, because I spend a lot of time asking questions: Can we do **this**? How bad would **this** be?

"The division is growing. We now have a squad in New York and one in San Francisco that are dedicated to computer crime. I would expect that in the next three or four years we will probably have another three squads."

COMPUTER FORENSICS

JOAN FELDMAN

This company in Seattle, Washington, is a great example of how creative people have to be in the world of computers because the best career path may not be marked; you may have to carve it out for yourself. Joan Feldman did that and ended up founding the company to fill a need no one else was addressing.

The company quickly started growing, Feldman stated in our interview. Now it includes a staff gathered from diverse backgrounds. The caseload quadruples every year, with Feldman herself working directly on six to eight cases at a time. Computer Forensics works to find evidence in electronic formats for use by attorneys involved in civil litigations. It retrieves and analyzes evidence stored in computers, stored on diskettes, even data stored in fax machines.

"If it's electronic, we go after it," said company president Joan Feldman. "We look at electronic data that people don't realize is kept, like at entry and exit security systems that need a passcard to go in and out of buildings. We work on cases involving contract disputes, fraud, sex discrimination suits, and product liability claims.

"We look for memos, or electronic mail messages, or spreadsheets, or database compilations. We look for lists of things people created in word processing. Sometimes we're looking for systems activity, and we want to make a note of the date and time that somebody was on a system. Sometimes we're looking at transactions, at logs that would list whether somebody was on the Internet and what sites they were visiting.

continues

"Computers are like big tape recorders in many ways. Not only are they recording the thoughts of people who are using them, they are also usually running a date and time stamp of their own activity. Sometimes this is critical because people want to know when somebody wrote or edited something, not just what they wrote.

"Am I a 'cybersleuth'? Well, I like to think of myself as a dumpster diver for the '90s. I spend a lot of time winnowing through other people's stuff, going through deleted files, recovering things they thought were long gone. I love the part of my job that is going after and finding evidence."

Feldman is not an investigator. She does not have a private investigator's license, but she is a forensic specialist. Although she is involved in collecting the information, she said the job is like working in a criminal investigation laboratory. The investigative work is really done by the attorneys who tell her what things they are looking for. Feldman is a form of interpreter for them, telling them where in the electronic universe they'd be most likely to find the needed information.

"We found evidence in one case of trade secret theft that was suspected in a company," she said. "We looked at backup tapes of employees' e-mail among themselves but didn't find anything there. Then we were given access to their computers' hard drives. On one of them, we found a deleted file, which we restored. That file was a presentation for the new company the employees were forming. The product they were touting in it was the intellectual property of my client.

"Another case we worked on involved an employee who was working for a competitor while working for our client. It was an interesting situation because his job was to find retail space, and he had accepted the same job with the direct competitor of my client. Here, we didn't find deleted files, but we did find a piece of a file embedded in another (a computer will sometimes place file fragments where it locates space in another file)." Feldman's team found a whole paragraph of lease agreement for the competing company. There was no way for the employee to explain it.

"In one case of alleged embezzlement," she reported, " a guy was ordered on the witness stand to turn his computer over to us. He was given a weekend to send it to us. Send it he did. We got it and it was spotlessly clean. There were no deleted files, no file fragments . . . but we could see that all of the files had been loaded in over the weekend. Even though, to trick us, he had put on files that went back five years, we saw that they were on a brand-new hard drive, which he had popped into the computer.

"It took all night to get my report to my client so she could use it in court the next day. Then the judge didn't realize the gravity of what the guy had done," Feldman said.

An added difficulty of prosecuting these cases, according to Feldman, is that many judges and jurists don't have the technical expertise of the individuals involved in the case. "There is about a 50/50 chance that you will get a judge who is aware of what any of the technical information is about," she stated. "They'll be inclined to do either of two things: either they'll give us everything we want because they don't want to listen to a technical explanation, or they won't give us anything we want because they don't want to listen to a technical explanation!"

Did Feldman expect to be doing this work? No. She worked in litigation and the traditional collection of evidence for a long time. For 20 years she followed paper trails, organizing fact patterns by putting together a mosaic of evidence. For the last five years she has been involved in what is stored electronically. By going into this line of work, by creating this field which didn't really exist except in law enforcement, she feels she has a lot more leeway for her imagination and her creativity. Feldman finds it very rewarding, partially because of the technology, which lends itself to mystery. She has always loved math, analytic problems, and puzzles, and is also a big mystery fan. She is inquisitive and curious, and finds that in doing this work, she gets to indulge all of that.

"High-tech stuff in movies looks much more interesting and easy than it is in real life, though. If you saw what my average day was like, you would agree that I wish I could put on a little cyber-gear helmet and explore some virtual reality. But most of what we do is sit around and try to figure out if we can find a drive for a tape that was created 10 years ago. We try to get things to work, gerry-rigging software solutions, tinkering with things so that we can get to the evidence we need. There's no Michael Douglas walking around here.

"I don't just have to find evidence, in many cases I have to make it readable, make it usable for the attorney or for the court. I also have to be able to talk to my clients and an attorney or judge and explain, in plain English, how we got what we got. I go into court and explain how I came to particular conclusions. I'm an expert witness."

Feldman does this with a bachelor's degree in sociology! All of her training has been either through attending day-long conferences or seminars, or just by doing it on the job. "But when I'm working in an area that requires a very detailed analysis of an operating system," she said, " it's always my practice to team with an expert who has educational credentials. That way we can turn over our evidence for further analysis without jeopardizing our clients.

"I'm incredibly scrupulous in record keeping and maintaining chain of custody (knowing who was in control of data at all times). I want to be able to be in a courtroom and be comfortable that I didn't contaminate anything, that I can account for all activity that may have occurred with a computer or with files, and that nothing I've done has damaged or affected any of the information. We have stringent rules and procedures that we follow."

Feldman has a staff and a collection of specialists who are responsible for the capturing of evidence and the analysis of it:

Senior project managers are people who are technically skilled and trained in the procedures for gathering evidence and analyzing it once they have found it. There are two types of senior project managers. One group includes an ex-Secret Service agent and an IRS agent/forensic specialist. These two individuals are most likely to go out and create "an evidentiary

continues

copy" of computers or to process a computer on the scene. They have law enforcement training and extensive forensic training.

Project managers at Computer Forensics follow a more traditional project management model—they have to have technical skills. They assemble the physical resources for a job, the right kind of computer, the right equipment and software. Then they organize a team of people, usually software engineers and support staff, like paratechnicals and paralegals, to review backup tapes and create printouts of the contents for their clients. They have to be in contact with the clients, answering their questions.

Technical support personnel in this company are usually certified Novell engineers. Sometimes Feldman needs to contract specialists in particular kinds of software.

Project coordinators are generally people with technical or paralegal experience who work on assembling information. In general, they support the project manager. They may prepare databases of findings for their clients.

"This is a real growth industry," Feldman concluded. "People need to be able to take the pressure of getting it right in a short period of time. It's also helpful to have three things: a legal background, a technical background, and a lot of courage."

Joan Feldman's company, Computer Forensics, brings the term "sleuth" up to date by searching for, and finding, evidence hidden in computers.

(Photo: Les Fetchko)

IBM Computer Emergency Team

AL FEDELI

A computer emergency response team is a center of technical wizards who deal with the intrusions, the viruses, the various threats and attacks that plague an organization's computerized information system. The IBM team provides service to IBM facilities worldwide.

The IBM Computer Emergency Response Team (CERT) came into being in 1988, when the company fell prey to a variety of destructive viruses. (At the same time, the federally funded CERT team was put in place at Carnegie Mellon University in Pittsburgh, Pennsylvania, to deal with such attacks on the Internet.) Al Fedeli heads up the team at IBM. Here is his interview with us.

"We deal with two categories of episodes: harmful codes and intrusions," he began. "Harmful codes, like viruses and worms, have the ability to spread widely throughout a corporation. Intrusions are attacks that can be launched from any site on the planet, and can effect multiple sites in a company. These classes of incident require central command and control if you want to manage them effectively. We use the biological analogy of the Centers of Disease Control. You wouldn't want them to limit their observable data to only one region of the planet."

Fedeli broke down the jobs involved in this kind of high-tech security work into five categories, classifying them from the ones with the most advanced requirements to the ones closest to entry level.

"At the top of the food chain is the scientific researcher," Fedeli said, "the person who generally has the advanced degrees and is qualified to do very sophisticated research work in modeling[1] the threat, getting out ahead of the threat, and analyzing the patterns of vulnerabilities in the system. The scientific researcher comes up with the long-term solutions to deal more effectively with these problems."

According to Fedeli, the scientific researcher is the person on the anti-crime side who is the high-priest of this work. It requires the highest skills, typically a Ph.D.

"The second-most skilled person," he continued, "is the technical guru, the technical expert, or the senior technical analyst, who usually has a masters degree in computer science or telecommunications. This person deals with the emergency intrusions, and is an intrusion or virus expert. He or she doesn't do science research, but has a thorough knowledge of incidents, operating systems, and network environments. The senior analyst has worked with live incidents, when the outcomes were matters of survival for the company being helped. This is a very important person, who has

continues

[1]Modeling means the creation of a mathematical model. If you have viruses that can be created in January, then there are two instances seen in March, then you may see 100 incidents in April and 1,000 in September. Modeling predicts the rate of spread of viruses and the effects on countermeasures that will reduce that rate to a controllable level.

proven that he or she can help in an emergency situation, can detect what is happening when a virus is spread, know who is intruding on whom, and what countermeasures will bring the situation into line."

Excellent "people" skills are a strong plus here, Fedeli noted. "Grace under fire is very important to this position. When you're helping someone out of a desperate situation, it is important to give senior management the confidence that they are in good hands. The senior analyst has to be thorough, systematic, knowledgeable, experienced, and has got to have the poise to say, 'Let's take the following steps. I've done this before and this is how I recommend we handle the problem.' Confidence is contagious, but it's not something that you develop overnight."

The third category is the product developer. This person understands the vulnerabilities of a system as described by a scientific researcher and also as described by the customer who may tell Fedeli's team, "I need an anti-virus product that will do X. I need a firewall that will do Y." The product developer, is a programmer who writes the code that produces the anti-virus software, firewall gateway, or other security tools.

Fedeli reported that the product developer is on a par with the fourth category, the technical investigator, technical administrator, and tester on an emergency response team. These people have the technical background, but not as extensive, and typically have undergraduate or masters degrees. They have expertise to gather information, correlate information, do proper investigations, interface well with customers, and deal with incidents in a disciplined fashion. They bring some skills at assessment and the ability to research and use other experts in helping diagnose and analyze situations.

The fifth category is helpdesk analyst. "The helpdesk is like a 911 number; the first contact people make when they are in a computer emergency situation," he explained. "It's basically a '7-by-24' situation, with people who are able to respond any time, day or night, seven days a week. The range of people in this position starts with somebody who answers the phone, has no knowledge of the technical work. This person is very professional at calmly listening to callers, asking questions that are scripted for him or her about the nature of a situation, and either passing on the call to someone else or keying the information into a database so that the next analyst up the chain can deal with it. The more training and information the helpdesk analyst has, the more closure you get at that point, so the better off you are."

Often people in technical positions try to educate the helpdesk analysts so that they themselves can work more productively. If the scientific researcher doesn't want to be bothered with every call and wants to spend more time on research, it's his or her job to pass information on to the next person in the chain. "The helpdesk analysts want to have the most information they can," Fedeli pointed out. "They can't do the same work as the heavy professional who has done this for the last 15 years, but they're going to work from text and from training they receive from others in the chain."

Two additional titles Fedeli mentioned are important security positions, although they are not necessarily involved in emergency response teams:

The security manager or policy administrator in a company is the person who manages the security discipline for a corporation. The security administrator is the individual responsible for administering the company's passwords and making sure that the local area network is properly managed.

AT&T NETWORK SECURITY

RICH PETILLO

Safeguarding information and the lines through which it travels is a big job for any company, but when you talk about this communications giant, it's truly monumental. Rich Petillo is the manager of network security for AT&T, to which he came with a technical background and much experience in this type of security.

"I'm responsible for interfacing with people of like responsibilities in other carriers across the U.S. and, really, across the rest of the world," he said in our interview. "I talk with MCI and Sprint, with people in British Telcom, as often as I do with people within my own company. I also manage the deterrent activities, which means, basically, the prosecution of people who steal long distance service from us, which is called theft of communications services."

Petillo worked on two sizable cases a few years ago in which subscribers' calling cards were being compromised at a very high rate. They were being used from overseas locations. In all, it involved over 160,000 cards being compromised and more that $55 million in losses to the telecommunications carriers in the U.S.

"We identified the problem in one case early on, brought it to the industry, and got the industry working on it," he said. "Ultimately, it culminated in the arrest of 12 people, two of whom were employees of other carriers, who were compromising cards of people who subscribed to their networks, then selling the card numbers overseas.

"In the other case, they used cards to dial up to offshore pay-per-minute messages. You would typically hear 'adult entertainment' on these lines. The message provider was compensated for every minute of calling, and it was with the calling cards that were stolen. We worked the case, brought it to the Secret Service, and worked together with other carriers. When it ended, we provided all the documentation for the trial and wrote the affidavits for the prosecutors. The individuals were arrested.

"One of these cases took only about two weeks from the time we identified the problem to the time the person was aware he was going to be prosecuted. This is fast, due to the excellent response we got from the Secret Service, with whom we often deal. The other cases took several months to piece together."

continues

Petillo's cases may need the work of two or three people, or up to a dozen or more, depending on factors like how many places in the world are involved. "I work with associate managers and managers of security, and people who administer the company's program for securing our critical network elements and our computers from compromise: the computer security specialist and the information protection specialist."

To fill jobs in this area, AT&T looks for people with computer science backgrounds, but they are not always required. Some of the most proficient people may or may not have had formal training in computer science. But AT&T and others looking for people to fill computer security positions generally would look for those with computer science backgrounds and criminal justice degrees.

There are some personal characteristics that make a person right for this kind of work. "Commitment is very important," according to Petillo. "Many of the best people that we know are driven. This is not the kind of job where you come in at eight and go home at five and forget about it. There's always a new challenge to meet, a criminal element with a new angle on stealing from the company.

"Tenacity. There are those who have the drive about peeling back the onion and finding where the crime is. You see it in the best policemen and private security people. People who are not willing to just shrug their shoulders and wonder why something happened, but are ready to roll up their sleeves and work on it. I refer to it as 'having the fever.' Someone who will stick with a problem and not give up until it's solved. The people we see who have that excel.

"We get lots of resumes from people with criminal justice backgrounds, and we find many people for our positions within our organization. People who come in contact with this kind of work say, 'Gee, this looks exciting.' I believe this is one of the most interesting positions you can have."

NEW JOBS IN THE FIELD

This set of up-close looks into specific organizations can give you a good idea of the types of jobs available in the broad area of fighting cyberspace crime. It is in no way meant to be a complete list of opportunities. In fact, many exciting jobs are still in the making.

Someone who is already a hacker, or has a suspicion he or she would like to be one—legally—may eventually become part of a team that breaks into organization's computer systems for a fee. One San Antonio firm, WheelGroup Corporation, performs just such break-ins, which they call "external assessments." They do this to locate weaknesses in the client's security and help them create stronger barriers.

A person who has the makings of a software engineer can become a cryptographer who creates programs to turn text into a hodgepodge of coded letters and symbols. These can only be read by people who either have the decoding programs or their own cryptography skills.

An accountant with highly developed computer skills and a nose for investigation can become a forensic accountant, specializing in locating irregularities in electronic data and gathering evidence that can be used in cases of fraud or white-collar crime. This is a growth field. In 1997, the FBI counted 460 forensic accountants among its agents, a number that had doubled since 1992. These statistics are borne out in private industry, where large accounting firms such as Price Waterhouse and Coopers & Lybrand have beefed up their forensic forces with two- to fivefold increases in the last five years.

PAY SCALES

As fields of endeavor go, computer security is among the better money-makers. And as in most fields, the longer a person stays in it, the better the pay becomes.

The 1996 salary survey of the magazine *Infosecurity News* indicates that, "A solid majority of respondents earn $50,000 or more a year. More than a third—36 percent—make $60,000 or more. Only 17 percent are under the $40,000 line."

The people responding to the survey had a variety of titles, mostly information-security related, plus titles in management information systems, data processing, corporate security, and EDP (electronic data processing) auditing. More than half stated that information security comprised at least half of the responsibilities of their positions. Eighty percent of the respondents were men.

Annual salaries, from a nationwide sampling, follow.

- **Information Security Director, Manager, Officer:** From under $25,000 (only 2% reported this) to over $100,000 (only 3% reported this). The largest grouping (28%) was in the $40,000 to $49,000 range.

- **Other Information Security:** From under $25,000 (1%) to over $100,000 (1%), with the largest grouping (34%) in the $50,000 to $59,000 range.

- **Management Information Systems Director, Manager:** From under $25,000 (3%) to the $70,000 to $84,000 range (23%). The largest grouping (26%) was in the $50,000 to $59,000 range.

- **Other Management Information Systems:** From under $25,000 (2%) to over $100,000 (2%). The largest grouping (52%) was from $30,000 to $49,000.

- **Corporate Security Director, Manager, Officer:** From the $30,000 to $39,000 range (13%) to the $85,000 to $99,000 range (13%). The largest grouping (52%) was from $40,000 to $59,000.

- **Other Corporate Security:** From the $25,000 to $29,000 range (5%) to $60,000 to $69,000 (15%). The largest grouping (35%) was in the $50,000 to $59,000 range.

- **EDP Auditors:** from the $30,000 to $39,000 range (3%) to over $100,000 (6%). The largest grouping (41%) was in the $50,000 to $59,000 range.

The survey pointed to what the editor, David Bernstein, called "the Eight-Year Hurdle." At that point, a large number of people in the field break through the $50,000 a year mark (48 percent of people with 5 to 7 years of experience were in that pay range, compared with 66 percent of those with 8 to 10 years). The message is that in this field you must learn on the job and that companies value personnel who do that learning.

Women lag behind men in salary, a fact that is not explained by lack of experience. Women must pass a 10-year hurdle, not an 8-year one, before more than half report earning $50,000 or more. Although many theories exist about the causes, inequality of pay and responsibility remains a problem in this as in other fields, and one which dims an otherwise bright outlook.

As Bernstein reported, "Although the six-digit salary remains out of reach for all but a few (4 percent), this is still a gain from three years ago. In short, the movement is in the right direction."

What's the best route to the top? According to the survey, which also tallied results regionally and by industry, the best way to ensure a $70,000 salary is to:

- put in eight years of experience
- get the word "director," "manager," or "officer" in your title
- work in information security rather than corporate security
- move to New England or the West Coast
- work for a manufacturing firm

NECESSARY EDUCATIONAL BACKGROUND

As indicated earlier, some organizations with positions in computer crimefighting require or prefer a high level of formal background in computer science. Others may prefer it, but are flexible, looking more closely at the kind of work experience an applicant has.

Going the more traditional route of education, colleges and universities nationwide have computer science degree programs. Looking into the programs closest to your home will give you an idea of what is actually available to you on a full-time, part-time, or continuing education basis.

Here we will look at some typical college programs as well as some of the certification programs available to people who are already working in the field.

At Ohio University, in Athens, Ohio, a BSCS degree (bachelor of science in computer science) requires 192 hours of course work, or four years of school on a trimester basis. Ninety hours consist of arts and sciences courses, including two years of foreign language studies or the high school equivalent. BSCS candidates take 12 computer science courses and a four-course math program in analytic geometry and calculus. The computer science courses are:

Introduction to
Computer Science I

Introduction to
Computer Science II

Introduction to
Computer Science III

Introduction to
Computer Systems

Introduction to Discrete
Structures

Organization of
Programming Languages

Introduction to Computer
Organization

Data Structures

Operating Systems and
Computer Architecture I

Database Systems I

Plus two electives chosen from:

Design and Analysis of
Algorithms

Computation Theory

Formal Languages and
Syntactic Analysis

Concurrent Programming

Parallel Computing I

Computer Networking

Software Design and
Development

Operating Systems and
Computer Architecture II

Database Systems II

Information Organization and
Retrieval

Artificial Intelligence

Artificial Intelligence
Practicum

Expert Systems

Special Problems in
Computer Science

Senior Seminar I, II, III

Computer Science
Internship

At Indiana University in Bloomington, Indiana, the BSCS is earned through 122 hours of course work, equaling four years of full-time studies on a semester basis. This includes a combination of courses from the College of Arts and Sciences and three semesters of foreign language studies or equivalent proficiency. There are also three required math courses. Core studies in computer science are:

Introduction to Computer Science

Introduction to Software Systems

Elements of Discrete Structures

Computer Structures

Data Structures

Fundamentals of Computing
Theory

Programming Languages

At Indiana, a BSCS candidate then selects six advanced computer science courses from the following:

Introduction to Artificial Intelligence and Computer Simulation

Introduction to Algorithm Design and Analysis

Compilers

Introduction to Operating Systems

Fundamentals of Computer Networks

Digital Design

Introduction to Computer Architecture

Database Concepts

Software Engineering for Information Systems I, II, III

Interactive Graphics

Seminar in Computer Science

Theory of Computing

Computational Complexity

Algorithms Design and Analysis

Introduction to Applied Logic

Programming Language Principles

Programming Language Foundations

Programming Language Implementation

Parallels in Programming Languages and Systems

Advanced and Distributed Computing

Hardware System Design

Computer Architecture

Elements of Artificial Intelligence

Knowledge Based Computation

Biomorphic Computation

Database Theory and Systems

Software Engineering I, II, III

Scientific Computing

Digital Signal Processing

Advanced Computer Graphics

Image Synthesis

Teaching in Computer Science

Advanced Algorithms Analysis

Topics in Algorithms and Computing Theory

Topics in Applied Logic

Advanced Concepts in Programming Languages

Programming Language Type Systems

Topics in Programming Languages

Very Large Scale Integration

Topics in Systems

Natural Language Processing

Computer Models of Symbolic Learning

Computer Vision

Topics in Artificial Intelligence

Software Engineering Management

Software Management Implementation

Topics in Database and Information Systems

Advanced Scientific Computing

Topics in Scientific Computing

Topics in Graphics and Human Computer Interaction

Many two-year schools offer programs designed entirely around computer training. These generally have more flexible scheduling, since they aim to fit around the work schedules of many of their students. Classes are typically available in the evening and on weekends.

For example, at the Milwaukee Area Technical College (MATC), students can take courses leading to associate degrees in computer information systems. They specialize in either data entry, microcomputer skills, or programmer/analyst skills. In comparison with a four-year college, this school does not require any studies outside the student's field of specialization, so there are no courses in such disciplines as writing, history, or foreign language. At this school, a student can work at his or her own pace, taking the courses as time permits. Aside from the more manageable time commitment of such a program, a student also may benefit from the college's job placement service.

To obtain certification in microcomputer skills at MATC, a student needs to take at least 12 credits from the following list (the first 12 are one-credit courses, those after them are two- or three-credit courses).

Introduction to Windows 3.1	Introduction to Paradox
Intermediate Windows 3.1	Introduction to FoxPro
Introduction to Windows 95	Introduction to MS Mail
Upgrading to Windows 95	Web Page Creation—HTML
Introduction to DOS	Internet and the World Wide Web—Part 2
Internet and the World Wide Web	Introduction to Power Point
Introduction to MS Word	Introduction to Freelance Graphics
Intermediate MS Word	Introduction to MS Project
Introduction to WordPerfect	Software Evaluation
Intermediate WordPerfect	Introduction to Quicken
Introduction to Lotus	Introduction to Quickbooks
Intermediate Lotus	Introduction to MS Works for Windows
Excel for Windows	Intermediate MS Works for Windows
Intermediate Excel	Programming BASIC
Introduction to Access	Visual Basic Programming
Intermediate Access	

Programs such as these teach specific computer systems and programs, their objective being to prepare the student for the particular needs of the workplace.

They also give students a firm enough basis in the workings of computers that they can do a great deal of further learning and problem-solving on their own, on-the-job.

The specifics of any degree program will change depending on the institution at which a person is earning that degree. We give you this look at current programs so that you can consider the level of skill, background, and motivation a person needs to pursue such a degree or certificate. This is not a quick, simple, or inexpensive path to getting into a career, but it is one that certainly offers a graduate many options, some of which can head toward fighting crime in cyberspace.

From the course titles you can see that computer security or information security are not addressed directly. Some schools, such as Golden Gate University, Purdue University, and Carnegie Mellon University, do have such courses of study. As interest and appreciation for the need grow, schools in your area are likely to begin offering them.

For people who are already working with computers, their quest is not so much to learn about how to use them as how to keep up with the latest advances—and how to protect their companies from the bad guys who are already using them. Industry associations aim at supplying professionals with this help.

"Generally, it's done in the form or workshops and seminars, as opposed to a college-type course," says Rich Petillo, AT&T's manager of network security. Security professionals in Petillo's field can contact the Communications Fraud Control Association (CFCA), which manages a professional accreditation process. The American Society of Industrial Security (ASIS) also has educational programs for security people.

The Institute for Certification of Computer Professionals (ICCP), the Information Systems Audit and Control Association (ISACA), The International Information Systems Security Certification Consortium (ISC²) (said "ISC-squared"), all are involved in the continuing education and certification of information security professionals.

Fighting computer crime is not like any other crimefighting. In other arenas you get protection with walls, locks, and weapons. Here, the tools are completely different. Here a crimefighter needs knowledge. The more you have, the better your chances are to protect your organization—and the greater your opportunities to move up the career ladder.

BIBLIOGRAPHY

BOOKS

Bintliff, Russell. *Police Procedural: A Writer's Guide to Private Investigators*. Writer's Digest Books, Cincinnati, OH, 1993.

Cohen, Paul and Shari. *Careers in Law Enforcement and Security*. Rosen Publishing Group, New York City, NY, revised 1995.

Connolly, Francis M. and George J. Mullins. *Police Sergeant/Lieutenant/Captain*. Arco, New York City, NY, 1991.

Cunningham, Wm. C., John J. Strauchs, Clifford W. Van Meter. *Private Security Trends, 1970–2000, Hallcrest Report II*. Butterworth-Heinemann, Woburn, MA, 1990.

Fischer, Robert J. and Gion Green. *Introducton to Security*, Fifth Edition. Butterworth-Heinemann, Boston, MA, 1992.

Hopke, William. *The Encyclopedia of Careers and Vocational Guidance*. 1993.

King, Dennis. *Get the Facts on Anyone*. Macmillan, New York City, NY, 1995.

Law Enforcement Exams Handbook. Arco, New York City, NY, 1996.

Mills, James, *Underground Empire*. Dell Publishing Company, New York City, NY, 1987.

O'Neill, Hugh, Hy Hammer, and E. P. Steinberg. *Police Officer*. Arco, New York City, NY, 1997.

Schmalleger, Frank. *Criminal Justice Today*. Prentice-Hall, Englewood Cliffs, NJ, 1997.

Stern, Kenneth. *A Force Upon the Plain: The American Militia Movement and the Politics of Hate*. Simon and Schuster, New York City, NY, 1996.

Stinchcomb, James D. *Law Enforcement and Criminal Justice Careers*. Career Horizons, Division of National Textbook Company, NTC Publishing Company, Lincolnwood, IL, 1996 (revised edition).

Travis, Lawrence F., III. *Introduction to Criminal Justice*. Anderson Publishing Company, Cincinnati, OH, 1995.

Warner, John W. *Federal Jobs in Law Enforcement*. Arco, New York City, NY, 1992.

Wright, John W. *The American Almanac of Jobs and Salaries*. 1993.

PERIODICALS

Behar, Richard. "Who's Reading Your E-mail?," *Fortune*, 3/3/97.

Bernstein, David S. "Infosecurity News Salary Survey," *Infosecurity News*, 3-4/96.

Calem, Robert E. "ENIAC and the 50th Anniversary of the Computer," *New York Times*, 2/14/96.

Clark, Bill . "A Call to Arms," *Security Management*, 10/95.

DeLucia, Robert C. "Breaking into Careers in Criminal Justice," *Journal*, Fall 1993.

Hansell, Saul. "Citibank Fraud Case Raises Computer Security Questions," *New York Times*, 8/19/95.

Johnson, Kevin. "Cracking the Mold of the FBI," *USA Today*, 3/20/96.

Johnston, David Cay. "Russian Accused of Citibank Computer Fraud," *New York Times*, 8/18/95.

Klein, Michael. "Celebrating the Grandaddy of Modern Computers," *Philadelphia Inquirer*, 2/9/96.

Lewis, Peter. "Cybervirus Whodunit: Who Creates This Stuff?," *New York Times*, 9/4/95.

Lewis, Peter H. "Losses from Computer Breaches are on the Rise, a Study Finds," *New York Times*, 11/20/95.

Littman, Jonathan. "Kevin Mitnick, the FBI's Most Wanted Hacker," *Computerworld*, 1/15/96. (Excerpt of book by Littman, *The Fugitive Game: Online with Kevin Mitnick*, Little Brown & Co., Boston, 1996).

Lohr, Steve. "Go Ahead, Be Paranoid: Hackers Are Out to Get You," *New York Times*, 3/17/97.

Markoff, John. "It Takes a Computer Hacker to Catch One," *New York Times*, 2/16/95.

Meyer, Michael, and Anne Underwood. "Crimes of the 'Net,'" *Newsweek*, 11/14/94.

Meyer, Michael. "Is This Hacker Evil or Merely Misunderstood?," *Newsweek*, 12/4/95.

Quittner, Joshua. "Cracks in the Net," *Time*, 2/27/95.

Snider, Mike. "E-mail isn't as private as you may think," *USA Today*, 10/10/95.

Stephens, Gene. "Crime in Cyberspace," *The Futurist*, 9/10/95.

PAMPHLETS, CATALOGUES, AND OTHER SOURCES

ABC Radio Network, "FBI, This Week," 7/5/96.

Butterworth-Heinemann, Publishers, "Security Books," a security catalogue. (The books in the catalogue range over the entire security field. They are for the interested reader who wishes to know more about a particular area within the private security field.) Address:

Butterworth-Heinemann Publishers
225 Wildwood Ave., Unit B
P.O. Box 4500
Woburn, MA 01801-2041

"Correctional Officers," Chronicle Guidance Publications, Inc., Moravia, NY, 1986.

"Court Reporter," Vocational Biographies, Inc., Sauk Centre, MN, 1985.

"Court Reporters," Chronicle Guidance Publications, Inc., Moravia, NY, 1987.

McClish, P. 1996, "Federal Law Enforcement Careers: An Employment Guide Listing 33 Law Enforcement Careers in the Federal Government."
   To purchase the booklet, state the title and send $9.95 to:

FCF Jobs
P.O. Box 2175
Brunswick, GA 31521-2176

"Probation and Parole Officers," Chronicle Guidance Publications, Inc., Moravia, NY, 1991.

United Nations, "International Review of Criminal Policy. N. 43/44, 1994," United Nations, New York, 1994.

WEB SITES

www.acsp.uic.edu/iaco/KV170411.htm, "Hollywood Movies Demean Correctional Officers," Nathan Kantrowitz.

www.acsp.uic.edu/iaco/KV170421.htm, "Unlocking the Prison Cycle for Women," Creasie Finney Hairston.

www.acsp.uic.edu/iaco/KV170413.htm, "Excellence or Mediocrity: Training Correctional Officers and Administrators," Sylvia G. McCollum.

www.acsp.uic.edu/iaco/KV170408.htm, "Joliet Correctional Center—An Internship to Remember," Amanda Larsen.

www.bop.gov.html, Federal Bureau of Prisons Employment Information Page.

www.corrections.com, Job Posting Page.

www.cs.indiana.edu, Indiana University Computer Science Department.

www.cs.ohiou.edu, Ohio University Computer Science Department.

www.dos.state.fl.us/fgils/agencies/fcc, Florida Corrections Commission.

www.fbi.gov, Federal Bureau of Investigation.

www.isaca.org, Informations Systems Audit & Control Association.

www.isc2.org, International Information Systems Security Certification Consortium.

www.ivory.educom.edu, Educom Review, Sept/Oct, 1994.

www.nafanet.com, National Association of Forensic Accountants.

www.spa.org, Software Publishers Association.

www.stpt.usf.edu:80/~greek/cj.html, Cecil Greek's Criminal Justice Page.

www.un.org., United Nations Home Page.

www.uwm.edu/Dept/CJ, Criminal Justice Program Home Page.